THE EVERYTHING

ONLINE JOB SEARCH BOOK

Find the jobs, send your resume, and land
the career of your dreams—all online!

Steven Graber

Adams Media Corporation
Holbrook, Massachusetts

Editor: Jennifer Wood
Researcher: Michael Paydos

An Everything Series Book.
"Everything" is a trademark of Adams Media Corporation.

Published by Adams Media Corporation
260 Center Street, Holbrook, MA 02343. U.S.A.
www.adamsmedia.com

ISBN: 1-58062-365-4

Printed in the United States of America.

J I H G F E D C B A

Library of Congress Cataloging-in-Publication Data
available upon request from the publisher.

This publication is designed to provide accurate and authoritative information with
regard to the subject matter covered. It is sold with the understanding that the publisher is not engaged in rendering legal, accounting, or other professional advice. If
legal advice or other expert assistance is required, the services of a competent professional person should be sought.
— From a *Declaration of Principles* jointly adopted by a
Committee of the American Bar Association and a
Committee of Publishers and Associations

Many of the designations used by manufacturers and sellers to distinguish their
products are claimed as trademarks. Where those designations appear in this
book and Adams Media was aware of a trademark claim, the designations have
been printed in initial capital letters.

Illustrations by Barry Littmann

This book is available at quantity discounts for bulk purchases.
For information, call 1-800-872-5627.

Contents

Chapter 5
Netiquette Fundamentals 43

Chapter 6
Building Your Resume 51

Chapter 7
Creating the Perfect Cover Letter 65

Chapter 8
Distributing Your Resume **93**

CONTENTS

Chapter 10
Networking 207

Chapter 11 ⬉
Getting the Interview 223

Chapter 12
Computerized Job Interviews 271

Chapter 13
The Job Offer 283

Glossary 289
Index. 297

Preface

With each passing day, a new area of our life and daily tasks is being made easier with the help of the Internet. When it comes to looking for a new job, the Internet is no slouch. From the early stages of preparing a strategy and writing a cover letter and resume to the final steps of interviewing and getting the job, the Internet can help job seekers in innumerable ways. Even some of the often overlooked but important details (getting directions to the office, sending thank you letters) can be made easier by being online.

Any way you slice it, searching for a new job is a time-consuming activity. But, with the help of this book and the Internet, you can be sure that you are making the most of your time. Why would you send out one paper resume when you could e-mail thousands in the same amount of time? Why would you spend the money on travel arrangements to interview with a company on the opposite coast when you could do it just as easily on the Internet? It's questions like these that beg answers; lucky for you, they're all answered right in this book.

If you've never actually thought about all the steps that are involved in searching for a new job, you might be surprised. This book outlines each step of the process and gives you detailed information on how to complete each one successfully. From where to put your name and address on a cover letter to questions you are likely to be asked in an interview (along with some good answers), this book will let you know how to best showcase your skills and impress an employer.

Regardless of what kind of computer experience you have, this book can help you navigate your way around the Internet's many career tools. If you are new to the Internet and the world of cyber-space (a "newbie," as you'll find out), there is a whole set of rules that you must follow to project the right image in your online communications. Chapter 5 reviews the rules of netiquette and tells you when (and when not) to apply certain techniques.

If you're a seasoned Internet surfer, you probably know many of the bigger jobs databases that are online and profiled in this book (CareerCity.com, Monster.com, HotJobs, etc.), but have you ever tried working the newsgroup angle to further your opportunities? Usenet newsgroups are really one of the Internet's best kept secrets; learn how to make them work for you and your career.

Remember, there is no room for mistakes when searching for a job. By knowing the right way to search for a job, as well as the common blunders to avoid, you're bound to find happy employment. And, with the speed of the Internet on your side, perhaps that new job is only a few days away.

Chapter 1
The Basics of Job Hunting

To win the perfect job, you've got to know how to play the job-hunting game. Regardless of which method of job searching you choose to employ (online or traditional), the rules of the game don't differ greatly. There are certain steps that always must be taken and specific rules of job search etiquette that always must be followed. Before deciding which method works best for you, it is a good idea to understand all the steps involved in a typical job search and decide whether or not you are ready to take on the enormity of the task at this particular point.

1. Defining Your Goals

The most difficult part of the entire process is figuring out what you actually want to do. Just because you went to school for a particular subject or earned a degree in a particular field does not mean that you need to stay married to that career for the duration of your life. It is not at all uncommon for one person to have five or more careers during his/her lifetime. As cliché as it sounds, you learn something new every day; you learn more about your strengths and weaknesses, your likes and dislikes with each new day that passes. When these lessons are applied to your career choices, they can be priceless bits of information.

When choosing or changing careers, there are two very important things to consider: First, while a particular industry or job title may *seem* glamorous or enticing, are you really prepared to take on the day-to-day duties that such a position would entail? Are you actually ready or willing to meet the demands of this job, or is it just a job title you think would impress your friends? Second, are you prepared to live the lifestyle that this job demands? For example, while the idea of becoming part of the road crew for a famous rock band sounds cool and will definitely have its perks, are you willing to spend most your life traveling on a bus from place to place? Many high profile and/or high-paying jobs often come with a strict "very-little-free-time" price tag. If you're not sure of the customary duties and tasks of a position, try and speak with someone in the field or a career counselor and learn more about them. That dream job could turn out to be a nightmare.

Okay, so you've determined that being a famous actor or a supermodel is out of the question (those long hours just aren't worth it)—now what? One of the easiest ways to begin figuring out what kind of career you would excel in is to sit down with a pen and a piece of paper and begin making a list. I know, it sounds elementary, but it works! Divide the paper into two columns and mark one column "Likes" and the other "Dislikes." Now it's time to draw on every work, personal, and out-of-body experience you've ever had. Think about the tasks that you liked performing as well as those that you could have done without, and assign each activity to the appropriate column. The most effective list should take at least a half-hour to compile. You won't use this piece of paper to determine your ultimate career goal *right now*; rather, this piece of paper is going to serve as your reference guide throughout the rest of the job search process.

Whenever you stumble across a job that sounds interesting or when you're being considered for a particular position, you can whip out this list and make sure that the job's duties are in line with your own objectives. Remember, just because *you've* always thought you'd be great in a particular occupation doesn't necessarily make it so. Just because you like to talk and people often come to you with their problems doesn't mean you'll make the world's best psychiatrist; don't forget all the science and medical training you'll need to master to pursue such a career. Career planning is really a science of its own; don't be afraid to seek out the help of career planning professionals and occupation specialists. Even if you can't find the time to meet with people during the day, there are several Web sites out there dedicated to helping you find a career that's right for you by offering advice, detailed information on what certain jobs and professions entail, and career and personality tests. Interested in checking a few out? How about these sites:

CareerExperience
www.careerexperience.com

Emode
www.emode.com

CareerPerfect
www.careerperfect.com

Experience Network
www.experience.com

Is This Career Right for Me?

Some people balk at the idea of career tests; and why shouldn't they? It is not always the case that a computer knows more than you do. Therefore, you should not always rely *solely* on what these tests or even a career counselor tell you. You should be open-minded though. If the results come back that you would make a fantastic "Land Title Examiner," why not take the time to figure out what this person actually does. Most industries and occupations probably have an organization that operates near you, if not on the Web. Chances are they also publish some sort of trade magazine or other publication that will give you more insight into this line of work. Take a few minutes and investigate an unknown career; you never know what you'll find out.

Mapping Your Future
mapping-your-future.org

Princeton Review Online
www.review.com

My Future
www.myfuture.com

Quintessential Careers
www.quintcareers.com

Personality & IQ Tests
www.davideck.com

University of Life
universityoflife.com

2. Developing a Strategy

While the focus of this book is using the Internet as your main job search tool, there are still many questions that remain as far as your strategy is concerned. For example, will you use the World Wide Web to search out currently available job postings, or will you use it simply to gain more information on companies that you hope to work for? Will you focus your attention on Usenet newsgroups, or will you omit them completely? Regardless of the media platform, there are several different job-seeking techniques that you may employ.

The most common techniques include:

- Answering a help wanted advertisement
- Employing a recruiter or employment service firm
- Calling on personal contacts
- Sending unsolicited resumes directly to employers (a.k.a. Direct Contact)

While each of these methods can certainly be employed if you choose to search for a job the traditional way (i.e. circling ads in the Help Wanted section of your local newspaper; sending a nice little letter on your personalized stationery), the Internet can also aid you and — usually — help you accomplish these goals more quickly. We will get more into the benefits of an online search in Chapter 2.

Answering a Help Wanted Advertisement

There are, currently, tens of thousands of Web sites around the world dedicated to helping you—the average job seeker—find employment. What this means in numbers is that, with one click of the mouse, you actually have access to millions of job openings around the world. While online job postings are probably not the ads that come to mind when you think "Help Wanted," this is *precisely* what they are. Even the places where you would traditionally look for help wanted ads—newspapers and magazines, for example—have joined in the technological revolution. You can now access thousands of local and national print publications in an online format, all from the comfort of your computer desk. Yet, at the same time, the majority of the job sites out there are independently operating jobs databases that can only be found online.

Employing a Recruiter or Employment Service Firm

Like the many print publications that have made their text available to online subscribers, many of the world's businesses have done the same. This includes several recruiting firms and other employment services. Many of today's largest recruiting firms like Management Recruiters International (*www.brilliantpeople.com*), Manpower (*www.manpower.com*), OfficeTeam (*www.officeteam.com*), and Kelly Services (*www.kellyservices.com*) have gone online . . . and they've brought their existing job opportunities with them. While not *every* recruiting/employment firm has taken to the Web, there are certainly enough to keep you busy for hours (possibly days) on end. In addition to these firms, the extensive use of the Internet has paved the way for the creation of new employment service businesses that can *only* set up shop in cyberspace, namely resume posting sites. As employers from all around the world can gain access to these resume databases and search out the specific skills they require, these sites can increase the visibility of your resume exponentially . . . not to mention the chances of your being hired. Such sites will be discussed further in Chapter 8.

Which Method to Choose

While responding to help wanted advertisements is probably the most popular way to search for a job—both online and off—the Direct Contact method actually boasts twice the success rate of the other aforementioned options. This is not to say that you *shouldn't* respond to help wanted ads or that you should *only* employ the Direct Contact method, but you should try and mix it up a bit. Try out both of these options and see which one works best for you!

Calling on Personal Contacts

With the entire world moving at breakneck speed, the days of finding the time to call up and chat with friends and family are almost obsolete. Mark Youngworth, a marketing manager for an always-busy *Fortune* 500 company, says that "If it weren't for e-mail, I would have lost touch with virtually every business and personal contact I have . . . including my family." Hence, e-mail has become an acceptable and anticipated way to keep in touch with everyone you know. "E-mail lets me reply to someone's message or question whenever it is convenient for *me*, allowing me to focus more time and thought on that particular person and the information that they need," continues Youngworth. So, while calling up an old high school chum, your parents' best friend, or your cousin's dog groomer's sister-in-law's babysitter to inquire about a possible job or acquaintance is definitely an acceptable thing to do, using e-mail will allow that person the courtesy to answer your question when his/her schedule allows. Plus, if you're not really good at making small talk or asking questions of someone you don't know all that well, sending a message via e-mail will allow you the opportunity to word your introduction and/or question appropriately.

Sending Unsolicited Resumes Directly to Employers

Chances are, when you log on to a company's Web site, there will be an entire section dedicated to current job opportunities that exist within that organization. So what should you do if the company of your dreams is not actively recruiting people in your field or your geographical area right now? *Send a resume anyway!* Just like looking through the want ads can sometimes be a last resort for you, *placing* a help wanted advertisement is often the last straw for an employer. Generally, employers like to promote from within the company before hiring an outside candidate. They also like to find out if any current employees (employees they trust and respect, of course) know of any worthwhile candidates that might fit the bill. If none of these attempts pans out, the employer will usually go through the resumes that are currently on file in their Human Resources or Personnel office. This is where the Direct

Who? What? Where? When? and Why?

One thing you should be prepared for when using the Direct Contact method of job searching is the waiting period. After all, depending on any given company's needs, it could be months before they are looking to employ someone with your qualifications.

One of the biggest mistakes people make is sending off a batch of resumes without making a note of where they are going. Be sure to keep a running list of all the places you send your resume to so that, if and when they do call you, you remember why it was you applied there in the first place. Start a notebook and keep track of the following:

1. The company name and address
2. The individual or department name you addressed it to
3. The date you sent your resume
4. The reasons why you would like to work there

You may want to write a brief description of what the company does so that, during an unexpected phone screening, you can speak with authority about a company and ask relevant questions—even if it's been 10 months since you sent out your resume.

Working 9 to 5

If you're looking for a new job but are currently employed, resist the temptation to give a potential employer your contact information at work. If you're afraid you'll miss a call, invest the $20.00 in an answering machine. If the only e-mail account you have is the one at work, set up a new account with one of the many companies that offer e-mail for free. Forget the fact that if an employer were to call you at work you would probably feel and sound completely awkward; giving out your work number so that you may try to find another job shows a complete lack of respect or loyalty to your current employer, painting a not-so-pretty image for a potential employer.

Contact approach comes into play. If you have already sent in your resume <u>and</u> you are qualified for the position, it is very likely that the employer will call you in for an interview before he/she places an ad, saving them time and money in the process and eliminating the amount of competition that you will be facing for the job. As so many small and big companies alike are occupying domains on the Web, you can easily find a number of companies that suit your needs and qualifications. Employing the help of a search engine can be particularly useful if you want to find out information on companies in your area. How to best utilize your time and make the most efficient use of search engines will be discussed in Chapter 4.

3. Developing Your Resume

Okay, so you know what you want to do and how you're going to go about getting there, so now what? Well now it's time to develop one of the most crucial elements to a successful job search: THE RESUME! While resumes are discussed in much more detail in Chapter 6, you should be aware of the two main purposes of your resume. First and foremost (and most obviously), your resume is the piece of information that lets a potential employer know what your skills are and whether or not—on the most basic, skill-based level—you would be a good fit for the company. For this reason, your resume must be as detailed and informative as possible without reaching too far beyond a one-page limit. The second function of the resume is to be as attention grabbing and attractive as possible. This is not meant in a purely aesthetic way (if you plan to create an electronic resume, pretty fonts and cool-looking graphics should be the furthest thing from your mind). Since many resumes are automatically fed into an applicant tracking system, your resume must be one step ahead of the game: it must include the skills, buzz words, and characteristics that an employer might seek out when researching potential employees. Even if you choose to use the traditional paper and envelope job search method, chances are good that at least one of the companies to which you send your resume will scan the hard copy into one of these tracking systems and search it later by keyword.

4. Writing Your Cover Letter

While many people shrug off the idea of a cover letter as a mere nuisance and don't deem it a necessary part of the job search process, they're wrong. After interviewing several recruiters and hiring managers, it was determined that if there is no cover letter, then there is no interview. Taking the time to write a personalized (not mass-produced) cover letter lets the employer know that you are interested in the position that they have to offer, not just any position that will bring home a paycheck. The cover letter can also be a great way to expand upon your resume and offer up a bit of your personality. If you don't think that your writing skills are really up to par, it is imperative that you find a few friends or family members who know good grammar and are willing to read over your cover letter and make suggestions. Even if you've got what it takes to be the next Pulitzer Prize–winning author, it's still a good idea to have a few trusted individuals look over your cover letter; editing one's own work can be a very difficult task. Cover letters will be discussed in greater detail in Chapter 7.

5. Applying Your Strategy

You've got your resume and cover letter together, now it's time to start sending it out. Since you've already developed your strategy, you should be all set to let the game begin. Of all the steps, this is certainly the easiest one. If you have created an electronic resume and are using the Internet to search out available positions, it is possible for you to send out tens and even hundreds of resumes at a time (depending on how quick your fingers are). Working online will also help you to employ *each* of the strategies listed previously. For example, while you may not have anyone to contact regarding your future in a particular field right now, Internet newsgroups and

Character Flaws

While certain characteristics are always highly regarded in any career (things like loyalty, honesty, etc.), chances are a hiring manager won't take the time to seek them out when running a resume search. Instead of wasting half the page explaining what a wonderful and creative person you are, make sure to slant your resume towards the goals that you have attained. Unless you are a mind reader, there's no way of knowing exactly which words an employer will seek out. If you know the industry and the position well enough, you should be able to throw in some pertinent skills and buzz words that an employer would be interested in. Just keep in mind that a potential employer is much more likely to search out nouns than anything else. So skip the "boisterous" and go with the "Bachelor's Degree."

networking make it easy to find people who may be willing to talk with you further.

6. Waiting . . . .

Waiting to hear from interested employers can seem like the longest part of the entire task. It can also become the most frustrating if you do not start hearing back as soon as you had hoped. Remember, finding a new job can take several months. Even being called in for an interview does not mean that the job is yours. You have to remember to always be patient and always be prepared. Many employers like to call a person and screen them over the phone before calling them in for a personal interview. You need to be ready to wow them with your answers and experience at any time of day. If you're registered with an employment service or posted your resume on a resume posting site, you should expect calls at all times. Because it is the recruiter's job to fill a position as much as it is yours to find one, recruiters will often jump at the chance to contact a potential match for the job they are trying to hire for. This is not to say that a recruiting firm could or should call you at midnight (that's completely unacceptable, regardless of how badly you want the job), but, because these people often work longer hours and even occasional weekends, it's not unheard of to get a call on a Saturday afternoon. Make sure that you don't become stagnant after one day of hard job searching. Finding a job is a difficult game to win, you need to continue sending out resumes and contacting potential employers for as long as you are looking for new employment.

7. Getting the Interview

Getting a call to come in and interview with a company can be one of the most exciting and nerve-wracking parts of the entire experience. So many questions abound about what to say (and

How Should I
Address an Employer?

Many people make the mistake of assuming too much at the beginning of their cover letter. They may address a hiring manager by his or her first name, or they may simply address the letter "Dear Sir."

When you are contacting a potential employer for the first time, make sure you are addressing them with respect. Unless the hiring manager is a close friend or family member, you don't know them well enough to call them by their first name. DO: *Dear Mr. Smith,* DON'T: *Dear Buck.*

If you don't know whether a woman is married or not, address her as *Ms.* not *Miss* or *Mrs.* Second, if you only know the department name to which you are sending your resume, do not address the letter to one particular gender, as you never know who will be reading it and you never know whom you may offend. DO: *Dear Human Resources Manager*, DON'T: *Dear Madam.*

what not to say), what to wear, what time to arrive, etc. Relax! As nobody interviews for jobs on a very regular basis, it is natural to have lots of questions. While many of these questions are answered in Chapter 11, there is one main point of the interview to keep in mind: You have already impressed this person with your resume; now all you need to do is show him or her you can do the job! Sounds easy enough, right? Okay, so maybe it's not that simple. Still, like an author's pile of rejection letters, every failed interview (or any interview where you *didn't* get the job) can serve as a learning lesson. If you can pinpoint exactly what you think you did wrong, try to avoid it the next time. Often it is the case that you did very well in your interview, but you still weren't offered the job. Remember that just because you didn't get *this* job doesn't mean that you won't get *a* job.

8. Getting the Job

For every job you *do* get offered, it's likely that there are several you did *not* get. Still, there's nothing more gratifying than getting a call from that company you loved and hearing that they loved you too! Better still, you'll be relieved to know not only that all your hard work has paid off but, more importantly, that you won't have to endure any more of this job search rigmarole. Congratulations!

Chapter 2

The Benefits of an Online Job Search

N ow that you've got the basics of job winning down it's time to convince you why you should use the Internet to help you. While it can't offer you advice or be there as a shoulder to cry on, your computer can still be your best friend—when it comes to finding a job at least. The benefits of making the Internet part of your job search repertoire are undeniable.

Time

Once you have a resume intact, what are the steps you need to take in order to mail it out? First off, you have to print a fresh copy of your resume and your cover letter. You then have to sign the cover letter, address the envelope, slap on a stamp or two, and stick it in the mailbox. This in itself could take anywhere from five to ten minutes. Tack on to that the time it will take via regular mail to actually reach the desk of the hiring manager, and we're talking at least two to three days of time.

If sending a resume via e-mail or pasting your qualifications into an internal resume system, applying to that same job online should take anywhere between five seconds and two minutes. And just how long will it take for the resume to actually reach the hiring manager's desk? Assuming the e-mail address is delivering the information directly to this person, anywhere between five seconds and two minutes.

Cost

Look back over the steps of sending out a paper resume and you'll see that signing the resume, addressing the envelope, and stamping the envelope are three of the four steps. Having a resume that gets noticed requires two important things: a higher-quality and heavier stock of paper and a matching envelope. Drop by any local office supply store and you'll see that this stationery doesn't come cheap. Add to that what it will cost—eventually—to replace the ink cartridge in your computer and the cost of mailing, and you're talking a good $.50 per resume.

Aside from the monthly fees that are already being accrued for Internet access at your home, library, or wherever you are using a computer, there is absolutely no cost to send your resume via e-mail. Let's say that you are applying for 20 different positions: If employing a paper resume, the cost to you will be approximately $10.00. The cost to the Internet user? Absolutely free!

Opportunity

In any form of job searching, you need to have a plan of attack. Are you going to search the classifieds in a few local papers? Planning to call a mail list service to pinpoint certain companies? Want to scan through the yellow pages and see if anything pops out at you? Determined to apply to every job listing in the latest edition of the trade papers? These are all fine options, but they're also quite limited.

By searching online, you can not only search your local newspaper, but the local newspapers of cities all across the country and all around the world. In essence, you are making the world your marketplace and are opening yourself up to any opportunity that may arise, whether it is in Hometown, USA, or Tokyo, Japan.

Need another reason to visit cyberspace?

Convenience

The Internet and all its many resources are open 24 hours a day, 7 days a week. No matter what time of day or night it is, you can access millions of job listings, get advice on how to best approach the job market, and perhaps even network with other insomniacs (or people in another part of the world).

Competence

Even the most illiterate of computer users can learn how to use the Internet, and usually in just a few minutes. By communicating with an employer electronically or even relaying that you found out about them on the Internet or learned about their opening on a job site, you are demonstrating that—on the most basic level—you are computer savvy.

Chapter 3
Internet Basics

You can't watch television, read the newspaper, browse through a magazine, or listen to the radio without hearing a "dot com" tag line attached to every company, person, or product you come into contact with. You never hear anyone say "I'll call you!" anymore, it's all "I'll e-mail you." Feeling a bit left out? It's understandable. If you're new to the Internet, grasping such a complicated and intricate phenomenon can be a bit overwhelming. Understanding what the Internet is and what it is all about is the key to harnessing some sort of grasp on it . . . if anyone can grasp that much information.

What Is the Internet?

You can tell an Internet novice by the questions they ask: "You mean, you can actually buy things on the Internet?" "You don't need to pay for a subscription to that magazine to read it?" "You can watch a movie right on your computer?" The Internet has led to a whirlwind of innovations; you can do, see, learn, and buy just about anything on the Internet. At its core, the Internet is a world-wide networking system where people from every corner of the world can communicate with one another. They do so not only for business reasons, but for personal communication as well.

A Little History

The Internet was first developed as a stroke of genius on the part of the United States Department of Defense. Created by their Advanced Research Projects Agency (the Internet was actually referred to as the ARPANET in its infancy) in 1969, the Internet was developed as a means of communication between the agency, military contractors, and several research-oriented universities. Because it had no main central computer, the Department of Defense was most impressed by the fact that the network would be able to withstand nuclear attack. But what impressed its users—namely, the universities—was the speed and ease with which this enormous amount of information could be accessed. As more and more universities became part of the network, ARPANET began to take on a very academic slant. Because there was so much information being exchanged, the ARPANET eventually divided into two separate networks: one that would continue with the original military intent and one that could be used in academia.

The National Science Foundation also became interested in spreading the word about this phenomenon; they set up five different supercomputer centers that connected to the ARPANET. In 1986, they even set up their own network of computers, called the NSFNET, with smaller regional networks at the helm. It was around this time that the term Internet came into use, and that countries beyond the United States wanted a piece of the action.

When the ARPANET went kaput in 1990, the National Science Foundation decided to take control of the Internet and do away with the restrictions that had previously been placed upon it, namely, prohibiting the use of Internet space for profit. In lifting these precincts, the National Science Foundation changed the face of not only the Internet, but also how the world communicates, *forever*! With this newfound marketplace, Internet service providers began to spring up from all around with a new audience in mind . . . the general public!

The Internet, Piece by Piece

While many people often use the terms "Internet" and "World Wide Web" interchangeably, this is incorrect. Let's use one of those good old SAT analogies to explain the World Wide Web's relationship to the Internet: A quarter is to a whole as the World Wide Web is to the Internet. The World Wide Web is one of the four separate parts that make up the Internet. In its entirety, the Internet is composed of:

- Telnet
- Gopher
- Usenet
- The World Wide Web

To Capitalize or Not to Capitalize? That Is the Question!

One of the biggest causes for confusion when someone is writing about the Internet is which words are capitalized and which words are not. As you have just learned that there is only <u>one</u> Internet, it would make sense that this word always be capitalized; as we are referring to a singular entity, the Internet is a proper noun. The same can be said for all four components of the Internet. Thus, when speaking of Telnet, Gopher, Usenet, and the World Wide Web, you should always capitalize.

Telnet

Telnet is the smallest part of the Internet, and it's getting smaller every day. It becomes most useful when looking for a job in the federal sector; it can also be a good place to connect to other areas of the Internet, like a Gopher server, for example.

Gopher

Developed at the University of Minnesota, Gopher was created by academics and always seemed to cater to this collegiate crowd. Gopher really originated the idea of making the Internet a more user-friendly tool for non-computer-people. Gopher itself can be broken down into its two major search engines, Jughead and Veronica (*Archie* fans I take it). While Gopher can still be useful if you're looking for some sort of academic position, its popularity is fading as that of Usenet and the World Wide Web rises.

Usenet

Also known as the User's Network, Usenet is the area of the Internet where you can connect to tens of thousands of news-groups. Newsgroups are, essentially, online discussion groups; they are used to find out information, exchange ideas, inquire about a certain occupation, or just talk. Hence, Usenet is the place to go if you're looking to network online. In addition to these discussion groups, Usenet also posts many job openings; at last count, there were more than 100,000 jobs posted on Usenet groups. With so many groups to choose from, you're bound to find something that interests you.

The World Wide Web

Now we come to the granddaddy of all the Internet compo-nents—the World Wide Web. When people talk about "surfing the Net" or "getting a great deal online," they're referring to their travels around the World Wide Web. The Web has, by far, the largest number of job postings available. They even have what seems like an interminable number of career centers and other sites where you can get advice on how to best proceed with your job search (as if this book weren't enough).

What Types of Things Can I Do on the Internet?

Research Information

In keeping with the reason for its original development, the Internet is one of the best places to research a topic. Not only does it give you access to millions of publications and other informational Web sites, but it's also a link to libraries across the nation and all over the world. Think of the most extraordinarily random topic and chances are you'll find something about it on the Internet.

Communicate with Friends, Family, and Acquaintances

One of the best features of the Internet is that you can use it to keep in touch with friends and family (minus the colossal phone bill) as well as a tool to help you find some long-lost friends and acquaintances. Many Web sites will allow you to type in the name and any other information you may have on a long-lost friend (city and/or state they live in) in an attempt to track down their e-mail address. Yahoo's People Search (*people.yahoo.com*) is one such site that can help reconnect you with an old flame, a college buddy, or an out-of-touch family member. E-mail is also a very good way to do business and connect with clients, as they can see everything in writing. Best of all, you can attach pictures, articles, art, contracts, or anything else that may be important to your message. Want to send out a picture of your newborn to all the 478 people you know? It's simple to do with just the click of a button; they'll be admiring your tot in just a few seconds!

Make New Friends and Acquaintances

Chatting online is usually one of the areas that people are most skeptical of. (NOTE: If your online pal tells you he looks just like Brad Pitt or that she's the spitting image of Cindy Crawford, that's a sure sign that he/she is probably not being straight with you.) If meeting a new person in an online chat room doesn't appeal to you, there are certainly other ways in which you can utilize this

How Much Information Is There?

Skeptical as to how much information there *really* is on the Internet? Do a little experiment! Think of the most random topics imaginable and execute a search for them on the Internet. See if the search brings back any information and, if so, how well it relates to your topic.

easy person-to-person connection. Joining a newsgroup is a great way to keep abreast of all the latest happenings in your field of interest, your favorite sports, or just about anything else you can imagine. Newsgroups are an online community where people post questions and discuss important topics. While many newsgroups take a very serious tone and will offer some great reference sources where you can get information, several newsgroups are just for fun.

Buy Something

You hear it every day: "I just got the best deal online!" Isn't it time you experienced the thrill of online shopping for yourself? You can buy everything from your weekly groceries to your next home online; many companies have caught the online fever and expanded their business to inhabit a location in cyberspace. From your favorite stores at the local mall to the local car dealership, whatever you're looking to buy can be purchased over the computer.

Sell Something

If you'd rather be making money than spending it online, you're in luck. For every Web site that allows a person to make a purchase, there's somebody selling a product or service at the other end. For companies and individuals who were having trouble getting a physical business started in the real world, the advent of the Internet was a real lifesaver. Especially for those entrepreneurs who were a bit too cerebral to make it in the real business world, cyberspace is the only place where you can actually sell ideas. Add to that the fact that—whatever you're selling online—consumers all around the world can purchase your product and you've got a global marketplace in your hands.

Download Software or Other Information

If you're happy with your computer but just wish it had the ability to _____ (you fill in the blank), it's the Internet to the rescue. Downloading software lets you to enhance your computer's capabilities and allows you to do such things as filter objectionable material so that your kids will not view it, or access plug-ins so that your computer can play sounds or show videos.

Have Fun

Whether your idea of fun is a quick game of Solitaire, a heated Bingo competition, or a think-quick game of *Jeopardy*, the Internet allows you access to do all these things. There are even plenty of sites that are geared toward children, making an hour on the Internet a much better alternative than an afternoon of mindless television.

How Does It All Work?

While it would take far too long to explain (and understand) all the underpinnings of the Internet and how it works, what happens at the most basic level is that a computer uses a *client* (a software program that allows it to talk to another computer) to get in touch with a *server* (a central computer or software program that can provide your computer with certain services). Some of the main functions of a server are sending and receiving e-mail and offering access to the Internet. When you can hear your computer dialing up a number, it is actually calling another computer, referred to as a *host*. The host shares information with your computer, whether it be text and files that already exist on this computer or Internet access. When you type in a specific address, you are essentially executing a command to your browser that these are the files you want. The browser responds by making the page or site available to you in just a few seconds.

How Can I Get Internet Access?

If you want to gain Internet access on your own home or business computer, you must get in touch with an Internet Service Provider. This provider will then create an account for you (you'll be given a unique user name and password) from which you can access the Internet. But even when looking for an Internet service provider, you have two choices: you may choose to have a direct Internet connection through an Internet Service Provider (ISP) installed, or you may choose to go with a commercial online service.

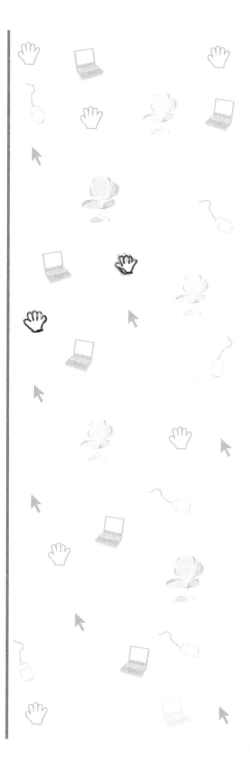

Internet Service Providers

Internet Service Providers do just that: they provide you access to the Internet with no frills. These are privately run companies with a much smaller subscription than that of commercial online services like America Online, hence access can be faster and service shutdowns can be fewer. Even without the support of an entire subscribed community behind you, you should be able to fend for yourself just fine with an ISP. Depending on the company and package you choose, an Internet connection can cost you anywhere between $10.00 and $20.00 a month plus phone usage (which, as connections are usually local, should be nothing). Check your local phone book for a list of Internet Service Providers in your area; don't call just one, shop around for the best price, plan, and service.

How to Choose an Internet Service Provider

While you should certainly consult your local Yellow Pages to find a list of Internet Service Providers in your area, you should certainly not choose one blindly. Be sure to call a number of different companies to find out which one will offer *you* the best service (just because your neighbor swears by one service does not mean it will be the best one for you). You should ask around though, and find out which ISP your friends, family, and coworkers are using. If one sounds good to you, ask about the kind of service they get: Do they experience trouble connecting? Are they often disconnected? Have they ever had to deal with technical support and, if so, how were they treated? You should also try and get a good idea of what type of service you are looking for. Do you plan on spending 50 hours online each week, or should two suffice? Can you afford to spend $20.00 for an optimal service, or is $10.00 all you can really afford? Following are some other good questions to keep in mind:

1) Find out if calling your POP (Point of Presence) is a local call. In order to avoid accruing astronomical telephone bills, it is important that your Internet Service Provider has a local POP. Do not assume that, just

because your POP is an 800 number, it is automatically free. New users have been surprised to find out that a purportedly "toll-free number" was costing them as much as $6.00 an hour.

2) Find out what an ISP's basic rate is. Be sure to ask how many hours this allows for. Then find out how much it would cost for unlimited access and try to determine which rate would be better for you. If you're not sure how many hours you'll be spending online each month, sign up for the basic rate (it's usually about half the price). If you find that you are exceeding your set hour limit within the first week or two, upgrade your plan to the unlimited access option.

3) Decide whether you want a local or national ISP. If you live in a large city or metropolitan area, chances are you can choose between either one. If you live in a more rural area, you may have to choose a local ISP. National ISPs are a bit more stable because they are often run by large companies like MCI, IBM, and Sprint; local ISPs tend to go out of business more often. Because they are run by large companies, national ISPs may offer better technical support, though local ISPs may be more attentive to your specific needs because they have such a small community of subscribers. If you travel a lot for work or pleasure, and you plan on taking the Internet with you, choosing a national ISP is the smart choice; national ISPs tend to have a POP in all major cities along with a bunch of 800 numbers for smaller towns.

4) Make sure that your chosen ISP is willing to provide you with all the software you will need to connect to the Internet, including a Web browser, connection software, an e-mail program, a newsreader, and an FTP program.

5) Ask if there is any setup charge to establish an account. With so many companies offering no setup charge, it would just be a waste of your money to pay one.

6) Speak with the members of the sales and support staffs and make sure that they are courteous and attentive. Find

Before You Make a Decision . . .

If the idea of an online "community" is a comforting thought, you should be aware of one thing: just because a commercial online service offers all these pretty little features free with membership does not mean that they cannot be accessed elsewhere on the Web. There are plenty of places to get free e-mail accounts, free Web page hosting privileges, and free access to discussion groups. Yahoo! is only one example (*www.yahoo.com*). Before you shell out big bucks to be a part of an enormous online community, talk to other people who have been using the Internet for quite some time. If you can save yourself a good deal of money by getting a direct Internet connection (and cost is an issue), you may opt for the latter option.

out whether or not they offer 24-hour technical support, 7 days a week. It would be a shame for you to experience a problem late Friday night and not be able to reach anyone until Monday morning. As you may prefer to e-mail your questions and problems to the technical support staff (telephone wait times can often be 30 minutes or more), find out how long it generally takes them to respond to e-mail inquiries.

7) Find out what the fastest modem speed is that a particular ISP can accommodate. Find out how fast your own modem is and make sure that an ISP can support that.

8) Find out what percentage of newsgroups your ISP includes. If particular categories are omitted, find out which ones; you don't want to find out that your particular interest group was not covered by your chosen service only after you've made a commitment.

9) Research the ISP itself. Ask them to send you written promotional materials on their company, read articles on them in the business and technology section of your local newspaper, and check out their Web site. Make sure that everything looks okay before deciding to go ahead with your decision to use this company.

10) Take advantage of a free trial offer. Better yet, take advantage of *several* free trial offers. See which services allow you the easiest access and best customer support. Find out what times are the peak hours for usage and then try and get online at that time to gauge the difficulties you may have.

Still Not Sure of the First Step to Take?

If everything you've heard about Internet Service Providers sounds good so far, but you're still not sure how where to begin, there are many places on the World Wide Web that could probably help you out. Try some of the following Web sites.

The Directory
www.thedirectory.org

ISP Check
www.ispcheck.com

ISP Finder
ispfinder.com

ISP Menu
www.ispmenu.com

The List
thelist.internet.com

Nettainment
www.netts.com

Online Connection
www.barkers.org

The Ultimate Web ISP List
www.webisplist.com

National ISPs

1.ConnectTo.Net
1.connectto.net
888/217-5498

1-2-3-Internet Me!
www.123internetme.net
888/426-7793

1-800-ACCESS
1800access.net

AIS Network Corporation
www.solutionprovider.net
847/882-0493

A+Net
www.aplus.net
877/A-PLUS-NET

AT&T WorldNet
www.att.net
800/967-5363

Blue Ribbon
www.blueribbon.com
800/788-1298

Cayuse Networks, Inc.
www.cayuse.net
253/891-0774

Concentric
www.concentric.com
800/745-2747

Connect-ED
www.connect-ed.net
615/367-4404

EarthLink
www.earthlink.net
888/EARTHLINK

EISA
www.eisa.com
877/EISA-EISA

FLASHNET
www.flash.net
888/FLASHNET

GTE Internet
www.gte.net
888/GTE-NET1

Globalynk Internet Solutions
www.globalynk2000.com
719/596-0322

IDT Corporation
www.idt.net
800/409-2870

InteReach Internet Services
www.intereach.net
888/343-8300

Internet 4 Families
i4f.com
888/654-8288

MCI WorldCom Internet
www.mciworld.com
877/MCI-LOOKUP

MindSpring
www.mindspring.net
888/MSPRING

Qwest Communications
www.qwest.com
800/860-2255

RCA Worldnet
www.rcaworldnet.com
800/976-1644

Spire
www.spire.com
888/55-SPIRE

TOAST.net
www.toast.net
888/TOAST-ME

WebTV Networks
www.webtv.net
800/GO-WEBTV

Regional ISPs

Ameritech
www.ameritech.net

Bell Atlantic
www.bellatlantic.net
800/NET-2026

Bell South
services.bellsouth.net

Erols Internet
www.erols.com
888/GO-EROLS

Eskimo North
www.eskimo.com
800/246-6874

Pacific Bell Internet
public.pacbell.net
800/708-4638

Southwestern Bell
public.swbell.net

US West
www.uswest.com
800/244-1111

Commercial Online Services

When people think of "going online," they tend to think of a commercial online service. Television commercials bombard the airwaves, telling you how easy it is to use America Online, CompuServe, or the many other services there are out there. In addition to an Internet connection, commercial online services will offer you other perks like a free e-mail account, Web page, discussion areas, chat rooms, personal shopping and other such services. In essence, they are trying to create a sort of cyber community, which they want you to be an active member of. If you're just starting out and are new to the Internet, knowing that you'll be part of an online community can be comforting. What is definitely comforting about commercial online services is that each and every one of them offers parents ways in which they can filter their connection so that children cannot access unsuitable material via the Web. Many people like to switch to a direct connection through an ISP once they feel they have mastered the Internet. Depending on the service plan you purchase, a commercial online service will cost you around $20.00 a month plus phone usage (again, because there are so many local servers, this should be a free local call). Who are some of the biggest commercial online services? Read on to find out . . . .

- **America Online,** *www.aol.com*
  Founded in 1985, America Online is the world's largest provider of interactive services, boasting a community of more than 22 million members. In addition to its own community, its company (America Online, Inc.) operates CompuServe, Netscape Navigator and Communicator browsers, and AOL MovieFone. The America Online software is very easy to install and even easier to use. The site's content is extremely well organized and simple to navigate. AOL subscribers get free e-mail accounts, free Web pages, and access to a variety of great chat sites and virtual shopping malls. Price plans range from $5.00 a month to just over $20.00.

- **CompuServe, *www.compuserve.com***
  Founded as a computer time-sharing service in 1969, CompuServe was the first service to offer e-mail and technical support to individual computer users in 1979. In 1980, they became the first service to offer online chatting capabilities and in 1998, CompuServe was purchased by America Online Inc. With approximately two million subscribers, CompuServe targets an adult market with various professional careers that only allow them a limited amount of time on the Internet. CompuServe aims to provide these people with a fast and easy-to-use Internet connection. The most popular CompuServe plan offers 20 hours of Internet access for under $10.00 per month.

- **Microsoft Network, *www.msn.com***
  Owned and operated by the Microsoft Corporation, Microsoft Network was introduced in 1995. Some of the benefits of MSN include free e-mail with spam filtering; access to Expedia, one of the Internet's best discount travel sites; and Encarta, an online encyclopedia. While service will run you about $22 a month for unlimited access, the information and services can be obtained for free just by visiting the above-referenced Web site.

- **Prodigy, *www.prodigy.com***
  Founded in 1990, Prodigy was one of the first companies to begin offering Internet services to individuals. The company fell a bit out of favor as new commercial services began to assert themselves and offer advanced services, but Prodigy wasn't afraid to respond to the competition. After reinventing themselves and their service, they are one of the nation's leading providers of Internet access and they are experiencing one of the nation's fastest rates of growth. The service offers a great money-back refund offer of $16.50 per month when you pre-pay for one year.

Free Internet Access

If you haven't got a computer or you can't afford to go online, there are plenty of ways to gain access to the Internet absolutely free:

- **Libraries:** Most public libraries now have a whole slew of Internet-ready computers for your convenience. Because these computers are for the community as a whole, there are often time limits of 30 minutes or so placed upon their usage (assuming there are others waiting to get online). To maximize your time online, ask a librarian when these computers experience the least amount of traffic and make it a point to go then. If you're new to the Internet, there should be some well-trained staff members who can help you get started and answer any questions you may have.

- **Schools:** Everyone from grade schoolers to college seniors is getting wired. Knowing what an important and ubiquitous resource the Internet is and will continue to be, schools are teaching their young early in the ways of the Web. Whether you're just learning your ABC's or you're working on your senior thesis, students can drop by their school library and/or computer center and gain unlimited access to the Internet.

- **Cyber Cafes:** They're popping up on every corner, and now you can frequent them for more than just the coffee. Cyber cafes are becoming a very popular place to access the Internet. Cafes vary in policy; some are much like a library and offer a set amount of time (if someone is waiting) absolutely free, others will let you linger as long as you like . . . as long as you pay the hourly price.

- Other places where you can access the Internet (though where you wouldn't necessarily have time to surf the Web) include:
    Airports
    Shopping Malls
    Hotels
    ATM-Style Kiosks

Warning: Unethical Road Ahead

When people think of all the places where they can gain free Internet access in an unhurried environment, one of the first spots that comes to mind is WORK! Please bear in mind that—especially considering the subject matter of this book—cruising the Internet during work time is a **completely unethical** pastime, and one that is not taken lightly by employers. Keep in mind the fact that it is very easy for employers to monitor what an employee is doing when he/she is online. Fooling around on the job when you're looking to change companies is the worst thing you could do; while searching for a new job is certainly a time-consuming activity, it is an endeavor that should be saved until after the work day has ended.

Is there any way for me to get free Internet access at home?

There sure is. In exchange for some demographic information or perhaps the agreement to carry a company's banner (sometimes with no catch whatsoever), many companies are beginning to offer free Internet access to the general public. Many Internet sites will provide you with a list of these company names and how you can go about acquiring your free access. Some such sites include:

Internet Service Providers Offering Free Access

Address.com
www.address.com

Bluelight
www.bluelight.com

dotNOW!
www.dotnow.com

1st Free Internet Access
www.1st-free-internet-access.com

1st Up
www.1stup.com

Free ISP
www.isps-free.com

Free ISP Internet Access Network
www.free-isp-internet-access.net

Free Internet
www.freeinet.com

FreeNSafe
www.freensafe.com

iFreedom
www.ifreedom.com

Juno
www.juno.com

NetZero
www.netzero.com

HELP THIS WAY

Chapter 4

Buying
a Computer
and Getting
Started

So You've Decided to Buy a Computer . . .

Congratulations! Having your own computer can help you in more than just the search for a new job; a computer can help you keep your finances in check, organize your calendar, keep you entertained, alert you to important dates, and so much more. Though the decision to purchase a computer is certainly a wise one, it is not something to be taken lightly or to be done on an impulse. As a good computer can easily run you several thousand dollars, you would be well served to know a little bit about what you are looking for and to research your options. While price is always a factor, don't be tempted to jump at a real "steal" that you heard about from an advertisement or even a friend. First and foremost, you should only buy your computer from a reputable dealer. There are plenty of stores in your local neighborhood and in cyberspace who are ready to couple a fair price with a trusted name; these are the only places you should consider when looking to make such a huge investment.

Following are some Web sites that can help you get started finding the information you will need:

Best Buy
www.bestbuy.com
888/BEST-BUY

CompUSA
www.compusa.com
800/COMP-USA

Buy.com
www.buy.com

Computers4Sure
www.computers4sure.com

Circuit City
www.circuitcity.com
800/251-2665

Cyberian Outpost
www.outpost.com
877/OUTPOST

Compaq
www.compaq.com
800/888-0220

DataVision
www.datavis.com
888/888-2087

Dell
www.dell.com
800/WWW-DELL

Egghead
www.egghead.com
800/EGGHEAD

Gateway
www.gateway.com
800/846-4208

IBM
www.ibm.com
800/772-2227

MicronPC
www.micronpc.com
888/224-4247

MicroWarehouse
www.warehouse.com
800/397-8508

OfficeMax
www.officemax.com
800/283-7674

Staples
www.staples.com

One of the biggest advantages to shopping at a store with a recognized, reputable name is that the salespeople are extremely knowledgeable about the merchandise. If you tell them what it is you are looking to do, they should help you find a computer that fits your needs as well as your budget. If a salesperson seems more interested in getting the most expensive computer in your cart than helping you find the computer that you really need, don't be afraid to walk out of the store. Just like buying a car, you are making a huge investment; in fact, you'll probably own your computer longer than you will your car, so you want to make sure that it is a purchase you'll be happy with for years. Being comfortable with your salesperson is just as important as getting a good deal.

Knowing Your Modem from Your Monitor

While you certainly don't need a degree in computer science to buy a reliable computer, it does help to know a little bit about what you're talking about. If you can't tell your modem from your monitor, you're more likely to get talked into something more advanced (and expensive) than you need. Before purchasing a computer, make sure you know the Dos and Don'ts.

Computer Buying Dos

DO buy your computer from a reputable store, manufacturer, or Web site.

DO make sure you put your receipt in a safe place; many places will not repair a computer for a person who cannot provide proof of purchase.

DO purchase an extended warranty, if available; computer repairs can be just as expensive as an entire system.

DO make sure you get a money-back guarantee of some sort; 30 days or more is probably your best bet, as you should be able to gauge in that amount of time whether or not the computer is working properly.

DO ask lots of questions before you buy; an inquisitive buyer is a smart buyer.

DO read all the fine print about the features included and the warranty you are being offered, especially if the price seems very low.

DO make sure that a monitor is included, as they can cost several hundred dollars on their own.

DO make sure you understand the warranty completely; know if it is full or limited, where repairs will take place, the duration of the warranty, under what conditions the manufacturer will make repairs, and what steps need to be taken in order to get the computer fixed.

DO find out whether a computer will need to be shipped (by you) to the manufacturer for repairs; computers usually need to be shipped in the original box and packing materials and the shipping charges are left up to you to pay (they can be very expensive).

DO contact the appropriate party (usually the manufacturer or the retailer) if you are experiencing any problems.

DO be sure to document every interaction you have with the manufacturer and/or retailer regarding problems with your computer; keep track of the date, person with whom you spoke, telephone number, the problem itself, and the solution you were offered.

DO contact the Federal Trade Commission's Consumer Hotline if the manufacturer and/or retailer fail to help you with problems, even with your warranty; they can be reached at 202/326-3128 and will be happy to tell you the agency to contact in your own state.

DO buy a surge protector and plug your computer into it to protect it against electrical surges; make sure that there is a certification mark ("UL-Approved") on the packaging and product itself.

Computer Buying Don'ts

DON'T buy from an unknown company, manufacturer, or Web site; you'll be the one crying when you can't get your computer fixed because a company no longer exists.

DON'T pay for a computer with cash or a check; using a credit card offers you added protection should you want to challenge the company's charges. Many credit card companies even offer an extended warranty when you use their card to make a large purchase.

DON'T buy a computer with a warranty that is "at the company's discretion." All this means is an extra headache for you; as the company would rather not spend their money to fix your computer, the repairs that will fit within the parameters will be few.

DON'T let the salesperson tell you what you need or talk you into buying the most expensive and technologically advanced machine; nobody knows your needs better than you, no matter how often you're told differently.

DON'T be afraid to ask any question that pops into your mind, no matter how embarrassed you feel.

DON'T jump at the first good deal you see; be sure to shop around as prices don't usually vary too drastically between retailers.

Where to Begin: Using Search Engines

So you've got your shiny new computer and you're already wired to the Internet. Where should you begin? Internet beginners can best get a hold of the Internet by learning about and trying out a few of the many Internet search engines.

A *search engine* is a World Wide Web-based software program that allows you to search out specific topics, words, and phrases on the Web and in newsgroups. Once retrieved, the search engine will display your results as links. You can click on any of these links to be brought to the specific page that houses your information. To get you acquainted with the power of the Internet (and to quickly learn how to weed out bad links), pick a number of random topics and type them into the search engine's home page. Click on a number of the links and see what kind of information you can find. No matter how obscure the search terms, chances are the search engine will turn up more than one result. For more information, statistics, and facts regarding Internet search engines, visit **Search Engine Watch** at *www.searchenginewatch.com* or **AllSearchEngines** at *www.allsearchengines.com.*

Popular Search Engines

All the Web, All the Time
www.alltheweb.com

Google
www.google.com

AltaVista
www.altavista.com

GoTo
www.goto.com

DirectHit
www.directhit.com

HotBot
hotbot.lycos.com

Excite
www.excite.com

I Won
www.iwon.com

GO Network
www.go.com

Lycos
www.lycos.com

Magellan
magellan.excite.com

MyWay
www.myway.com

Northern Light
www.northernlight.com

Snap
www.snap.com

WebCrawler
www.webcrawler.com

Yahoo!
www.yahoo.com

With so many different search engines, how will I know I'm choosing the best one? Chances are, whichever search engine you choose, you'll come up with many of the same results. It all depends on whether you're looking for a search engine that turns up the highest quantity of results, or the one that retrieves the highest quality results. Let's experiment by trying to execute the same search on a number of different search engines. For each of the below listed search engines we will run a search for "Jobs in Alaska" and see the kinds of information the search engine retrieves. Since each Web site has its own way of retrieving information (Web sites vs. Web pages; Web sites vs. new articles), you may still want to experiment to see which search engine is the best at bringing up the information you need.

SEARCH ENGINE RESULTS

AltaVista	110 Web pages found
Direct Hit	10 Web sites; 10 Web pages; and 10 related searches
GO Network	1 Web directory; 308 Web pages
I Won	90 Web sites
Lycos	4 popular sites; 477 Web sites; 1,904 news articles
My Way	496 Web sites
Northern Light	4,598 matching items
WebCrawler	1 Web directory; 38 Web pages
Yahoo!	2 Web sites; 462 Web pages

English-Internet Translations

Search engines are very sensitive little guys; the choice of whether or not to use quotes or use the word "and" can make all the difference in the world. Should you want to know a rough translation of what it is you are typing, look to the following English to Computer Translation Table:

You Type: Careers and Jobs
Translation: Retrieve all sites with the words "careers" or "and" or "jobs"

You Type: "Careers and Jobs"
Translation: Retrieve all sites that contain the exact phrase "Careers and Jobs"

You Type: "Careers" and "Jobs"
Translation: Retrieve all sites with the words "careers" or "jobs"

What have we learned from this experiment? We've learned that the numbers can differ greatly from search engine to search engine though, for the most part, they are retrieving much of the same information. For example, all of the above-listed nine search engines listed each or all of the following Web sites in their first 10 retrievals: *Alaska Fishing Jobs, Cool Works, Alaska Jobs Center, Seafood Jobs,* and *Action Jobs.* If you're looking for a little more juice to get your search going, try using one of the Internet's many meta search engines.

Meta search engines have the ability to search multiple search engines at one time. Instead of going back and forth between Yahoo!, Snap, and AltaVista, you can search all three at once, and in the same short span of time. Some of the Internet's most popular meta search engines include:

Ask Jeeves
www.askjeeves.com

Mamma
www.mamma.com

The BigHub
www.thebighub.com

MatchSite
www.matchsite.com

C4
www.c4.com

MetaGopher
www.metagopher.com

GoToWorld
gotoworld.com

1Blink
www.1blink.com

InfoZoid
www.infozoid.com

SherlockHound
www.sherlockhound.com

IQSeek
www.iqseek.com

RedeSearch
www.redesearch.com

Ixquick
www.ixquick.com

Zworks
www.zworks.com

E-Mail

Once you've got the whole search engine thing mastered (it shouldn't take more than an hour or so), it's time to move on to the next necessary tool: **e-mail!** You've heard countless conversations end with the phrase "I'll e-mail you!" Now it's time to get in on the action. Having an e-mail account (and using it) is an essential part of using the Internet. Many companies won't even let you log on to their site without submitting your name and e-mail address.

While many Internet Service Providers will provide you with an e-mail account upon signing up (some will provide you with multiple accounts), there are plenty of places to get free e-mail once you're on the Web. Even if you do have an account, you may decide to set up a second e-mail account for career correspondence only. This is a particularly good idea if your current e-mail user name is something a little too cutesy . . . or scary! *pookybear@email.com* may seem cute when your significant other sends you a message, but an employer may see it as being a little lame. Similarly, *KingOfGoth@email.com* might be an appropriate place for your fellow Sex Pistols' fan club members to send the latest gossip, but an employer might not care to respond.

But let's not go too far; if you are planning to set up a new e-mail account so that you can e-mail ABC Company a copy of your resume, don't be so enthusiastic that your user name somehow becomes *ILoveABCCompany* or *ABCCompany's#1Fan*. A simple *jsmith@email.com* is certain to suffice.

Another thing to watch out for is the e-mail company you use. With so many out there, choosing one can be dizzying. However, while you don't want your user name to appear too out-of-the-ordinary, the same can be said for the e-mail domain. Some of the companies that offer free e-mail may not represent the best corporate image. Imagine applying for your first job in the public relations field with *yourname@anti-social.com* as your e-mail address. Or how about that future social worker who uses *yourname@cruelintentions.com* as their professional e-mail account? The FBI may not think that *yourname@chickmail.com* has got what it takes to survive their training. Again, these are free e-mail accounts that you should not hesitate to

use on a personal level; but when it comes to the professional world, how you present yourself is extremely important.

Where Can You Get a Free E-Mail Account?

Address.com
www.address.com

AmExMail
www.amexmail.com

Angelfire
www.angelfire.com

Computermail
www.computermail.net

Email Choice
www.emailchoice.com

Excite
www.excite.com

Fiberia
www.fiberia.com

Flashmail
www.flashmail.com

Hotmail
www.hotmail.com

Mail.com
www.mail.com

MailChek
www.mailchek.com

Net@address
netaddress.usa.net

WowMail
www.wowmail.com

Yahoo!
www.yahoo.com

Chapter 5

Netiquette Fundamentals

Before you hop aboard the information superhighway, don't forget to take your road map. Unless you want to offend those other travelers you meet along the way and forge "foeships" rather than friendships, it's best to know a bit about netiquette.

Netiquette Defined

A shortened form of "Network Etiquette," using proper netiquette entails knowing the accepted rules of Internet communication. In addition to helping you come across as a good **netizen** (an Internet user who employs the rules of netiquette), using proper netiquette will help you avoid the common mistakes that many **newbies** (one who is new to the Internet) frequently make and keep you from offending anyone. While some of these basic rules may not seem to apply to your purposes (finding a job via the Internet), it is important to know *all* these rules in the case that you begin communicating with a potential employer via e-mail.

Basic Thoughts to Keep in Mind

While it is easy to make new friends on the Internet (as well as some enemies), it is also easy to forget that you are communicating with an actual person, with real feelings and real emotions. When meeting someone in cyberspace, you should behave the same way you would if you were meeting him or her on the street.

- **Always show respect.** Just as in real life, you should always show respect and thanks for the time someone has taken to write you, answer a question, etc. In the same respect, you should respect their time. Hence, if someone has taken the time to write you or respond to a question of yours, it is okay to send a quick note saying "thank you." However, these quick notes can often turn into a game of e-mail tag, where the other person feels compelled to send a "Your Welcome." Don't let this happen to you, especially if you're hoping to get a job out of these communications. If sending a thanks, a simple "Thank you so much for your time. I look forward to speaking with you soon." will do. Make it short and sweet, and make sure it has closure.

- **Check out the FAQs.** If you should have a question on a Web site or in a newsgroup, make sure that your query isn't already answered in the site's designated FAQs (frequently asked questions) section. Not *all* sites have FAQs, but most do.

- **Fast doesn't mean lazy.** While e-mail is certainly a *quicker* way to exchange information and keep in contact, it is not meant to be the *lazy* way to do so. You should maintain all of the basic letter-writing rules that you learned in elementary school: address the letter properly (DO: Dear Mr. Smith, DON'T: Hi Mr. Smith), and make sure to separate paragraphs. While every e-mail program may format differently, the least you can do in helping to maintain a semblance of uniformity is to put a space between paragraphs, thus ensuring that the entire letter won't run together.

Technical Details That Should Not Be Overlooked

Because e-mail is a much quicker way to communicate, people often make the mistake of spending much less time looking over their e-mail correspondences. The truth is, because e-mail is so technologically advanced, it is much more prone to the pitfalls that go along with being so far in advance. People often overlook the technical details of their e-mail correspondence before sending them, and wind up sending a message that looks like it could have been written by a toddler. While keeping in mind all the above-referenced thoughts, there are also several technical details you should check on before hitting that "Send" button and sending your mistakes into cyberspace.

- Make sure your caps lock button is off. WRITING IN ALL CAPS DENOTES THAT YOU ARE YELLING; you don't want to scare anyone off, do you?

- All e-mail should be in ASCII format; this is a form of written communication that does not allow for special formatting, making it easy to read regardless of the writing program the recipient is using.

- Do not send attachments unless they have been specifically requested or you have requested permission ahead of time. Due to the proliferation of viruses and Web hackers, many people are hesitant to open any unsolicited attachments for fear that they will damage their computer. Also, depending on the speed of one's computer, they can take an awfully long time to download, leading to much frustration (especially if it is a document—like a resume—that could have just as easily been sent in the body of the text).

- If someone does request that you send a written attachment, make sure that what you're sending will be in a readable format. For example, if you are using Word 2000 and the recipient is using Word 6.0, they will need to have conversion software so that they can read it. Sending a plain text or word pad document is a better way to do it.

- If someone does request that you send a picture or other graphics-based attachment, make sure that you send it in a format that takes up the least possible amount of space.

Though many programs automatically default to a bitmap format (.bmp), this is a format that can waste a lot of space. Try converting it to .jpeg format or a .tiff file.

- Avoiding sending messages with a bunch of HTML tags, as they don't make much sense to much of the Internet-surfing world.

- If you are replying to a message that was sent to you, make sure that you are the primary recipient of the message, and not the carbon copy (cc:) recipient.

- When replying to a message that was sent to a group, make sure you are only responding to the message author and not the entire group (unless, of course, that is your intention).

- If sending a message to a group, make sure you can do this blindly. This means that when recipients are reading the message, the e-mail addresses of everyone else in that same group are not made available to them. Aside from violating one's privacy, this can take up a lot of unneeded space.

- Do not use symbols in the text of your message, as they can often appear as something else in the final letter that is being read.

- Make sure to always enter a subject heading, especially when communicating with somebody new who might not recognize your name right away. If applying for a position, note the job number or position title in the subject heading. Likewise, if you are replying to a message, make sure that the noted subject is actually representative of the message you are sending.

- When sending any information that needs to be encrypted (or asking someone to send you a secure document), make sure that you and/or your company are employing some sort of encryption technology. If you are not sure whether or not you are using a secure server, pick up the phone and call the information in.

As a Common Courtesy to Your Recipients . . .

- If you are sending a message that will take a while to read (e.g., 100 lines or more), indicate that it is a long message in the subject header by simply typing in the word "LONG" before or after the subject.

- If you receive a message about a VIRUS ALERT, check a few online news pages or send it along to a few close friends to see if it has any credence. Unfortunately, there are far too many people around with the technical skill and the time to kill to create scares like this amongst the cyberspace community. Don't help them realize their pathetic attempts at notoriety by forwarding the message along without checking to see whether or not it is real.

- Do not engage in any online "flaming" (heatedly attacking someone—someone you don't know, by the way—through the Internet). Do not respond to anyone else who is engaging in flaming. This is another example of people with too much knowledge and not enough work to do. The general idea is that if the entire practice is ignored, it will eventually go away.

- Finally, whatever you do (and no matter how superstitious you are), do not further the already overabundance of chain letters and other junk e-mail that begs to be forwarded (no, there is no Good Times virus and the Neiman Marcus cookie thing is a scam). Not only is it a complete waste of your time and energy, but it's also a waste of the recipient's time who then must proceed to trash it!

Still, with the Internet being a relatively new medium, every day brings new questions as far as what is right and what is wrong when trying to practice proper netiquette. Many newspapers and magazines (*People*, for example) have frequent columns that address these concerns. For the latest in netiquette, you can always go to your favorite search engine and just type in "netiquette."

Netiquette Symbols and Abbreviations

While using the symbols and abbreviations listed below is completely informal and unprofessional in a job search, you never know who will respond to you, or what they'll write. So that you're not in the dark about the many "emoticons" (punctuation that is used to express a feeling) and abbreviations that are frequently used in friendly (read: **not professional**) discussion groups and e-mail messages, below are some of the most frequently used.

ABBREVIATIONS		**EMOTICONS**	
BCNU	Be Seeing You	:-)	SMILING
BG	Big Grin	:-(	FROWNING
BRB	Be Right Back	>:-(	ANGRY
BTW	By the Way	;-)	WINKING
FOAF	Friend of a Friend	:-o	YELLING
F2F	Face to Face	:-@	SCREAMING
FWIW	For What It's Worth	:-●	KISSING
GTG	Got to Go	:-/	CONFUSED
IMHO	In My Humble Opinion	:-D	SURPRISED
LOL	Laughing Out Loud	:-&	TONGUE-TIED
ROTFL	Rolling on the Floor Laughing		
SEG	Super Enormous Grin		
TIA	Thanks in Advance		
TTFN	Ta-Ta for Now		
TTYL	Talk to You Later		
VBG	Very Big Grin		
YNF	You're Not Funny		

Chapter 6

Building
Your Resume

While constructing a resume has never been anyone's favorite pastime (at least no one who will admit to it), it is—obviously—the most important tool you can have when looking for a new job. Even if you aren't actively seeking employment, keeping your resume up to date is important as the workplace is such an unpredictable place (plus, you never know when a great opportunity will arise; it's usually when you least expect it). Though the advent of the Internet has made sending out your resume a task that can be completed much more quickly, it has not made the creation of the resume itself any faster. In fact, because it's a good idea to have both a hard copy resume and an electronic resume, it's almost safe to say that all this technology has made the resume creation process a bit lengthier.

Even if the Internet has made the process of *creating* a resume a bit longer, it certainly makes up for it in other ways. In the time it would take for one resume to leave your hands and reach an employer's desk through regular mail (a minimum of two days), you could send out more than 17,000 resumes by e-mail (assuming each resume took approximately 10 seconds to send . . . and that you did nothing but send resumes for the entire two days). If you consider all the cost that goes into creating that same paper resume (paper, ink, envelope, stamp), you're looking at approximately $.50 per resume. As free access to the Internet is readily available through a number of services and phone charges are usually local, sending a resume via e-mail should cost you nothing. If you need any more convincing, go back to Chapter 2, where the benefits of conducting an online job search as opposed to a paper one are discussed in depth.

Why Do I Need a Paper Resume?

While sending your resume via e-mail is a much easier way to do it, the Internet does not eliminate the need for a paper resume altogether. First, it is traditionally part of the job interview etiquette to bring along a second copy of your resume. Sure, they've already got it, but what if someone misplaced it? Or what if it is stored on a computer and something is wrong with the printer? Everyone has minor catastrophes like this in their lives; companies are no exception. It's better to be over-prepared than under-prepared, thus, bringing a paper copy of your resume to a job interview is the number one reason why you need one.

While many companies may have the technological know-how to post a job online, that doesn't mean they have the ability to accept resumes online. They may not even have e-mail accounts, a Web address, or Internet access in the workplace. Just because you hear about an opening online doesn't mean you can apply for the job online. When you look at a job listing's application instructions and see that you are to "mail or fax" your resume to a certain location, you'll be happy you have one handy.

Finally, one of the ways that companies are advancing, technologically, is with the use of scanners. Instead of soliciting new resumes via e-mail or online resume posting sites, many companies scan the hard copies of the resumes they receive into an *applicant tracking system* to be searched out later. When a position becomes available, the hiring professional can then search out the particular skills and training they are looking for, and the tracking system will retrieve all the qualified candidates that have been added into the applicant tracking system.

Even if you are sending your resume via e-mail, it is very likely that your qualifications will also be fed into an applicant tracking system. Yet, while it is a good idea to have two different *types* of resumes, they need not differ much in appearance, as it is likely they'll be entered into the same type of tracking system. Though the idea of a paper resume often conjures up ideas of fancy fonts and neat-looking graphics, the paper resume that *you'll* need (also known as a scannable resume) does not concern itself with such visuals. The point of the scannable resume is to be so chock full of accomplishments and industry buzz words that any search of the database will call your name up as a matching candidate. And, as it is likely that your electronic resume will be fed into the same type of system, this should be the ultimate point of the electronic resume as well.

Resume Format: Scannable and Electronic

While it is true that your resume should always aim to grab the attention of the person reading, in the case of the scannable and electronic resumes, that person is a computer. Still, you can catch a computer's attention by following these rules:

Length

Unless there are some sorts of extenuating circumstances (a world of relevant experience, etc.), scannable and electronic resumes should abide by the one-page limit that is so often imposed upon traditional resumes. Sure, it might be difficult to gauge the length of a resume when sent via e-mail, but the recipient will certainly know when they've been reading it for too long . . . and see no end in sight.

While you definitely want to make mention of all your most impressive accomplishments in school, work, and in your community, you don't need to list every minute detail on your resume. When you're changing jobs at the age of 40, the fact that you were president of your class as a sophomore in high school has no relevance to a potential employer. If anything, listing such impertinent achievements can work against you; it will give the impression that you haven't had any accomplishments since then!

Font

While changing the font size has always been the easiest way to manipulate information into fitting a specific space limit (A few pages short? Change it to an 18-point font! A few pages too long? No problem, just make that font an even 6 points!), this trick doesn't really fly in the job market. A 12-point font is an acceptable size. If you're just a bit over the one-page limit, changing it to an 11- or even a 10-point font isn't frowned upon. But—whatever you do—do not go over 12 points! Anything over 12 points looks unprofessional and garish.

For many people, choosing a font type is a lot like choosing an outfit: it's something they mull over for hours. Well, rest assured that when it comes to choosing a font to "match" your resume, the choices are definitely limited: $\mathcal{PRETTY}$, BOXY, **WAVY**, and pretty much anything else nontraditional should be out of the question. Times or Helvetica fonts are a good choice because of their clear and distinctive lettering.

Using certain style techniques—italics and underlining, for example—can also be detrimental to the overall understanding of the resume. The computer reads the actual *styling* as another word, and the overall point of the resume can be misunderstood as certain achievements are overlooked. While most scanners will recognize boldface type, it's best to check with the particular company you're applying to first. If boldface isn't an option, one way to tactfully separate major section headings (Experience, Education, etc.) is to use all capitals. Though, even with these style exceptions, you should employ them sparingly. For example, even if a scanner will recognize boldfaced characters, avoid using it with such items as your name and address. If an employer likes what he or she sees, they will actively seek out your name and phone number; there is no need to make it jump off the page.

Graphics

In the same way that you want to avoid any strange fonts or styles, you also want to avoid using any unusual graphics that may cause a scanner to misread your resume. While the absence of decorative fonts may lead you to want to use all sorts of those symbols that your writing software is likely to offer (the symbols found in Wingdings and Webdings), this is a definite no-no. It is even likely that lines and shading will be read as jumbled resume text. Finally, don't stray from the traditional page layout—a one-column format.

Abbreviations

Just because a particular abbreviation is widely accepted and thrown around in your particular field doesn't mean a scanner will recognize it. Commonly used abbreviations—terms like A/R or A/P for accounts receivable and accounts payable, respectively—are usually okay to use. Degrees (BA, MFA, MBA) are usually accepted with or without periods, as are state abbreviations. If you're not

sure whether an abbreviation is known as common knowledge or just in your field, spell it out. The best rule to follow? When in doubt, s-p-e-l-l i-t o-u-t!

Spacing

White space can't be mistaken as a jumbled word; however, two lines that have been formatted to sit dangerously close together can read as mixed-up text. Rather than run the risk of a scanner error, be sure to leave plenty of space between sections.

Paper

Unlike a traditional resume, if you're asked to send a paper resume specifically for scanning purposes, fancy paper is only a waste of your money. Standard 8½x11-inch paper of regular printer quality is fine to use.

Printing

Like the paper itself, you should treat the printing of a scannable resume as you would any other important document. Make sure that it is crisp and clear, with no visible marks or any sort of printer error. Send originals only, as photocopies can lessen in sharpness, and always *mail* your resume for scanning, do not fax it. Finally, if your resume is more than one page long, use a paper clip to attach them together rather than a staple. The mark that is left from the staple is likely to confuse the computer.

Resume Content: Scannable and Electronic

The information you include in a scannable or electronic resume is not much different from the information you would include in a traditional resume; the only real difference between the two is the manner in which you present it. While the mark of a good traditional resume has always been the employ of lots of great action verbs—words like *coordinated, implemented,* and *developed*—such words are relatively unimportant to an electronic resume. As a hiring manager's main concern is whether or not you have the basic skills to perform a job, they're more interested in education level, computer familiarity, and other such skill-based information. All in all, hiring managers are much more likely to search out nouns than they are to search out verbs, traits, or any other type of word.

Knowing which keywords are likely to get sought out is critical to the creation of an attention-grabbing electronic or scannable resume. If you work in the industry already, think about the many buzzwords that get thrown around all day and try and incorporate them into your resume. If you are trying to break into a field, read the industry trade magazines and speak to people to find out which skills are likely to be sought after. Even if you don't know somebody in the business, read several help wanted ads in your desired field; you're likely to find that many of the advertisements sound similar. Why is this? It's because they're all after the same candidate and the same skill set. If you have the skills that they are seeking (and have proven so in your past experiences), make sure to list them somewhere on your resume.

Name

Your name should appear at the very top of the resume. Your address, telephone number, and e-mail address should be listed immediately beneath your name. If you are a student, be sure to list both your home and school contact information and be sure to indicate each as such. If you split your time between two residences, be sure to do the same. For the easiest-to-read results, put your name on the far left side of the page and give each bit of information (name, phone number, e-mail address, etc.) its own line. Be sure to put parentheses around your area code—this is the format that most computer systems are used to.

Summary

Also known as a "keyword summary," the summary is the place where you get to pitch yourself as a potential employee in 30 seconds or less. The summary is, more or less, an abridgment of all that you have accomplished in life thus far. Often written as a series of concise keyword phrases, the summary tells all your skills,

Restating versus Repeating

While reading through a series of help wanted ads in your particular field is a particularly good and easy way to get to know an occupation and the skills it entails, plagiarizing an entire ad is not the way to go. If company ABC is looking for "a detail-oriented problem-solver with strong leadership skills who is not afraid to take initiative," the worst thing you can do is send them a resume repeating the entire description. "Dear ABC Company, I am a detail-oriented problem-solver with strong leadership skills who is not afraid to take initiative." Instead, think of the help wanted advertisement as your "cheat sheet" of sorts. You know what the company wants, now all you need to do is figure out how to present your skills so that they fit this description.

achievements, and experience right up front. Why is this necessary? There are two reasons why a keyword summary is imperative to any electronic or scannable resume.

First, computers are often limited in the amount of information that they can read at any given time; if your resume is too long, the computer may very well stop reading it at some point. By having a keyword summary, you can ensure that all your skills are being considered when an employer runs a search of the database, regardless of whether or not your entire resume was entered.

Second, when a resume created for electronic purposes does reach the hands of an actual human, they may very well just glance over the summary to decide whether or not to pursue a candidate any further. Like the search engine that calls up a lot of extraneous links, applicant tracking systems and resume posting sites can do the same thing. While the brief link description is often what determines whether or not we pursue that Web site, the keyword summary serves the same function for an employer. The keyword summary should follow your contact information on a resume.

Objective

Unless you are applying for a very specific position, you might be better off omitting an objective in your resume. While this is a good way to define what it is you would like to do in and for a company, it can also work against you by limiting the other positions you might be considered for. If you do decide to include an objective, make sure to keep it general. Be sure to include the particular field or industry you are looking to work in (an entry-level position with a well-established publisher), but not a specific job title or way-too-specific company description (a senior associate editor with a 12-year-old publishing company that specializes in fishing magazines). You should also try to include a few keywords in your summary to increase your chances of a match. If you decide to list an objective, it should come after your keyword summary.

Experience

If you have been out in the real world for any amount of time, your work experience should immediately follow your keyword summary (or your objective, should you choose to include one). You will want to list your work information chronologically, starting with your most recent or current position and working backwards. For each job entry, be sure to include your title, company name, company location, and dates of employment. For each entry, highlight your most important achievements and responsibilities. Again, pay particularly close attention to the words that you are using to describe your experience; if and when you can apply a keyword, do so! Like the keyword summary, work experiences can be listed with sentence fragments. If you want to separate each of the responsibilities at a particular job, you may do so with spacing or by using dashes in place of bullets (again, these are a stylistic tool that can be difficult for a computer to read). If you are a recent college graduate, you want to highlight your educational experience instead of your work experience (if you have any). That said, recent college graduates should list "Education" before "Experience."

Collegiate Activities

Many colleges are now offering students the chance to get some hands-on work experience in an academic setting. College students who've engaged in some sort of worthwhile activity through their schools (associations, organizations, etc.) should certainly include this on their resume. If necessary, provide a brief description of the activities and your responsibilities, the same way as you would for a work entry. While internships are often arranged through school for credit, they can be considered "Work Experience." Listing these activities after your work experience is probably the most appropriate way to do it.

Education

Again, if you are a recent college graduate, this section of your resume will immediately follow your keyword summary (or your objective, should you choose to use one). If you have been in the workforce for any period of time, "Education" will follow your "Experience." In addition to listing any degrees, licenses, permits, and certifications you may hold, this section can also be used to highlight any relevant course work and/or academic honors or

awards you may have received. Just because you didn't graduate from a particular school or program does not mean that you should not list it. Education is education; just because you do not have a piece of paper that asserts your mastery of a subject does not mean that you can't list it. Be sure to include the name of each school attended, location, dates attended, and year of graduation.

Associations

In addition to any formal education and/or training you may have received, employers are interested in any organizations or associations you may be affiliated with. Though it might sound surprising, many recruiters often search out this bit of information when performing a more advanced search for applicants. This section only needs to list the name of the association; it should follow the "Education" section if you're not a student and the "Experience" section if you are a student.

Personal Data

Many people think it is a good idea to include personal information such as hobbies and interests . . . . IT'S NOT! Personal information is irrelevant to the purpose of an electronic or scannable resume, and it takes up way too much space. Also, you should not include such personal data as your birth date, marital status, religion, or nationality. As it is unlawful for companies to even inquire about this type of information (because of discrimination), there is no need for you to volunteer such personal details on your own.

References

It used to be the case that potential employees would take up half the page with the contact information for their references. Next, it became more acceptable to just say "References Available upon Request." In the case of scannable and electronic resumes, neither of these options is necessary. References are often a mandatory part of the job application process and one that employers will ask you for. Instead of wasting the time of whomever it is reading your resume (a computer, a scanner, an actual person), it is best just to

A Few Resume Basics

One quality that can make or break a resume is correct spelling, punctuation, and grammar. First and foremost, it is imperative that you use your spell check before distributing a resume. It's there for a reason, and this is precisely it. Many companies see incorrect grammar or spelling on a resume and/or cover letter and attribute that to a lack or caring or inattention to detail. The result? The job goes to someone who took the time to have someone else look over their resume and to spell check it on their computer.

Still, you can come out on top if you know some of the more common inaccuracies that appear on resumes time and time again . . . .

- Be sure that when describing your work experience, you remember that "years" is possessive and, thus, must have an apostrophe. DO: "with over five years' experience" DON'T: "with over five years experience"
- When discussing your degree, there is no need to say a "BA degree in . . . " Using the word "degree" after stating your degree is just plain redundant. DO: "BA in Psychology" DON'T: "BA degree in Psychology"
- It is standard editorial practice to use a comma after each item in a series; please make sure you do so on your resume. DO: "Wrote, produced, and directed . . . " DON'T: "Wrote, produced and directed . . . "
- There is no need to use a colon after a subhead. As the purpose of the subhead is to set the section apart from the rest of the resume and describe the information that follows, a colon is unnecessary. DO: "WORK EXPERIENCE" DON'T: "WORK EXPERIENCE:"

skip mention of your references altogether. Instead, type up a list of references that you would like to use to bring along to job interviews, etc. When a potential employee asks for your references, you can hand them a neatly typed copy or fax them the same list.

Need More Information?

For more information on developing your resume and lots of invaluable resume-writing tips, the following Web sites offer priceless bits of information:

America's Employers
www.americasemployers.com

Knock 'Em Dead
www.knockemdead.com

Damn Good
www.damngood.com

#1 Resume Writing Service
www.free-resume-tips.com

eResumes
www.eresumes.com

The Riley Guide
www.rileyguide.com

Sample Scannable Resume—Experienced Professional

Virgil Starkwell
150 West Allen Street
Cambridge MA 02138
(617) 555-5555
virgils@email.com

SUMMARY
Accounting manager with eight years' experience in general ledger, accounts payable, and financial reporting. MBA in Management. Proficient in Windows, Lotus 1-2-3, and Excel.

EXPERIENCE
MALCOLM CORPORATION, Newton MA
Accounting Manager, 1996–present

Manage a staff of six in general ledger and accounts payable. Responsible for the design and refinement of financial reporting package. Assist in month-end closings.

Established guidelines for month-end closing procedures, speeding up closing by five business days.

Implemented team-oriented cross-training program within accounting group, increasing productivity of key accounting staff.

DAKOTA & SOPHIA COMPANY, Wellesley MA
Senior Accountant, 1993–1996

Managed accounts payable, general ledger, transaction processing, and financial reporting. Supervised staff of two.

Developed management reporting package, including variance reports and cash flow reporting.

Staff Accountant, 1992–1993

Managed accounts payable including vouchering, cash disbursements, and bank reconciliation. Wrote and issued policies. Maintained supporting schedules used during year-end audits. Trained new employees.

EDUCATION
MBA in Management, Northeastern University, Boston MA, 1994
BS in Accounting, Boston College, Boston MA 1992

ASSOCIATIONS
National Association of Accountants

Sample Scannable Resume—Recent College Graduate

Virgil Starkwell
150 West Allen Street
Cambridge MA 02138
(617) 555-1212

SUMMARY
Accounting major with two years' internship experience in general ledger, accounts payable, and financial reporting. Proficient in Windows, Lotus 1-2-3, and Excel.

EDUCATION
BS in Accounting, Boston College, Boston MA, 2000

WORK EXPERIENCE
MALCOLM CORPORATION, Newton MA
Internship, 1999–present

Assisted accounting manager in general ledger and accounts payable. Supported staff of six in month-end closings.

DAKOTA & SOPHIA COMPANY, Wellesley MA
Internship, 1998–1999

Assisted senior accountant in the management of accounts payable, general ledger, transaction processing, and financial reporting.

Helped to develop management reporting package, including variance reports and cash flow reporting.

Learned about accounts payable including vouchering, cash disbursements, and bank reconciliation. Helped to write and issue policies.

COLLEGE ACTIVITIES
Association of Accounting Majors
Founder

Future Accountants of America
President

ASSOCIATIONS
National Association of Accountants

Career City
CUTTING EDGE CAREERS

CAREERS.N33.COM

Interview

Topics:

Question:

Answer:

Chapter 7
Creating the Perfect Cover Letter

Is This Business or Is It Personal?

When writing a cover letter, there are two different styles to choose from: business (also known as block style) and personal. In a business style letter, all of the letter's elements (return address, salutation, body, and complimentary close) begin at the left margin. In the personal style cover letter, the return address, date, and complimentary close begin at the centerline of the page, and each paragraph is indented. When choosing which style is right for you, keep in mind how awkward the spacing in an e-mail can be. For this reason, if you are sending your cover letter via e-mail, it is best to use a business style. If you are sending your cover letter along to be scanned, either style is fine.

In the ever-evolving and fast-paced world of Internet job searching, taking the time to personalize your resume with a cover letter may seem out of place—IT'S NOT! Yet, as necessary a part of the job search process as a cover letter is, it is also the most overlooked. If you've ever had the experience where you've been in an interview or engaged in a conversation with someone and you think of just the right thing to say—one hour after the fact—then you should certainly appreciate the role of the cover letter.

The cover letter can serve as many different things: it can be the introduction to you as a person and not just you as a job seeker, or it can help explain and/or clear up any part of your resume that you think may be misunderstood. For example, if you have a bit of a lapse in employment because you took time off to raise a family, the cover letter can bring this fact to light. By personalizing the letter, you can also help to further illustrate why you would be the perfect match for the specific company you are applying to, not just any company in your field. Should you have a contact within the company or know a friend of the hiring manager, the cover letter offers you the opportunity to state this fact and do a bit of networking. The cover letter is all these things and more.

While the cover letter can certainly do wonders for your career and the way in which you are perceived by a certain company, if can also backfire horrendously. If written sloppily or without thought, a cover letter can also serve to tarnish your image in the eyes of a company. While you want the cover letter to be informative and to go one step beyond what the resume says, you don't want to give away too much information. What you're essentially trying to do is market yourself and grab an audience. If you can learn how to write a good sales pitch, you can learn how to write an effective cover letter.

Aside from some technical details, the cover letter that you send via e-mail and the one that you send through regular mail are exactly the same. The only thing you need to watch out for with an electronic cover letter is that there is no strange spacing, styling, fonts, etc. The cover letter should be as plain looking as your resume. If you use an 11-point Times New Roman font on your resume, you should do so on your cover letter as well. The most important thing to remember is that the cover letter is there simply to tie together the package that is you; if an employer likes what they see, you will be called in for an interview.

Format

The first thing an employer will notice about your cover letter, before having read your excellent use of grammar and perfect execution of a few five-syllable words, is its appearance. The Internet has a funny way of rearranging sentences and paragraphs in a document, making them look completely different from how you had intended. It is important that you don't try to get too fancy and, in the process, damage the overall neat presentation of your cover letter.

Return Address

Your return address should appear at the top margin, without your name. Depending on whether you have chosen to use a business style or personal style, the information will either begin at the left margin or start at the centerline. The only abbreviation that should appear in the return address is the state abbreviation. Anything else is unacceptable. Be sure to include your phone number in this information as well, as it is quite possible that your cover letter and resume could get separated at some point, and you want to make sure it's easy to contact you.

Date

Immediately following your return address, you should include the date that you are sending the letter. Again, depending on which letter style you choose, the date will either begin at the left margin or start at the centerline. The date should always start in the same place as your return address, just one line below. Make sure that you write the entire date out; don't abbreviate. DO: May 22, 2000 DON'T: 5/22/00

Cover Letter Blunders

"My experience as an Invintory specialist and Camp Councilor prove my abilities to work well at your software company."

• • •

"I am excited by the prospect of growing with {   } and look forward to discussing your needs."

Inside Address

A few lines below the date, you will want to include the inside address. This is the full address of the person and company to whom you are sending your resume. Be sure to write the addressee's full name on the first line. Subsequent lines should include the person's title, the company's full name, and the full mailing address.

As the most important part of the letter—the body—is what will follow the inside address, you want to make sure that it stands out. Generally, you should try and center the body vertically on the page. One way in which you can do this is by manipulating the spacing around the inside address. If your letter is short, you can begin the inside address anywhere from six to eight lines below the date. For longer letters, you may want to start the address just two lines beneath the date.

Salutation

The salutation should appear two lines below the inside address. The salutation should always begin "Dear Mr. So-and-So" or "Dear Ms. So-and-So" and be followed by a colon. Even if you have chatted with Mr. or Ms. So-and-So previously and they asked to be referred to as "Bob" or "Carol," a cover letter salutation is not the place to begin your first-name-basis relationship. In some cases, like when responding to a blind advertisement, you won't know either the name or the gender to which you're writing. In cases like these, a "Dear Sir or Madam" will do just fine.

Body

Obviously, the body of the cover letter is the most important part; this is where you get your chance to shine. Again, if you're using a business style cover letter, you'll want to start each paragraph at the left-hand margin; if you're using a personal style, you will want to indent with each new paragraph. You want to keep the letter succinct, but not too sparse. Including a cover letter just to say "I have enclosed a resume" is a waste of your time as well as the employer's. Three or four short paragraphs is an ideal length (assuming this fits on one page). Any cover letter that reaches more than one page in length could be considered self-indulgent and is not likely to get read (not completely, at least).

Content

Before sitting down and pontificating about all the many job seekers out there and why you are the best one for the job, stop and think: does anyone really want to read this? Before you actually write the cover letter, you should think about the most important things you would want to tell an employer were they to give you 60 seconds to pitch yourself as a candidate. If you know how to write a good sales pitch, you should have no trouble selling yourself as a potential employee.

Making It Personal

One of the best ways to get your cover letter noticed is to personalize it. If you are responding to a help wanted advertisement, you more than likely have a contact name to go along with the job description. Make sure that you address your letter to the specific person mentioned, not just "Dear Sir or Madam:" Not spending the time to personalize each letter and, instead, sending out a mass mailing of cover letters and resumes displays a bit of desperation on your part; you don't care where you get hired, as long as it's a job. Employers need to be coddled, too; they need to know that you are impressed with their organization and that you want to work there, not just anywhere!

If you are sending out an unsolicited resume, try to determine the appropriate person to whom you should address your cover letter. In mid-sized companies, a department manager is often involved in the initial screening process. In larger companies, your resume may have to go through the Human Resources or Personnel Department to be considered for employment; if this is the case, try to find out the name of the Human Resources Manager and address your cover letter and resume to this person. Simple details like this can really make a difference in the eyes of a potential employer.

Getting Over Your Phone Phobia

One of the most useful tools to use when writing a cover letter, even if you plan on sending it through the Internet, is the telephone. Before sending out a resume, you should call each company and verify the address and recipient's name, etc. If you are replying to a recent help wanted advertisement, this is unnecessary. However, if you are sending an unsolicited resume and/or responding to an outdated help wanted advertisement, it is best to call and double check that the information you have is correct. When faced with a person's name that could be either a man or a woman, that's another time you'll want to pick up the phone and call. What's more embarrassing: calling the company and asking if "Chris Smith" is a man or a woman, or sending "Christine Smith" a letter that starts "Dear Sir:"?

Getting Through

Constant change is just the nature of the business world, and you can bet this extends to the employees that work for these companies as well. In the time it takes for you to call and verify a person's name and title and the time it takes for your correspondence to reach their desk, someone new could be in this position. For this reason, it is important that you put a person's title as well as their name on any correspondence. It's kind of the "Joe Smith or Current Resident" philosophy; should the person you're mailing to not occupy that position any longer, a successor will know it's okay to open the mail.

Showcasing Your Knowledge

Sending your cover letter and resume to a specific person is not the only way in which you can personalize your application. Another great way to sell yourself to a company is to show them that you know what they do. Far too often, applicants send in a resume and cover letter claiming they would be a perfect match for the company when, in fact, they have no experience in the company's field. Before applying for a position, make sure you know what the company actually does and be sure that they hire for your type of work. This can get especially confusing in industries that are closely related, like advertising, marketing, and public relations. Just because many of the tasks performed by these types of companies are similar does not make them the same. Just because you have worked as a marketing assistant does not make you a shoe-in for a public relations position. When you do know what a company does, tailor the cover letter so that it applies to company ABC in particular. It also shows the company how hard a worker you are; if you're willing to put this much effort into a cover letter, imagine what you could do as a full-time employee.

Highlighting Your Accomplishments

The idea of the cover letter is not to repeat what can be seen in your resume, it's to give the employer a bit more insight into your capabilities and why you would make a good employee. One way to peak an employer's interest is to offer up one or two of your strongest accomplishments or achievements. Think of the one accomplishment you've made—in school or work—that you are most proud of, and briefly describe it in your letter. Showing pride in your work and offering up such a personal story will increase your chances of being remembered.

The Cover Letter: Piece by Piece

While following a certain cover letter recipe would be the easiest route to success, unfortunately, there isn't one. As each person is at a different point in his or her professional life and has accomplished different things, there is no way to tell someone exactly what to include without knowing his or her past. Yet, by following a specific four-paragraph model, creating the perfect cover letter can be made a bit easier.

First Paragraph

State the position that you are applying for. If you are responding to a help wanted advertisement, cite the source where you found the job description. *Example:* "I would like to apply for the position of child care director advertised in the *Daily Planet*." or "I am interested in applying for the position of child care director that is listed on the *CareerCity.com* Web site."

Second Paragraph

Indicate the skills and knowledge that you could contribute to this specific company and show how your qualifications would benefit them. If you're responding to an advertisement, talk about how your skills relate to the job's requirements. This is not a time for excuses or negativity; don't talk about the things you *can't* do! *Example:* "I am a licensed child care provider in the state of Ohio with five years' experience working in a private center, facilitating the care of over 50 children. In this capacity, I have been solely responsible for supervising 10 children, ranging in age from six months to five years. My duties include distributing meals and snacks, supervising playtime, and developing and instructing the children in a variety of educational and stimulating activities."

Third Paragraph

If possible (and true), illustrate not only how you meet the job's requirements, but also how you *exceed* them. You don't want to portray yourself as just another candidate, you want to show them that you are an exceptional candidate, and one that they would be lucky to employ. This is your chance to mention any of your biggest accomplishments and honors, and talk about instances where you've risen to a challenge or gone above and beyond the call of duty. If you have any testimonials or commendations that might be appropriate, you may want to quote a sen-

tence. *Example:* "I also have experience working with children in a range of other settings, having held positions such as private nanny, camp counselor, and gymnastics instructor. I am also the author of a children's book, *Home We Go!,* a book that Gregory Michaels from *Child Care Today* called "insightful and knowledgeably executed."

Fourth Paragraph

Close the letter by saying how much you look forward to hearing from the company. If you wish, you can also thank them for their consideration. Whatever you do, don't ask for an interview; it's a bit too presumptuous on your part. If an employer is interested in speaking with you further, *they'll* contact *you*; asking for an interview won't persuade them of anything. Don't tell them you will call them either; many job advertisements say "No Phone Calls" specifically for this reason. If you send your resume and have not heard anything after one or two weeks, a call is acceptable, though never necessary.

Complimentary Close

The complimentary close should be placed two lines beneath the body of the letter, aligned with your return address and the date. Keep the closing simple—a "Sincerely," will do just fine. "Yours truly," "Love," or any other line won't get you any closer to the interviewer's desk. If you're sending the cover letter to be scanned, you may type your full name three lines below the closing and sign above your typed name in black ink. If you are sending your cover letter via e-mail, typing your full name on the line below your closing is fine. Don't bother with a fancy computer-assisted signature, it will only wind up taking up additional space.

What Makes a Great Cover Letter?

Appropriate Writing Style

You always know just what to say and how to make people laugh uncontrollably. Come on comedians, you know who you are! While comical banter is fine for after-work cocktails or around-the-water-cooler chitchat, it has no place in a cover letter. You never know who will be reading you cover letter and you never know whether or not they'll have a sense of humor. That said, it's best to keep things on a professional level in writing style and tone.

Writing a cover letter in the appropriate style is a lot like a balancing act. The style should be formal but polite, and objective but persuasive. You want to sound enthusiastic, but not overzealous. You want to be sure to illustrate self-confidence in your abilities without coming off as arrogant or boastful. Above all, you want to maintain a constant respect for the employer. *Example:* "Currently, I am a writer for the *Vertov Film Journal,* a monthly entertainment magazine. In addition, I am capable of shooting, printing, and developing 35-mm, black and white film. In my last year at Villanova University, I researched, wrote, and edited a one-hundred-page senior honors thesis on the filmmaker Sergei Eisenstein. I enjoyed that project immensely, and would enjoy researching film and film-related literature on a daily basis."

Solid Evidence

Just because we say something is true does not necessarily mean it is so. It's unfortunate, but that's the way of the world; people want evidence of accomplishments and achievements, and the workplace is no different. Just because you tell a potential employer that you were an "indispensable asset" to your last company does not mean that that is, in fact, the case. What sort of corroboration do you have to prove that you were a key employee? By providing an employer with numbers and other key accomplishments, you are proving your worth. Again, the tone should be professional, not haughty. Example: "While General Manager at Cozy Restaurant, I supervised a team that increased revenues by 35 percent in 18 months." Even if your job is not numbers-driven, you can still provide some examples to demonstrate your skills. Example: "At Thompson Corporation, I advanced from telephone fundraiser to field manager to canvassing director within two years."

Autograph, Please

If you're sending out a resume to be scanned, you must sign the cover letter. PLEASE DON'T FORGET TO DO THIS! As with many other minor details, employers are likely to dissect this oversight. Instead of thinking you were in such a hurry to get hired by this particular company that you rushed the cover letter right into the envelope, they're more apt to think that you just didn't care enough to remember to sign it.

Skills Trouncing Traits

While being an extremely goal-oriented individual or a reliable, trustworthy employee are all things that any employer would be happy to find, this is something they must decide on their own. Again, just because you tell them that you are "loyal" doesn't mean they have to believe you. If you have a choice of listing specific skills or some of your many wonderful attributes on a resume, choose to list your actual skills. First of all, like a resume, an employer is much more likely to search out skills than they would an attribute. As you don't have much time or space to waste on your cover letter, reserve talking about your personal qualities until the interview. Example: A sentence like "I am fluent in C+, Pascal, and COBOL" is a much better choice than saying "I am a goal-oriented, highly skilled computer programmer."

Eloquent Language

You don't have to be a published author to write a good cover letter, but you do have to know what is eloquent and what is not. People often fail to recognize the power of the English language; by choosing just the right words, you can turn a mediocre cover letter into a persuasive sales pitch. Your language should be assertive and articulate, yet easy to read and polite. You should also make sure you're not being too long-winded. The best cover letters are those that do their job with the fewest words possible.

While electronic and scannable resumes don't allow for much in the way of action verbs, the cover letter is a different story. Using action verbs like "achieved," "devised," facilitated," "generated," and "implemented" as opposed to passive verbs like "was" and "did" is part of what makes a persuasive cover letter. Change any sentences like "I was responsible for streamlining . . . " to "I streamlined . . ."

Omission of Technical Terminology

While a future boss will probably be thrilled to hear you rattling off all the industry jargon and career-specific catch phrases, it is not a good idea to lace your cover letter with such language. As it

Cover Letter Blunders

"When I recently came across your add for a Engineer, I was excited."

• • •

"Realizing how busy are, I would greatly appreciate a chance to meet with you in person."

Thesaurus and Dictionary:
A Dynamic Duo

Since it may be necessary for you to get a little help with your cover letter in the eloquence department, always remember that a thesaurus and a dictionary are a writer's two best friends. What many people don't realize is that these two books complement one another; they are not competing reference tools, nor can they be used interchangeably.

For example, if you've used the word "create" far too many times in your cover letter, you can consult a thesaurus and find that "craft," "build," and "construct" are other words that could be used. Yet, what you'll also find is that words such as "establish," "conceive," and "give rise to" are also synonyms for "create." As any given word can have several different meanings, it is necessary to have a dictionary on hand as well. That way, when you find a synonym that you would like to use, you can make sure it makes sense in the context of the sentence.

is often the case that a resume will go through a human resources or personnel professional before actually reaching your department of interest, you want to make sure that the cover letter is reader-friendly, not just occupation-friendly.

Avoidance of Catch Phrases

After combing through enough help wanted ads and career-related literature, it's very likely that you'll be talking like a seasoned headhunter. Still, regardless of how much employment argot you pick up, resist the temptation to include them in your cover letter. You don't want to make your skills sound like an insincere mirror of the skills required for the job, though you do want the employer to know your qualifications. The best way to counter this tendency is to respond to the job description with evidence of your abilities. Example: If a job description calls for a "dedicated achiever with proven leadership skills," make sure to mention that fact that you "supervised a staff of 20 and increased the number of projects completed before deadline by 50 percent."

Mentioning Pertinent Information

Here's the scenario: you're currently living in Seattle and you're responding to an ad in New York. Unless you mention in your cover letter your willingness to relocate, an employer might be confused that you didn't understand the position clearly. This does not mean that you wouldn't be called in to interview, but by making mention of your readiness to relocate, you have already answered the question for the employer.

So that there is no misunderstanding or wasted time exchanged between employer and candidate, many companies will request that you forward your salary requirements. If this is the case with a job you are applying to, it is best to respond to this in your cover letter, with a salary range. If you're really interested in a particular position and are willing to take a dip in salary, you can also mention that salary is "negotiable."

Action Verbs

If you're struggling to come up with an interesting way in which to present yourself on paper, consider using some of the following action verbs to spice up the language in your cover letter.

Achieved	Directed	Launched	Resolved
Administered	Discovered	Maintained	Restored
Advised	Distributed	Managed	Restructured
Analyzed	Eliminated	Marketed	Revised
Arranged	Established	Mediated	Scheduled
Assembled	Evaluated	Monitored	Selected
Assisted	Examined	Negotiated	Served
Attained	Executed	Obtained	Sold
Budgeted	Expanded	Operated	Solved
Built	Expedited	Ordered	Streamlined
Calculated	Facilitated	Organized	Studied
Collaborated	Formulated	Participated	Supervised
Collected	Founded	Performed	Supplied
Compiled	Generated	Planned	Supported
Completed	Headed	Prepared	Tested
Computed	Identified	Presented	Trained
Conducted	Implemented	Processed	Updated
Consolidated	Improved	Produced	Upgraded
Constructed	Increased	Proposed	Wrote
Consulted	Initiated	Provided	
Controlled	Installed	Published	
Coordinated	Instituted	Purchased	
Created	Instructed	Reduced	
Designed	Integrated	Regulated	
Determined	Interpreted	Reorganized	
Developed	Interviewed	Represented	
Devised	Invented	Researched	

Vigilant Proofreading

Aside from being a plain embarrassment, misspellings and other mistakes are enough to take you out of the running for employment consideration. Especially if something obvious is misspelled (like your name, the position you are applying for, etc.), proofreading errors can be very costly. You should be extremely cautious when proofreading your resume; check it as many times as makes you feel comfortable, and enlist the help of several friends (preferably ones with strong English backgrounds).

Even if you have a built-in spell checker on your computer, remember that most of these don't proof for grammar, and will not recognize misused words. Most programs do not recognize incorrect punctuation either, so it is important to pay particular attention to these things when you proof the cover letter yourself. Make sure you are using the correct forms of "there," "their," and "they're"; and "to," "two," and "too." Be sure that words aren't missing a letter—"I currently wok for ILG Incorporated" instead of "I currently work for ILG Incorporated." Also proof carefully to make certain letters within specific words did not get mixed up to create a new meaning. How embarrassing would it be to see that you wrote "I barley have a minute" instead of "I barely have a minute"?

If and when you do find mistakes, do not fix them with a pen, pencil, or White-Out. Make the changes on the computer and reprint a copy of the letter. Before you send a cover letter via e-mail, make sure it has been carefully proofed, because once you hit that SEND button there's no retrieving it.

Cover Letter Pitfalls to Avoid

Along with all the many elements that comprise a great resume, there are several blunders that you should try desperately to avoid. Although many of them seem far too obvious, they happen far too often! The following examples have been adapted from actual cover letters. They epitomize "the wrong way to write a cover letter." Needless to say, none of the applicants wound up getting the job in these cases.

Stating Unrelated Career Goals

One of the most important things an employer wants to hear is how dedicated an employee you will be when hired. The last thing he or she wants to hear is that you are merely looking for a job to pass the time, and that you're not interested in the available opportunity as a career move. Make sure you express a genuine interest in the position and all that it entails.

WRONG: "While my lifelong goal is to become a famous actor, I am currently exploring the possibility of taking on some proofreading work while I await my big break."

RIGHT: "I am extremely interested in your available proofreading position, and I am confident in my ability to make a long-term contribution to your capable staff."

This is not to say that you should lie about your goals and abilities; but there is no need to take yourself out of the running by telling an employer about your lifelong dream that may never come true. Basically, what you're telling the employer is that the available position is an acceptable job to tide you over until something better comes along. Aside from being narcissistic, comments like that are completely unmannerly.

Using Clichés and Obvious Comparisons

In everyday conversations, clichés and obvious comparisons run rampant. While their intention is to further illustrate a point or feeling, all they really serve to do is make your speech uninteresting. The purpose of the cover letter is to help you stand out from an already crowded pool of applicants—that is the real "light at the end of the tunnel." Don't eliminate yourself from the running by using the same, trite expressions that half the other applicants have already employed. If you're feeling tempted to say that you're "as smart as a whip," think about what it is you are really trying to convey. At the heart of the letter, what is it that distinguishes you from the rest of the applicants? Find an eloquent way to state *that* and use that sentence instead.

Obvious comparisons aren't as immediately recognizable as many clichés, but they're BAD, BAD, BAD all the same. What you may think is an in-the-know kind of business term may, in fact, be

Details, Details, Details

Can and May
WRONG: "I may be reached at 555/555-5555."

RIGHT: "I can be reached at 555/555-5555."

Fused Participle
WRONG: "I appreciate you taking the time to speak to me."

RIGHT: "I appreciate your taking the time to speak to me."

just as trite as a cliché. Comments like "I am a people person," "I'm a jack of all trades," "I wear many hats," "I am honing my skills," or "I'm a multitask-oriented kind of person" can be just as detrimental to the overall effect of your letter.

Creating Wasted Space

Ideally, a cover letter will be brief but to the point; there's nothing a potential employer hates seeing more than wasted space. As the cover letter should be short in the first place, there's no reason—if you're a qualified candidate—why there should be wasted space or irrelevant information. Like the "Hobbies & Other Interests" that have no place on a resume, superfluous information should not appear in your cover letter. If you're applying for a job as a sales manager, the employer wants to know about your relevant experiences in business, school, etc.

WRONG: "As my resume illustrates, I possess the business experience and educational background to succeed as the sales manager of your software division. In addition, I am an avid dancer and was named the Disco King of Omaha in 1979."

RIGHT: "I have several years' experience in developing sales and marketing strategies. I have been involved in a number of employment situations, including a self-owned business, in which I successfully applied sales techniques, including cold calling, telemarketing, and prospecting. In my first two years at Nojunk Software, I increased the client base by 25 percent. While at the Hoffman Corporation, I was part of a sales team that generated a record-breaking $10 million in one year. In addition, I have held numerous positions where I supervised and developed personnel and assisted in facilitating daily operations."

Sending Form Letters

One technique that is *never* a recommended strategy is sending a mass mailing, where you send a form letter to a large number of companies. The many reasons why this is a bad idea should be obvious. The key to winning an employer's interest is to try to make a personal connection. By employing the certain techniques described earlier, you should be able to personalize your cover letter

Cover Letter Blunders

"Dear Smada Corporation, I am very excited about the possiblity of working for Regal Corporation after reading all about you on the Internet."

• • •

"Although my background is slight (see resume), I think I can offer you a genuine interest in a job as an desktop publishing assistant."

enough to make it speak to not only the individual reviewing it, but the company as a whole. That said, sending the same letter to various companies is in no way helping you to *personalize* your applications. Each cover letter that you send should be tailored to the company to which you are sending it; a cover letter should demonstrate not only your desire to work for that company in particular, but your familiarity with their business and company philosophy.

Demonstrating Your Fabulous Comic Timing

Tempting as it may be to showcase your comedic skills, unless you're applying for a position as a comedian, keep the amusing anecdotes and other "funny" stories to yourself. Sharing such personal information with a stranger indicates a lack of respect and lack of seriousness. The tone of your cover letter should always be professional, polite, and respectful.

Giving Erroneous Company Information

If you feel the need to mention your familiarity with a company's products or services, make sure you do your homework. Giving erroneous company information to a person who *actually works for the company* can be pretty embarrassing. Telling a reference book editor how often "I read your magazine" is not the best first impression to make. On the other hand, *pretending* to know something about a company by using vague and general statements can be equally off-putting to an employer. Saying something like "I know an awful lot about your company" or "I am quite familiar with your product line" may signal that you don't have a clue about what this company does.

Being Too Desperate

Regardless of how far behind you are on your rent, you should never sound desperate in a cover letter. While enthusiasm is always highly regarded, sob stories and desperate pleas for employment are just plain pitiful. Determination is good; desperation is bad!

WRONG: "I really, really need this restaurant manager job so that I can pay my rent and eat something other than a bag of potato chips for dinner."

Cover Letter Dos and Don'ts

Don't Philosophize
DON'T: "Dear Mr. Smith:

Finding the right person for the job can be a difficult, costly, and frustrating experience."

DO: "Dear Mr. Smith:

I would like to apply for the position of research assistant advertised in the *Daily Times*."

RIGHT: "I have continually heard many favorable reviews of Ristorante, and I have always enjoyed my own dining experiences there. I would be interested in joining your management team and hope that you will give me the opportunity to discuss this further."

Being Fanatical

While being too desperate is a bad thing when it comes to cover letters, being too enthusiastic can have a negative impact as well. It's okay to be passionate about your career, you just want to make sure that you don't go overboard in your declaration of excitement. Again, determination and enthusiasm are key to winning an employer over; being fanatical about a position can make an employer apprehensive and ill at ease. Describing such excitement is also one place where clichés can often come into play.

WRONG: "I am sending my resume in response to your recently advertised position of account executive at your advertising firm. I have just a few words for you: Your Search Is Over! Since the time I was a child, I have sat in front of the television set for at least five hours a day, just flipping from commercial to commercial. Advertising is in my blood, I can feel it pumping. That said, you'd be crazy not to consider me *the* answer to your needs."

RIGHT: "I am very interested in the Account Executive position listed recently in *Advertising Times,* and I am including my resume as an application. I am familiar with many of the accounts Ads Plus has worked on, and would love the opportunity to contribute my own ideas and creativity to your efforts."

Stating the Obvious

When a new job opportunity arises, it's completely understandable that you're excited about it. One mistake that people often make (and one that can be a bit bothersome to employers) is a tendency to "dumb down" their resume or make statements that are completely obvious. Applicants treat the cover letter as the Cliff

Notes to their resume. Anything that can be learned from just looking at the resume should not be restated in the cover letter.

WRONG: "Hello! My name is Fiona Pickles. I am a graduate of Syracuse University and I am currently working for WBAD Radio in Topeka, Kansas. The reason I am writing is because I would like to be considered as a suitable applicant for your current On-Air Promotions Director. This is a position that I saw advertised on the *Tuscaloosa Times* Web site at *www.tuscaloosa-times.com* on Monday, May 22."

RIGHT: "Please accept this letter as an application for the On-Air Promotions Director position advertised in the *Tuscaloosa Times*. My confidential resume is enclosed for your review."

Including Personal Photos

Though this is a common mistake, it's a pretty easy one to avoid: unless you are applying for a position as a model, actor, or other performing arts position, it's completely inappropriate and unnecessary to include a picture of yourself.

Confessing Your Shortcomings

Job seekers often treat cover letters as a confessional; they tend to volunteer their weaknesses right off the bat in an attempt to deflect an employer's objections. The reason this is such a bad thing to do is that the purpose of the cover letter is to illustrate your strengths, not illuminate your weaknesses. If you are applying to a field that you have no actual experience in, you want to highlight your past experiences and skills that you have learned that could in some way help you in this new career.

WRONG: "Although I have no experience in feature film making, I have always liked movies and think that I would enjoy working as a production assistant because of my deep interest."

RIGHT: "In my experiences at B.E. Ellis Publishing, I was continually faced with the challenge of managing a project from start to finish and coordinating all the people and activities that go into making a book a success."

Cover Letter Dos and Don'ts

Don't Be Longwinded

DON'T: "I understand that a brief letter such as this one cannot fully inform you as to my true personality, charisma, and professional goals, and it is for this reason that I welcome the opportunity to speak with you, whether it be for a preliminary telephone conversation or a face-to-face meeting."

DO: "I thank you for taking the time to review my credentials and look forward to speaking with you in the future."

Misrepresenting Yourself

Lying on an application or during an interview is always grounds for dismissal, even after you've been working for a company for quite some time. Hence, you should never, *ever* misrepresent yourself or your experiences on a resume or in a cover letter. If you accomplish something that you think is important, say so, and offer the information up in the best possible light. Now is not the time to be modest, as there are plenty of other applicants that won't hold back. Don't feel the need to boast to the point of exaggeration and, in the process, misrepresentation. Remember, all information *can* be verified, so stick to the facts.

WRONG: "In June, I a graduated with honors from The School at the Art Institute of Chicago. In the course of my studies, I played three varsity sports, and was the President of 15 major on-campus organizations while concurrently holding four jobs and an Internship. Since beginning my freelance photography career three months ago, I have won several hundred artistic competitions and am considered by many to be the nation's best photographer under the age of 40."

RIGHT: "After graduating with honors in June from The School at the Art Institute of Chicago, I have been lucky enough to maintain a consistently busy freelance career. In August of 2000, the editors of *Photography Now* named me one of the "Most Promising Newcomers.""

Making Demands

As you are the one looking to an employer for help, now is not the time to ask "What can you do for me?" You should never make demanding statements or be presumptuous in what you ask and tell an employer.

WRONG: "Let's meet next Wednesday at 4:00 P.M., when I will be available to discuss my candidacy further."

RIGHT: "I welcome the opportunity to meet with you to further discuss my qualifications and your needs. Thank you for your time and consideration."

Forgetting to Enclose Your Resume

Well, you keep *referring* to the enclosed resume, but the employer can't seem to find one. Rather than spend their own time making you aware of this fatal oversight, an employer is much more likely to move on to the next candidate who *did* remember to include her or his resume. When sending your resume via e-mail, this can be a particularly costly mistake, as the last thing you want to do is send a second message with the subject heading "Ooops!"

Including Personal Information

Again, like in a resume, there is no need to include personal information in your cover letter. Not only is it illegal for an employer to ask you such personal questions such as your age, marital status, race, and religious affiliation, but it's completely irrelevant to what you can do in the workplace . . . *any* workplace.

Employing Third Person Pronouns

Like the applicant that refers to themselves as a "natural born" applicant, candidates who refer to themselves in the third person can make an employer ill at ease. Is the applicant actually *writing* the cover letter? Does the applicant refer to him/herself as "Joe" or "Barbara" in normal conversation? How many personalities does this person actually have? These are the kinds of questions that float around an employer's head when they read a cover letter where the applicant refers to him or herself in the third person rather than the first. What you may think is a cute or creative approach to presenting yourself and your qualifications may come off as just downright discomfiting to an employer.

WRONG: "Johanna Malkovich is a highly qualified sales executive with over five years' experience in the business. She is extremely intelligent and possesses strong communication skills, both written and oral. She also comes with an extensive client base."

RIGHT: "I am a highly qualified sales executive with over five years of relevant experience in the business. I possess strong com-

munication skills, both written and oral, and have an extensive client base."

Employing an Inappropriate Tone

Before sending your cover letter and resume off, you should carefully review each sentence and make sure that it could not be misconstrued in a way that could cost you this opportunity. Dissect each sentence to determine whether or not an employer could mis-interpret what it is you are saying, and recruit a friend to come in and do the same. If you have *any* question about a sentence's wording, rewrite it immediately. Make sure to walk a definite middle line between extremely formal and completely informal, opting for a polite and professional tone that is always respectful.

Using a Gimmick

Sure, you're trying to sell yourself in the job market, but unlike in advertising, gimmicks don't often work. Being tempted to send in a video resume or singing telegram may *seem* like a good idea, but it's not! Employers will be much more impressed by a well-crafted letter that clearly pinpoints all your achievements and qualifications than by your lovely singing voice. Straying from the norm can immediately label you a complete eccentric, a label that is not likely to get you hired in many companies (though it's one that will probably make you remembered, though not to your advantage).

WRONG: Sending your resume attached to a bathing suit that claims "I'm diving into the applicant pool!"

RIGHT: Sending a properly-formatted and well-written resume along with an eloquent cover letter expressing your interest in the available position.

Making Typographical Errors

When you're sending out dozens of applications, it can be easy to make a mistake. Just remember how costly one mistake can be when it comes to looking for employment; many hiring managers are likely to reject a cover letter that contains errors, even those that you may deem minor. One experienced book editor, on the prowl for new employment, made the mistake of spelling his own name wrong while, at the same time, discussing his monomaniacal attention to detail! But don't just think it's your own name you have to watch out for; many hiring managers take offense when their own name or the name of their company it spelled wrong or referenced incorrectly. Some of the most common mistakes job seekers make are as follows:

- Misspelling the hiring contact's name or title in the inside address or salutation or on the envelope.
- Forgetting to change the name of the company you're applying to each time it is used in your cover letter. For example, the hiring manager at PETA might not be too thrilled to hear how enthusiastic you are about working for Just Fur You magazine.
- Indicating your interest in a specific position and mentioning a different position in the body of your letter. For example, one candidate who was applying to a position as a Telemarketing Manager later referred to her excitement about the Marketing Analyst position.

Making Messy Corrections

If, after reviewing your cover letter, you find some sort of mistake (*any mistake*), you **must** rewrite the letter. There is never an excuse for making corrections directly on the cover letter, regardless of whether you've used white out, scratched the mistake out with a pen, or have attached a Post-It with a brief note. What would an employer think about such a tactic? Probably that you are a) unprofessional, b) lazy, or c) unprofessional *and* lazy!

Forgetting Your John Hancock

If you're sending a hard copy of your resume, don't forget to sign it. All too often, people forget this minor but important detail. Make sure that you sign the cover letter with blue or black ink and do not use a script font as a substitute for your signature.

Cover Letter Dos and Don'ts

Don't Share Your Delusions of Grandeur

DON'T: "As a recent graduate of Pine Ridge College with a degree in political science, I am currently launching my career as a city manager assistant in hopes that I will eventually be elected to the United States presidency where I can eliminate the national deficit as well as put an end to the problems of homelessness, war, and world hunger."

DO: "I would like to apply for the position of city manager assistant due to my strong interest in many civic and governmental issues."

Some Final Dos and Don'ts

DO

- Make sure your phone number, street address, and e-mail address are on the cover letter as well as the resume in case the two get separated.
- Make sure your cover letter is brief (no more than one page) and to the point.
- Emphasize all that you have to offer a company.
- Proofread, Proofread, Proofread!!
- Sign your name on a scannable cover letter; type your name on an electronic cover letter.

DON'T

- Reiterate the same information that can be extracted from your resume; give the employer a glimpse into who you are and what you can do.
- Overuse the personal pronoun "I."
- Send a generic cover letter.

Sample Scannable Cover Letter
Responding to an Advertised Opening

150 West Allen Street
Cambridge, MA 02138
(617) 555-5555
virgils@email.com

May 22, 2000

Mr. Jackson Leslie
Head Nurse
Henderson Hospital
101 Henderson Road
Quincy, MA 12345

Dear Mr. Leslie:

I am responding to your *Nursing News* advertisement for a clinical research nurse.

I am a dedicated professional capable of working with physicians and nursing, laboratory, and professional specialty groups. I have a Bachelor of Science in Nursing and more than fourteen years of responsible experience, ranging from staff nurse and charge nurse to clinical research nurse with a major teaching hospital. My graduate studies have focused on epidemiology and international health. My experience encompasses sound knowledge of nursing quality assurance programs and in-service education programs. Throughout my career, I have worked on studies involving psoriasis, cardiology, AIDS, sickle-cell anemia, amyloid, diabetes, and oncology.

I hope that, after reviewing my resume, we can speak further about the position and my qualifications. I thank you for your time and consideration.

Sincerely,

Virgil Starkwell, R.N., B.S.N.
Virgil Starkwell, R.N., B.S.N.

Sample Scannable Cover Letter
"Cold" Letter to a Potential Employer

150 West Allen Street
Cambridge, MA 02138
(617) 555-5555
virgils@email.com

May 22, 2000

Mr. Jackson Leslie
Human Resources Director
Henderson Publishing Company
101 Henderson Road
Quincy, MA 12345

Dear Mr. Leslie:
I have four years' of publishing experience including two years' of scholarly journal experience in social science, physical science, and engineering, that I would like to put to work at Henderson Publishing Company.

Specifically, I am seeking a position as an associate editor, project editor, or the equivalent in new book or journal development and administration. My qualifications include the following:

- Developed a new book series in sociology through all phases of publication, from author contract negotiation to the creation of a series marketing plan.
- Acquired *Earth Day Every Day*, which was nominated for the Fortmiller Foundation's Prize and is already an academic bestseller.
- Participated in a dynamic engineering program that included the launch of three new journals: *Physical Science*, *Micro Journal*, and the *Journal of Alternative Energy*.
- In addition to a strong background in English literature and the social sciences at the University of Notre Dame, my training has included courses relevant to a position in medical publishing: anatomy, physiology, medical terminology, nursing procedures, biology, and radiographic physics.

I thank you for taking the time to review my credentials and hope to get the opportunity to speak with you further.

Sincerely,

Virgil Starkwell
Virgil Starkwell

Sample Electronic Cover Letter
Responding to an Advertised Opening

150 West Allen Street
Cambridge, MA 02138
(617) 555-5555
virgils@email.com

May 22, 2000

Mr. Jackson Leslie
Director of Social Services
Henderson Agency
101 Henderson Road
Quincy, MA 12345

Dear Mr. Leslie:

I am responding to your advertisement in the *Star Times* in search of a Case Manager. My interest is in pursuing and expanding my professional career in the motivation and guidance of juveniles to achieve positive objectives and personal dignity. It is this goal that has prompted me to forward the attached resume for your review and consideration.

Please note that I have directed and dedicated my efforts, both academically and through the Co-op program at Fordham University, to working with juveniles and prison inmates, guiding them through innovative programs in self-preservation. These programs required extensive communication and interaction with boards of trustees, agency personnel, and the Neighborhood Watch campaign. In addition, I have acquired excellent customer/client relations and communications skills, as well as a sound knowledge of office procedures, in a variety of full-time and part-time positions.

I would welcome a meeting to learn more about your work at Henderson Agency and how I could contribute to your success.

Sincerely,

Virgil Starkwell
Virgil Starkwell

Sample Electronic Cover Letter
"Cold" Letter to a Potential Employer

150 West Allen Street
Cambridge, MA 02138
(617) 555-5555
virgils@email.com

May 22, 2000

Mr. Jackson Leslie
General Manager
Henderson Hotel
101 Henderson Road
Quincy, MA 12345

Dear Mr. Leslie,

In the interest of investigating career opportunities with your company, I am enclosing my resume for your consideration and review.

During the past six years, my positions have ranged from sous chef to executive chef of a restaurant continually rated in the top 100 restaurants and institutions nationwide. As you will note from my resume, my earlier experience includes country clubs, hotels, resorts, and four-star restaurants.

Because of my ability to organize, train, and work effectively with personnel in quality, high-volume restaurants, I am able to maintain a conscientious, highly productive workforce. I have expertise in coordinating activities and directing the indoctrination and training of chefs and other kitchen staff to ensure an efficient and profitable food service.

In addition to being an honors graduate of the Culinary Institute of America, I have received several national and regional awards for my creative culinary skills.

I hope to hear from you if you have need of someone with my qualifications.

Thank you for your consideration.

Sincerely,

Virgil Starkwell
Virgil Starkwell

Chapter 8
Distributing Your Resume

Now that you've got your computer-friendly resume and cover letter ready, the question becomes "Where should I send it?" Without being asked for your electronic or scannable resume specifically, there are three ways in which you can begin circulating it: applicant tracking systems, electronic employment database services, or posting your resume via the Internet.

Applicant Tracking Systems

Applicant tracking systems and in-house resume databases are becoming more and more common in many of today's companies. When an applicant sends in his or her resume, it is automatically entered into this database, regardless of the person's qualifications and whether or not the company is currently hiring for the desired position. Once your resume has been entered, you essentially become a potential candidate for any position that might open up in that company. Rather than spend the money placing a help wanted advertisement, the hiring manager submits a search request using specific keywords and skills. Based on the criteria, the system then brings up a number of matching candidates who might be a good fit for the job and the manager takes it from there. Applicant tracking systems and in-house resume databases will accept both scannable paper resumes as well as electronic resumes sent via e-mail.

Advantages and Disadvantages
Advantages
* Computers are a completely unbiased audience.
* A computer won't be likely to misplace your resume.
* Even when you don't get the job you originally applied for, your qualifications may be suitable for another position in the future, and the computer can alert the hiring manager to this fact.
* You only need to send one resume to a company, even if you are interested in several positions.

Advantages and Disadvantages of Posting Your Resume Online

+ Your resume can be on the employer's desk just minutes after a job has been posted.
+ The cost to you is reduced a great deal by sending your resume through the Internet.
+ Employers from every corner of the world can see your resume and consider you for a potential employee.
- Your privacy can be at risk if you're not careful where you send your resume.

Disadvantages

- Since a computer is looking for specific keywords, it may be more difficult for a recent college graduate or job changer to find a job this way.
- While computers don't have feelings, they are rather sensitive; should you send in an imperfect resume for scanning, it may reject the entire thing rather than overlook your one mistake.

Electronic Employment Database Services

The only difference between an applicant tracking system and an electronic employment database service is that the latter is not in-house; it is a business, run by a third party. You would submit your resume the same way as you would to an applicant tracking system, except you won't know which companies are reviewing your resume. Recruiters and other employment agencies often employ electronic employment databases; when a company calls in a job description, the recruiter can then search their own database to see if they have an applicant matching the employer's needs. Many of these services do require payment, though there are some free ones out there. Prices are generally $50.00 and under. So, it's up to you; if you have the money and are willing to take a chance, check out some of the sites listed below and see which one will work best for you.

CareerXpress
www.careerxpress.com

The Resume Wizard
therezwiz.com

Resucom
www.resucom.com

Resumes Direct
www.tier21.com

Resume Blaster
www.resumeblaster.com

ResumeXPRESS
www.resumexpress.com

Resume Dart
resumedart.com

ResumeZapper
resumezapper.com

Advantages and Disadvantages of Electronic Employment Database Services

+ Candidates have the potential to showcase their skills to hundreds of companies and positions after sending only one resume.
+ It is less time consuming than searching these employers and/or positions out on your own.
- In general, companies don't rely solely on this type of technology.
- Some services can be costly.

Posting Your Resume via the Internet

Posting your resume via online technology consists of more than just finding a resume posting site. Sending your resume via e-mail, or posting it with a commercial online service or newsgroup are all ways that would be considered part of this category. Obviously, when sending your resume through cyberspace, you will want to employ the electronic resume and not the scannable one.

While some resume posting services *do* charge a fee, there are enough free ones out there that you shouldn't have to pay any money to post your resume with a reputable Web site. Check out some of the sites listed on the following pages to find some of the best of the Web.

One way to avoid lots of superfluous phone calls from recruiters and employers in undesirable areas is to post your resume on a geographically specific Web site. That way, recruiters and employers who view your resume will be well aware of your geographical preference. In any given state or metropolitan area, there is bound to be a local career site where you can post your resume. Check out the listings that follow.

Insider Tip

One piece of information that you should put in your cover letter or on your resume (even if just a one-line comment) is whether or not you are looking to relocate. If you would like to stay in a particular area, be sure to indicate that somewhere so that you aren't getting calls from Tokyo when you don't want to step foot outside of Toledo.

Big Money = Big Companies

While the Internet has provided a much more efficient way of looking for work and employees, this does not come without cost. While most job sites are free to job seekers who want to look at job boards, they're certainly not always free to employers looking to fill a position. Companies often have to shell out big bucks to place a help wanted advertisement on a Web site or to view the resumes in an online database. Thus, the majority of companies that can afford such tactics are usually the largest and wealthiest companies around.

In a random sampling of more than 50 *Fortune* 100 companies, more than 85 percent of these companies had their job postings listed on Monster.com, one of the Internet's biggest (and most expensive) job sites. While this is great news for those who want to work for a larger company, job seekers hoping to work for a smaller start-up company may want to stick to smaller sites.

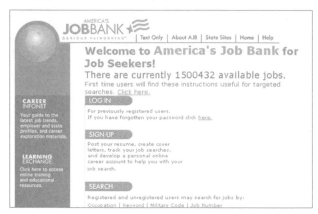

America's Job Bank • *www.ajb.org*

CareerAvenue • *www.careeravenue.com*

CareerBuilder • *careerbuilder.com*

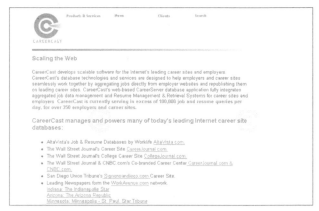

CareerCast, Inc. • *www.careercast.com*

CareerCity.com • *www.careercity.com*

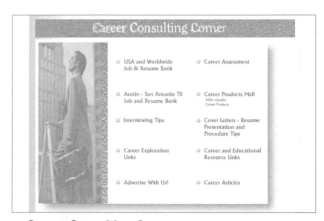

Career Consulting Corner • *www.careercc.com*

CareerEngine • *www.careerengine.com*

Careerfile • *www.careerfile.com*

CareerMart • *www.careermart.com*

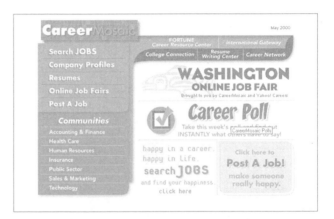

CareerMosaic • *www.careermosaic.com*

CareerPath • *www.careerpath.com*

CareerShop • *www.careershop.com*

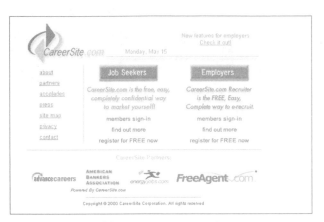

CareerSite • *www.careersite.com*

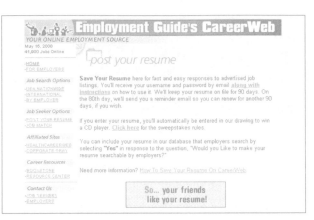

CareerWeb • *www.cweb.com*

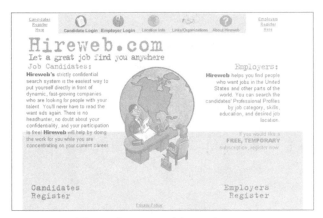

Hireweb • *www.hireweb.com*

HotJobs • *www.hotjobs.com*

HotResume • *www.hotresume.com*

The Internet Job Locator • *www.joblocator.com*

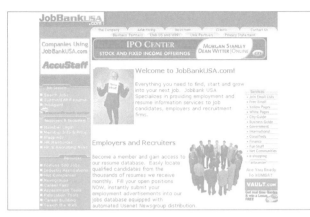

JobBank USA • *www.jobbankusa.com*

JobDirect • *www.jobdirect.com*

JobExchange • *www.jobexchange.com*

JobOptions • *www.joboptions.com*

Jobtrak • *www.jobtrak.com*

Monster.com • *www.monster.com*

6FigureJobs • *www.6figurejobs.com*

US Resume • *www.usresume.com*

Alabama Jobs
www.alabamajobs.com

Arizona Jobs
www.arizona-jobs.com

Arkansas Employment Opportunities
www.bigemployment.com

Atlanta Job Resource Center
www.ajrc.com

California Employment
californiaemployment.com

The California Online Job Network
www.cajobs.com

Carolina Jobs
www.carolina-jobs.com

Colorado Online Job Connection
www.coloradojobs.com

Delaware Jobs
www.delaware-jobs.com

Florida's Preferred Jobs
florida.preferredjobs.com

Georgia Jobs
www.georgia-jobs.com

Hawaii Jobs
www.hawaii-jobs.net

Idaho Jobs
www.idaho-jobs.com

Illinois Jobs
www.illinois-jobs.com

Indiana Jobs
www.indiana-jobs.com

Iowa Jobs
www.iowa-jobs.com

Job Force NY
www.jobforceny.com

Jobs in Alaska
www.jobsalaska.com

Kansas Jobs
www.kc-jobs.com

Kentucky Jobs
www.kentucky-jobs.com

Las Vegas Jobs
www.lasvegasjobs.com

Louisiana Jobs
www.louisiana-jobs.net

Maine Jobs
www.maine-jobs.com

Maryland Jobs
www.maryland-jobs.com

Massachusetts Jobs
www.massachusetts-jobs.com

Michigan Jobs
www.michigan-jobs.com

Minnesota Jobs
www.1-jobsmn.com

Mississippi Jobs
www.mississippi-jobs.com

Missouri Jobs
www.missouri-jobs.net

Montana Jobs
www.montana-jobs.com

Nebraska Jobs
www.nebraska-jobs.com

Nevada Jobs
www.nevada-jobs.com

New Hampshire Jobs
www.newhampshire-jobs.com

New Jersey Jobs
www.newjersey-jobs.net

New Mexico Jobs
www.newmexico-jobs.com

New York Jobs
newyork-jobs.net

North Dakota Jobs
www.northdakota-jobs.com

Ohio Jobs
www.ohio-jobs.net

Oklahoma Jobs
www.oklahoma-jobs.com

Oregon Jobs
www.oregon-jobs.com

Pennsyvania Jobs
www.pennsylvania-jobs.com

Rhode Island Jobs
www.rhodeisland-jobs.com

South Dakota Jobs
www.southdakota-jobs.com

Tennessee Jobs
www.tennessee-jobs.com

Texas Preferred Jobs
texas.preferredjobs.com

Utah Jobs
www.utah-jobs.com

Vermont Jobs
www.vermont-jobs.com

Virginia Jobs
www.virginia-jobs.com

Washington DC's Preferred Jobs
dc.preferredjobs.com

Washington Jobs
www.washington-jobs.com

West Virginia Jobs
www.westvirginia-jobs.com

Wisconsin Jobs
www.wisconsin-jobs.com

Work For You Nebraska
www.nebraskaworkforyou.com

Wyoming Jobs
www.wyoming-jobs.com

Privacy on the Internet

Privacy on the Internet has been a growing concern for years; you've heard stories about it, you've seen movies about it, now it's time to learn the facts. As e-mail and other electronic transmissions need to be sent through a variety of channels before reaching the intended party, it is quite possible that an uninvited third party could somehow intercept your personal message. Hence, you should always assume that the information you are sending could be monitored. Another way in which people can unknowingly jeopardize their privacy on the Internet is by responding to a variety of ads and solicitations that you have not researched fully. The "dream job" that you are applying to could actually be the makings of a really good scam.

There are several ways in which you can retain anonymity while working online. One way to prevent your personal information from getting into the wrong hands is to use an encryption program. By encrypting a message, you make it unreadable to unwanted parties and extremely difficult to encode, even to the most practiced expert. PGP or "Pretty Good Privacy" is one such program that you can use. With over million users, PGP is also one of the most respected encryption programs. You can download PGP for free on many Internet locations. For more information, visit *www.pgp.com*. For more information on retaining anonymity on the Web and being able to surf safely, there are plenty of Web sites that focus on keeping you informed. EPIC (*www.epic.org*); Policy (*www.policy.com*); PrivacyPlace (*www.privacyplace.com*); and Privacy Times (*www.privacytimes.com*) are just a few.

There are also several Web sites out there that focus on helping you discern the legitimate Web sites from the scams. If you are concerned about the legitimacy of a particular Web site, check out Cyber Patrol (*www.cyberpatrol.com*) or SurfWatch (*www.surfwatch.com*) for more information. Learning more about a Web site before posting *any* information is always a good idea, and it's a particularly vital step if you are looking to post your resume on the Internet. Aside from using a patrolling Web site, it's also a good idea to do a little research of your own. You should get as much

information and as many testimonials as you can by visiting a company's Web site and running a search for the company name on a search engine. If you still have questions, don't be afraid to call the company and ask. If the person with whom you're speaking doesn't sound like they're being straight with you or if they don't seem to want to help you, choose another site to post your resume. While most sites are completely legitimate, you always have to be aware of the people out there lurking with interminable Internet know-how and a wrongful agenda.

Chapter 9

Searching for Jobs Online

For one book to claim that it knows all the places to search for a job on the Internet is a complete overstatement. Every single day, new career-related Web sites are being created and older sites are disappearing into the depths of cyberspace Siberia, never to be seen again. Just as ever-changing as the job market is, the Internet job marketplace is a continually evolving area. Still, even if the same site you visited last month is no longer on the Web, there is never a lack of career resources to be found and utilized.

The main way in which one would go about searching out jobs online is to visit one or several of the thousands of online job databases. You've heard their names on television and radio and have seen their ads in newspapers and magazines; now it's time to figure out what they're really all about and find the ones that work best for you.

Nationwide Sites—United States

America's Employers

Web Address: *www.americasemployers.com*
Number of Job Listings: More than 100,000
Industries Included: High-Tech; Computers; Engineering; Medical; Legal; Education
Location of Jobs: United States; Some International
Frequency of Updates: Daily
Search By: Company Name; Job Category; Keyword; Location; Other
Resume Database ☑
Employer Profiles ☑

Summary: Offers tips on job searching and interviewing, an employment agency database, a job search forum chat room, and the "Linkin Library," which connects job seekers to other career-related Web sites. A comprehensive site with listings from Usenet newsgroups and newspapers.

America's Job Bank

Web Address: *www.ajb.org*
Number of Job Listings: More than 1,000,000
Industries Included: All
Location of Jobs: United States
Frequency of Updates: Daily
Search By: Job Category; Job Code Number; Keyword;
Location; Military Occupational Code
Resume Database ☑
Employer Profiles ☑

Summary: Links to state, employer, and private agency
Web sites; offers cover letter services; has a job search
resource library. A joint service from the United States
Department of Labor and state employment offices, this
is an immense database of jobs culled from the combined job databases of 1,800 state employment offices.
The listings contain detailed information including a job
description and educational and work requirements.
Many also contain the salary range.

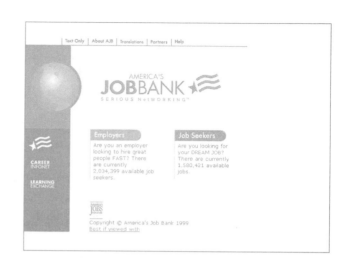

American Jobs

Web Address: *www.americanjobs.com*
Industries Included: All
Location of Jobs: United States
Frequency of Updates: Daily
Search By: Company Name; Job Title; Keyword;
Location
Resume Database ☑
Employer Profiles ☑

Summary: A good, basic career site.

Best Jobs USA

Web Address: *www.bestjobsusa.com*
Number of Job Listings: More than 20,000
Industries Included: All
Location of Jobs: United States
Frequency of Updates: Daily
Search By: Job Category; Keyword; Location
Resume Database ☑
Employer Profiles ☑

Summary: Newsgroup listings, articles from the monthly publication *Employment Review* online, and several other career-related resources such as relocation and salary information. An excellent site that provides a plethora of services and information. *Employment Review* offers a wealth of career advice to individuals and recruiting advice to employers. There is also information about Best Jobs Career Fairs, offered in more than 40 cities nationwide, as well as links to other employment-related sites.

The Black Collegian Online

Web Address: *www.blackcollegian.com*
Number of Job Listings: More than 10,000
Industries Included: All
Location of Jobs: United States
Search By: Company Name; Keyword; Location
Resume Database ☑
Employer Profiles ☑

Summary: Each job description has an option to have that description e-mailed to you. The site also includes general information concerning minority issues. This site is the online version of the *Black Collegian* magazine that is distributed to college career centers twice a year (the online version is updated regularly). A large percentage of the jobs listed are from major corporations like CIGNA, Deloitte & Touche, Lockheed Martin, and Pfizer.

Boldface Jobs

Web Address: *www.boldfacejobs.com*
Number of Job Listings: More than 750
Industries Included: All
Location of Jobs: United States; Some International
Frequency of Updates: Daily
Search By: Industry; Location
Resume Database ☑

Summary: Boldface Jobs links to other job sites, recruiters, and employment agencies. For a nation-wide site offering all types of jobs, there aren't a whole lot of listings. Nevertheless, with a direct approach, job seekers can quickly uncover many matching jobs. This site is most recommended for those seeking a job in a larger metropolitan area in a major industry.

BusinessWeek Online Career Center

Web Address: *www.businessweek.com*
Industries Included: All
Location of Jobs: United States; Some International
Frequency of Updates: Daily
Search By: Job Category; Keyword; Location; Salary

Summary: *BusinessWeek*'s "Personal Search Agent" is a job-hunting tool that searches the online job database and automatically e-mails job seekers new openings that match their employment preferences. Tools such as a cost-of-living calculator are also included. As the online version of *BusinessWeek* magazine, this site offers extensive information on the economy and job market. Hundreds of past articles pertinent to both job seekers and employers are archived through the "Selected Stories" link.

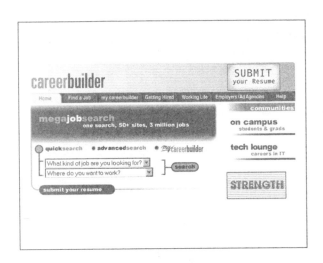

The CareerBuilder Network

Web Address: *www.careerbuilder.com*
Number of Job Listings: More than 4,000,000
Industries Included: All
Location of Jobs: United States; Some International
Frequency of Updates: Daily
Search By: Job Category; Keyword; Location; Salary; Skills; Type of Position
Resume Database ☑
Employer Profiles ☑

Summary: Offers advice and information on career planning as well as writing a good cover letter. Listings link to each sponsoring company's Web site. CareerBuilder provides the monthly e-zine *Achieve*, which offers articles and columns about job hunting, the workplace, and starting a business. There's also a free personal job search agent, which allows you to use up to five search agents (so you can choose different criteria) for the same e-mail address—you describe the job you want, and CareerBuilder notifies you when it has found it.

CareerCity.com

Web Address: *www.careercity.com*
Number of Job Listings: More than 4,000,000
Industries Included: All
Location of Jobs: United States; Some International
Frequency of Updates: Daily
Search By: Job Category; Keyword; Location; Job Description; Job Title; Country
Resume Database ☑
Employer Profiles ☑

Summary: Offers a wealth of career information from bestselling job-hunting and career books; free resume posting to a large, up-to-date resume database; and a search engine with links to over 27,000 companies featuring job listings on their Web sites. CareerCity.com also includes information on ordering career-related books and software, and a "Feature of the Day" column with career-related articles to help you with your job search.

Career.com

Web Address: *www.career.com*
Industries Included: All
Location of Jobs: United States; Some International
Frequency of Updates: Daily
Search By: Company Name; Job Category; Location; Keyword
Resume Database ☑
Employer Profiles ☑

Summary: Links to company home pages, virtual job fairs, and companies that have entry-level opportunities listed on this site. Career.com is especially good for technical positions, though the number of positions in other areas continues to grow. All the job listings contain the dates they were posted, making it easy for job hunters to gauge how long the listings have been floating around. The special area covering employment opportunities for new graduates is a great feature, as is the section featuring this week's "Hot Jobs."

Career Connection

Web Address: *www.connectme.com*
Number of Job Listings: More than 4,000
Industries Included: All
Location of Jobs: United States
Search By: Job Title; Keyword; Location; Date Posted
Resume Database ☑

Summary: Career Connection offers a section of career-related articles that touch upon issues such as using the Web in your job search, negotiating a great salary, and the most common mistakes that job seekers make. The information is timely and informative and definitely worth a look, even if you don't find a matching job.

Career Exchange

Web Address: *www.careerexchange.com*
Industries Included: All
Location of Jobs: United States; Canada
Frequency of Updates: Daily
Search By: Job Category; Keyword; Location; Position Type (part-time, full-time, contract)
Resume Database ☑

Summary: Additional services include a "People-Match" e-mail service and the "Conference Room" career forum. Career Exchange provides various career resources including relocation services, a salary calculator, and more. Jobs posted to this site are also listed on related newsgroups and on Yahoo! Classifieds.

Career Exposure

Web Address: *www.careerexposure.com*
Industries Included: All
Location of Jobs: United States; International
Frequency of Updates: Daily
Search By: Company Name; Industry; Keyword; Location; Salary
Resume Database ☑
Employer Profiles ☑

Summary: Essentially, Career Exposure compiles the thousands of job listings from large corporate Web sites, and presents them on their own Web site. The quality of the listings indicates that their aim to help both employers and job seekers is working. The Career Exposure Biz Center offers some great advice and information on the latest trends in the job marketplace and the latest happenings in the business world.

CareerLink USA

Web Address: *www.careerlinkusa.com*
Industries Included: All
Location of Jobs: United States
Search By: Job Category; Keyword; Location
Resume Database ☑

Summary: CareerLink USA can e-mail job seekers' resumes directly to employers, or employers can conduct their own resume search on this site. They even provide links to a limited number of other career-related Web sites.

CareerMagazine

Web Address: *www.careermag.com*
Industries Included: All
Location of Jobs: United States; Some International
Frequency of Updates: Daily
Search By: Job Category; Job Title; Keyword; Location; Skill Set
Resume Database ☑
Employer Profiles ☑

Summary: Includes career-related news and articles from publications such as the *National Business Employment Weekly,* and information on networking and interview preparation. Offers dozens of links to other employment-related sites include salary guides and an employment agency directory. CareerMagazine's "On Campus" section is tailored college students, while their "Diversity" section focuses on workplace diversity and minority opportunities. CareerMagazine offers numerous other career resources to job hunters, such as the World Wide Web Resume Database and career articles.

CareerMart

Web Address: *www.careermart.com*
Number of Job Listings: More than 1,000
Industries Included: All
Location of Jobs: United States; Some International
Frequency of Updates: Daily
Search By: Company Name; Location; Job Category; Keyword
Resume Database ☑
Employer Profiles ☑

Summary: CareerMart is full of links; they offer links to some of today's top publications on their "Newsstand" as well as useful links to top employers across the country and to the Web pages of universities, colleges, and community colleges nationwide. That said, CareerMart is an especially appealing site to students and recent graduates.

CareerMosaic

Web Address: *www.careermosaic.com*
Industries Included: All
Location of Jobs: United States; Some International
Frequency of Updates: Daily
Search By: Job Title; Company Name; Location; Keyword
Resume Database ☑
Employer Profiles ☑

Summary: Contains several international job databases, including International Gateway, which features thousands of job opportunities worldwide. CareerMosaic also offers a searchable database of job listings from Usenet, and links to hundreds of sponsoring companies. It also includes information for college students such as job opportunities and programs (College Connection), online job fairs, and a Career Resource Center, which gives job hunting advice as well as information on industry trends. Whether you're looking for job opportunities close to home or across the globe, CareerMosaic is one site you should definitely try. Job hunters of all experience levels can find advice and tips on everything from writing a computer-friendly resume to managing their career.

CareerNET

Web Address: *www.careernet.com*
Industries Included: All
Location of Jobs: United States; Some International
Frequency of Updates: Daily
Search By: Company; Job Category; Keyword
Resume Database ☑
Employer Profiles ☑

Summary: In addition to a large number of job postings, CareerNET offers a variety of career-related news and information. Their monthly newsletter, *careerSOURCE*, offers some great tips on job searching as well as a list of featured books that just might be able to help you out. Book covers even link to amazon.com for easy purchasing. If you're still not convinced, check out some of their great testimonials that are posted online, or add your own!

CareerPark

Web Address: *www.careerpark.com*
Number of Job Listings: More than 1,000
Industries Included: All
Location of Jobs: United States
Search By: Company Name; Job Category
Resume Database ☑
Employer Profiles ☑

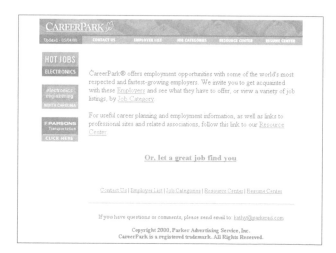

Summary: Not being able to search by location makes this site difficult to navigate if you're looking to work in one specific geographical location. However, CareerPark does offer a number of good links to employer, organization, and other career-related Web sites through their online Resource Center.

CareerPath

Web Address: *www.careerpath.com*
Number of Job Listings: More than 300,000
Industries Included: All
Location of Jobs: United States
Frequency of Updates: Daily
Search By: Company Name; Industry; Job Category; Keyword; Location; Newspaper Name; Posting Date
Resume Database ☑
Employer Profiles ☑

Summary: CareerPath contains information on participating newspapers and the areas they cover, including links to each individual newspaper's home pages. CareerPath also offers a Web-based job search, with more than 10,000 open positions, and a career management section, which includes company profiles, industry news, and more. CareerPath's job database is composed of the daily employment ads from nearly 100 major city newspapers including the *New York Times*, *Chicago Tribune*, *Hartford Courant*, *Boston Globe*, *Washington Post*, *Denver Post*, *Los Angeles Times*, and *Miami Herald*. Thus, the quality of the job listings will depend on the companies that placed the ads. This is a great service for anyone considering relocating to a major city, and a great resource for researching the job market in another region. The Web-based jobs database also holds a wealth of opportunity, and a more general search will definitely field better results with this database.

CareerShop

Web Address: *www.careershop.com*
Industries Included: All
Location of Jobs: United States
Frequency of Updates: Daily
Search By: Job Category; Keyword; Location
Resume Database ☑
Employer Profiles ☑

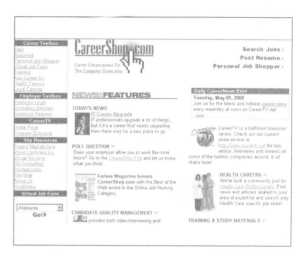

Summary: Offers a Deja News newsgroup search engine as well as an e-mail service that notifies you of new openings that meet the criteria you specify. CareerShop links to national and local job fairs, and training and certification programs. This is a good resource for job seekers and employers alike. This site is easy to navigate, and the e-mail service is beneficial to those who can't spend hours surfing the Web. In addition to its own listings, CareerShop searches more than 35 other career sites, including many major sites, using the criteria you select, to generate a good selection of jobs.

CareerSite

Web Address: *www.careersite.com*
Industries Included: All
Location of Jobs: United States
Frequency of Updates: Daily
Search By: Industry; Job Category; Location; Skills
Resume Database ☑
Employer Profiles ☑

Summary: Links to company profiles and job openings for specific companies. By filling out "My Profile," you get free access to the jobs database, e-mail notification of job openings you'd be interested in, and you can post an "anonymous profile" that can be viewed only by potential employers you approve of through e-mail. Job seekers are also able to search jobs based on their personal profile, getting a list of openings ranked according to best match. CareerSite has one of the best online resume/profile services for job seekers around. "MyProfile" is very user friendly and easy to access and edit; with one click you can access a page to write in a cover letter to a specific ad and have your resume sent along in tow.

The Employment Guide's CareerWeb

Web Address: *www.careerweb.com*
Industries Included: All
Location of Jobs: United States
Frequency of Updates: Daily
Search By: Company Name; Job Category; Keyword; Location
Resume Database ☑
Employer Profiles ☑

Summary: CareerWeb is packed with information and resources for job hunters. JobMatch (a personalized automated database search) and career assessment tests (found under "Career Inventory") are just two of the career-related resources you'll find on this site. Other resources include links to affiliates and other job sites, plus tips and advice on internships, resume writing, the job hunt, and more. If you register your resume, you can respond to advertisements with a simple click of a button. Also, check out the Career Doctor for columns on finding a job, self-employment, and more. Health care professionals and persons leaving military duty can also find helpful information on this site. If this Web site doesn't answer all your career-related questions, CareerWeb provides a list of books, software, and videos that can help you in your job search.

Career Women

Web Address: *www.careerwomen.com*
Industries Included: All
Location of Jobs: United States
Frequency of Updates: Daily
Search By: Company Name; Job Category; Keyword; Location; Salary
Resume Database ☑
Employer Profiles ☑

Summary: Career Women provides links to news and resources for professional women. Check out the site's advice and survey areas for more helpful information. Career Women is a part of the Career Exposure Network, which also includes Career Exposure, MBA Careers, and Diversity Search.

Classifieds2000

Web Address: *www.classifieds2000.com*
Number of Job Listings: More than 450,000
Industries Included: All
Location of Jobs: United States
Frequency of Updates: Daily
Search By: Job Category; Keyword; Location
Resume Database ☑
Employer Profiles ☑

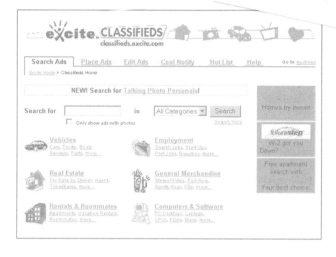

Summary: "Cool Notify" e-mail service informs job seekers of new postings matching their criteria; and a special section detailing opportunities with start-ups can be particularly appealing to those who don't like to go the large corporation route. Job seekers can search ads from employers, recruiters, or both. Visit their resource center for career advice and for the opportunity to research potential employers. Overall, Classifieds2000 is a fantastic job search Web site that offers a wealth of employment information in one place.

College Grad Job Hunter

Web Address: *www.collegegrad.com*
Types of Jobs Listed: Entry-level; Internships; Professional
Location of Jobs: United States; Some International
Frequency of Updates: Daily
Search By: Job Category; Keyword
Resume Database ☑
Employer Profiles ☑

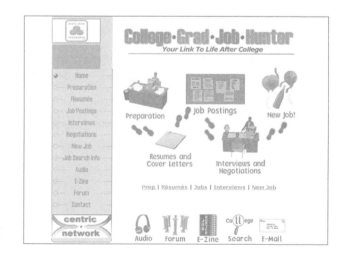

Summary: This attractive, well-organized site is geared toward recent college graduates. It offers a step-by-step guide to getting a job, with information on everything from resume preparation to interviewing tips to negotiating an employment offer. Information is adapted directly from the book of the same name, which you can read on the site. Actual job listings are limited, but those that are available are ideal for entry-level candidates, and many are from major employers such as Intel Corporation and Netscape. College Grad Job Hunter also links to a variety of other job-hunting Web sites. This site is an excellent choice for those new to the job market, while also providing opportunities for recent grads with a year or so of experience. Experienced job seekers are linked to CareerCity.com (*www.careercity.com*) which includes, in addition to more than one million job listings, a resume database and other career resources.

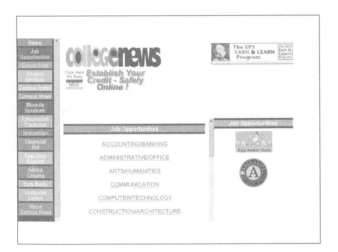

College News

Web Address: *www.collegenews.com*
Number of Job Listings: More than 250
Industries Included: Entry-level; Internships; Summer; Temporary Employment
Location of Jobs: United States
Frequency of Updates: Monthly
Search By: Job Category
Resume Database ☑

Summary: Offers extensive information relating to student life and college and career planning. This Web site is the online version of *College News*, an independent print publication that is distributed monthly to colleges and universities nationwide. In addition to questions about careers and employment opportunities, College News tries to answer questions that relate to the college experience in general: music, finances, dating, etc.

CollegeRecruiter.com

Web Address: *www.collegerecruiter.com*
Industries Included: All
Location of Jobs: Worldwide
Search By: Job Category; Location
Resume Database ☑
Employer Profiles ☑

Summary: This site focuses on students heading into graduation, or those who have recently graduated. Recruiters post jobs to this site for entry-level through experienced positions, as well as for part-time jobs and internships. Company information is provided through a partnership with Company Sleuth's Web site. CollegeRecruiter.com links to related sites and company e-mail addresses. The CollegeRecruiter.com bookstore offers a short list of books and links where you can get more information on finding the perfect job.

Cool Works

Web Address: *www.coolworks.com*
Number of Job Listings: More than 75,000
Types of Jobs Included: Seasonal employment at national parks, resorts, camps, and ski areas
Location of Jobs: United States
Frequency of Updates: Weekly
Search By: Company Name; Job Category; Job Environment; Location
Employer Profiles ☑

Summary: Cool Works provides information about volunteer opportunities and career placement information concerning recreational employment. The Web site does a good job of covering a unique market, seasonal employment. Links to colleges and various large career sites enable job hunters with an interest in these kinds of jobs to get a good glimpse of what is available.

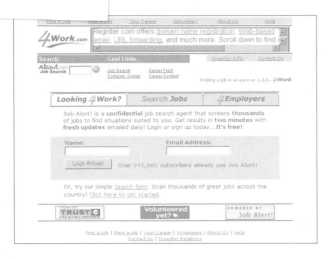

4Work

Web Address: *www.4work.com*
Number of Job Listings: More than 1,000
Industries Included: All
Location of Jobs: United States
Frequency of Updates: Daily
Search By: Keyword; Location; Job Type

Summary: While it doesn't have the additional career resources offered by Monster.com and other big Web sites, 4Work's jobs database is well worth the time of the search. Better yet, if you register your personal profile—name, e-mail address, skills— Job Alert! lets you know when an employer has posted an appropriate opportunity. The information includes both part-time and full-time positions, volunteer opportunities, and internships. 4Work also offers information on relocating, as well as links to numerous colleges and universities.

Freetimejobs.com

Web Address: *www.freetimejobs.com*
Types of Jobs Included: Freelance and Contract Jobs
Location of Jobs: United States; Some International
Frequency of Updates: Daily
Search By: Job Category; Keyword

Summary: The limited search criteria can make it difficult to narrow down your "favorite jobs." As a result of an apparently large database of jobs, searching can be difficult at times. Many of the jobs listed were also over two months old. You must register to "bid" on a job and create an online resume or applicant profile. Registered users have access to a message box, a folder for tracking bids, and convenient links to contact employers.

Go Jobs

Web Address: *www.gojobs.com*
Number of Job Listings: More than 5,000
Industries Included: All
Location of Jobs: United States
Frequency of Updates: Daily
Search By: Job Category; Keyword; Location

Summary: Other than a fairly large number of job listings, this site doesn't offer any other services to job seekers. Still, the number of quality listings make this site a good choice if you've specified the industry and area you'd like to work in.

Headhunter.net

Web Address: *www.headhunter.net*
Number of Job Listings: Approximately 200,000
Industries Included: All
Location of Jobs: United States; Some International
Frequency of Updates: Daily
Search By: Job Category; Keyword; Location; Salary; Skill Set; Job Type; Education/Experience
Resume Database ☑

Summary: The Candidate Resource Center offers extensive information on such topics as interviewing, finances, career assessment, training, and company research. Because the search database will allow you to search up to five jobs and five industries at once, you are likely to retrieve a large amount of employment opportunities.

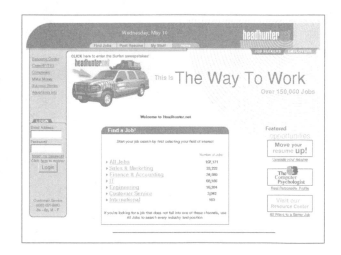

The Help-Wanted Network

Web Address: *www.help-wanted.net*
Industries Included: All
Location of Jobs: United States; Some International
Frequency of Updates: Daily
Search By: Keyword; Location; Posting Date
Resume Database ☑

Summary: The Help-Wanted Network is an especially great way to access newsgroup listings. This is not a large site, but it claims to offer access to 2.5 million job listings. As newsgroups are part of the retrieved links, such a high number is likely. The "Other Resources" section links you to a limited number of career Web sites, company Web sites, and more.

Hotjobs.com

Web Address: *www.hotjobs.com*
Industries Included: All
Location of Jobs: United States
Frequency of Updates: Daily
Search By: Company Name; Job Category; Keyword; Location
Resume Database ☑
Employer Profiles ☑

Summary: This straightforward job database keeps growing more popular by the minute. Perhaps it's because of the big name companies that choose to post their job openings here. This easy-to-navigate, no-frills Web site makes Hotjobs.com an ideal site for job seekers eager to dig right in. In addition to job listings, they offer a resume writing workshop, a job search agent, a message board, a "shopping cart" feature that allows job seekers to save relevant job announcements, and links to company home pages.

Internet Career Connection

Web Address: *www.iccweb.com*
Industries Included: All
Location of Jobs: United States; Some International
Frequency of Updates: Daily
Search By: Keyword; Location
Resume Database ☑
Employer Profiles ☑

Summary: The Internet Career Connection offers more than just job listings; with invaluable advice on the latest trends and most frequently asked question in job hunting, and a variety of links to other real and virtual career centers, this site offers a virtual smorgasbord of job-related data. Of particular interest to those interested in working for the government is ICC's federal job information section.

The Internet Job Source

Web Address: *www.statejobs.com*
Industries Included: All
Location of Jobs: United States
Search By: Date Posted; Job Category; Keyword; Location
Resume Database ☑
Employer Profiles ☑

Summary: The Internet Job Source is a particularly good site to visit if your job search is focused largely on location or government positions. The newspaper and magazine listings are great for accessing current news, be it focused on your career or getting local information on an area in which you'd like to live and work. The site provides links to over 20 state and area job source pages; as well as links to *Fortune 500* jobs and federal and state job listings. The Internet Job Source also features career-related news articles, links to major search engines and online news publications, and a free weekly newsletter.

JobBank USA

Web Address: *www.jobbankusa.com*
Industries Included: All
Location of Jobs: United States
Frequency of Updates: Daily
Search By: Job Type; Keyword; Location

Summary: The real draw of this site is its Jobs Meta Search Page. Not only can you search the JobBank USA database, but you can perform searches in the databases of several of the major World Wide Web job-hunting sites including Monster.com, CareerCity.com, and JobOptions. Of course, if you use only this job searching service, you'll miss out on the other valuable information these services provide, but if you're short on time and only want to check out job listings, JobBank USA is an excellent choice. Key features of JobBank USA include a job search e-mail service, career fair information, job-related newsgroups, an online newspaper that features tips and job openings for international job hunters, and the Jobs Meta Search Page.

JobDirect

Web Address: *www.jobdirect.com*
Industries Included: All
Types of Jobs Included: Entry-Level
Location of Jobs: United States
Frequency of Updates: Daily
Search By: Education Level
Resume Database ☑

Summary: JobDirect focuses its resources on recent and pending college graduates, at both the undergraduate and graduate levels. The service is unique; enter your resume into the JobDirect resume database and you will be e-mailed a list of new job openings that meet your experience. It's definitely worth a shot if you've been in school for as long as you can remember and are new to the workplace.

JobFind.com

Web Address: *www.jobfind.com*
Industries Included: All
Location of Jobs: United States; Some International
Frequency of Updates: Daily
Resume Database ☑
Employer Profiles ☑
Search By: Company Name; Job Category; Job Title; Keyword; Location; Salary

Summary: JobFind.com allows job seekers a more focused list of viable job options. Information includes listings of job fairs, current news articles, and MyJobFind, an automatic e-mail service that notifies job seekers of new matching listings.

Job-Hunt.org

Web Address: *www.job-hunt.org*
Industries Included: All
Frequency of Updates: More than once per week
Employer Profiles ☑

Summary: They call themselves "the job hunter's super list" and it's easy to see why. Job-Hunt.org is easily one of the most comprehensive sites on the World Wide Web. While they do not offer any job listings or resume databases themselves, they do provide plenty of links to where you can find such places on the Web. In fact, the number of links is really amazing. Search online resume banks, newsgroups, company profiles, and jobs specifically in academics, medicine, science, and engineering; browse through the database of recruiters; link to college and university career centers; or access online reference material and most (if not all) of the major, most informative career resources on the Web. This site has a very respectable company profile database and lots of research tools, which will benefit anyone from the entry-level employee to the most seasoned CEO.

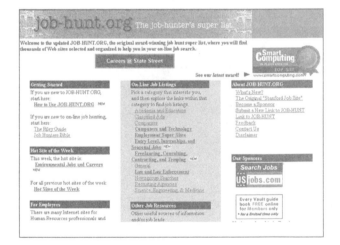

JobOptions

Web Address: *www.joboptions.com*
Industries Included: All
Location of Jobs: United States; Some International
Frequency of Updates: Daily
Search By: Job Category; Keyword; Location
Resume Database ☑
Employer Profiles ☑

Summary: JobOptions is another very useful site that is easy to navigate and offers more than simple jobs and resume databases. Especially unique to this site is its emphasis on serving both the job seeker and the employer, making this a great stop for people on both sides of the job search. The Web site offers more than enough employer profiles to keep you busy for a while as well as e-mail services for the job seeker and the employer alike—Job Alert notifies job seekers of new positions matching their criteria, while Resume Alert e-mails employers regarding freshly posted resumes that just may suit their openings. HR Tools covers a variety of human resource topics, and the Career Tools section offers tips on creating a resume, salary and relocation information, career news, and more.

The Job Resource

Web Address: *www.jobresource.com*
Number of Job Listings: More than 1,000
Industries Included: All
Types of Jobs Included: Entry-Level
Location of Jobs: United States; Some International
Frequency of Updates: Daily
Search By: Industry; Job Category; Keyword;
Location
Resume Database ☑
Employer Profiles ☑

Summary: The Job Resource has been around for a
while, and has led the way for many similar-minded
job search sites. They certainly get high marks for
design, focus, and quality. Geared toward graduating college seniors and recent graduates, this site
offers assistance in creating a professional-looking
HTML resume or an ASCII resume to be e-mailed.
They also offer online discussion forums for job
seekers as well as daily tips that can help keep you
motivated in your job search. In addition, employers
can search for candidates by college.

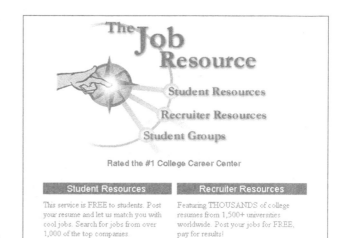

Jobs.com

Web Address: *www.jobs.com*
Number of Job Listings: N/A
Industries Included: All
Location of Jobs: United States
Frequency of Updates: Daily
Search By: Job Category; Job Title; Job Type; Location; Salary
Resume Database ☑
Employer Profiles ☑

Summary: Formerly the Resumail Network, this site is based on the Resumail software program. It claims to simplify the process of creating an online resume by allowing job seekers to simply fill in their career information (experience, education, etc.), while the software automatically plugs it into electronic format. Aside from making the entire computer-friendly resume a snap for job seekers, Jobs.com ensures that employers are getting a readable electronic resume. Both job seekers and employers must download the software from the site to either post a resume or read resumes. Jobs.com offers a special section for student job seekers that includes information on internships, entry-level jobs, and more.

The Job-Search-Engine

Web Address: *www.jobsearchengine.com*
Industries Included: All
Location of Jobs: United States; Canada
Search By: Keyword; Location

Summary: This is a great site for collecting multiple job listings. The Job-Search-Engine is, basically, a meta search engine that gathers applicable job listings from some of the Web's biggest sites including CareerCity.com, Career Mosaic, Headhunter.net, and Monster.com. By doing a search for keywords "computer programmer" in the US, for example, we received more than 2,000 listings (Note: the 2,000 listings were not necessarily unique listings). The Job-Search-Engine's Resource Center lists and links to several jobs sites, career services sites, and career-related newsgroups.

Jobtrak

Web Address: *www.jobtrak.com*
Industries Included: All
Location of Jobs: United States
Frequency of Updates: Daily
Resume Database ☑
Employer Profiles ☑

Summary: Jobtrak's primary distinction is that its job listings are geared directly toward college students, MBAs, and alumni through college career centers. Jobtrak has formed partnerships with more than 800 college and university career centers, MBA programs, and alumni centers nationwide to bring information from these sources to job seekers. In addition to job listings, Jobtrak offers a career forum, graduate school information, and a calendar of career fairs.

Jobvertise

Web Address: *www.jobvertise.com*
Number of Job Listings: More than 50,000
Industries Included: All
Location of Jobs: United States; Some International
Search By: Keyword; Location
Employer Profiles ☑

Summary: Companies use Jobvertise's free service to set up a jobs page on their own home pages. The Jobvertise site can be searched for jobs coming from those home pages, or job seekers can be directly linked to the company home pages. Jobvertise also links to other career sites, as well as communities and companies that use their service.

MBA FreeAgents.com

Web Address: *www.mbafreeagents.com*
Industries Included: Interim; High-Tech; and Business-Related Jobs for MBAs
Location of Jobs: United States; Some International
Frequency of Updates: Daily
Search By: Company Name; Job Type; Keyword
Resume Database ☑

Summary: Membership is required for this job-matching service for experienced MBAs from top business schools. The 39 schools included (Carnegie Mellon and Harvard Business School are just two of them) are all members of the International MBA placement group. According to the service, the majority of applicants meet one of the following criteria: one to 15 years out of business school, 30 years of experience, or an independent consultant who goes from one job to the next. Clearly, this site is not for all job seekers; however, it is a good example of a job-hunting Web site that focuses on a target audience and succeeds at it. Job seekers who qualify should register in the alumni members database, which is searched by employers and hiring managers. Networking tools include e-mail interaction between job seekers and employers/hiring managers, and a database of alumni members.

Monster.com

Web Address: *www.monster.com*
Number of Job Listings: More than 375,000
Industries Included: All
Location of Jobs: United States; Some International
Frequency of Updates: Daily
Search By: Company; Job Category; Keyword; Location
Resume Database ☑
Employer Profiles ☑

Summary: Monster.com (formerly the Monster Board) is one of the best and most well-known job-hunting resources on the Web. It's an easy-to-use, completely comprehensive, graphically entertaining site that provides job hunters with tons of valuable information. The job listings themselves are thorough and, if you have previously submitted your resume to the resume database, you can apply for positions with impressive ease. It really is a monster too, growing all the time through partnerships with other job-hunting sites. In addition to job listings, Monster.com offers Zones for different experience levels and specific fields (such as Health Care, Technology, and dot.coms); expert job hunting and career advice; a job search agent; and links to other career sites. There are also links to international sites like Monster Board UK.

NationJob Network

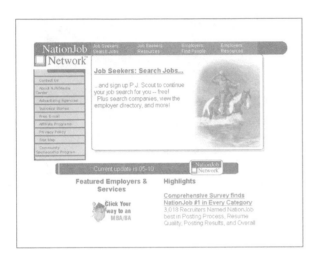

Web Address: *www.nationjob.com*
Industries Included: All
Location of Jobs: United States; Some International
Frequency of Updates: Daily
Search By: Company Name; Education; Job Category; Job Type; Keyword; Location; Salary; Skill Set
Employer Profiles ☑

Summary: Presented by NationJob, Inc., this site also lists its openings on America's Job Bank, Alta Vista Careers, and Yahoo! Classifieds. Specialty pages enable job seekers to research companies in a particular employment category or geographical area. The Community Pages section offers current, local job information for much of the country. NationJob Network's job search agent, called P.J. Scout, serves more than 325,000 job seekers per week. In addition to the traditional job search engine, NationJob Network offers a variety of specialty Web pages, and links to Web sites of many sponsoring companies (all of whom have current job openings posted).

Net-Temps

Web Address: *www.net-temps.com*
Number of Job Listings: More than 125,000
Industries Included: Administration; Engineering; Finance; Health Care; Human Resources; Sales and Marketing; Management
Location of Jobs: United States; Canada
Frequency of Updates: Daily
Search By: Job Category; Job Type; Keyword; Location
Resume Database ☑
Employer Profiles ☑

Summary: A good site with comprehensive job listings for those seeking exposure to recruiters' openings in a variety of fields. This site lists thousands of job listings from as many as 1,500 employment agencies. Placements found here are typically contract, temporary, and permanent.

Recruiters Online Network

Web Address: *www.recruitersonline.com*
Number of Job Listings: More than 25,000
Industries Included: All
Location of Jobs: United States; Some International
Frequency of Updates: Daily
Search By: Date Posted; Industry; Job Category; Keyword; Location
Resume Database ☑

Summary: For job seekers willing to work with recruiters, this site is a good choice as there's the potential to have thousands of recruiters help you with your job search. Recruiters Online Network is an association of over 7,000 recruiters. The site even offers a directory of its member firms by specialty and location, and allows the job seeker to view all the jobs posted by that firm.

USA Jobs

Web Address: *www.usajobs.opm.gov*
Industries Included: All; All Jobs are Government Positions
Location of Jobs: United States
Frequency of Updates: Daily
Search By: Date Posted; Government Agency; Job Category; Job Experience (GS Level); Job Title; Keyword; Location; Salary

Summary: Operated by the United States Office of Personnel Management, USA Jobs is the U.S. government's official site for jobs and employment information. It contains a wealth of information on applying for federal jobs, federal salary and benefits, student employment, and more. Job listings are neatly divided into the following categories: professional; clerical and technical; trades and labor; senior executive; entry-level; worker-trainee; and summer positions. You can also conduct an alphabetical search of available jobs, or search for a specific GS level. The site offers online career transition assistance provided by the United States Department of Labor, and various government information resources.

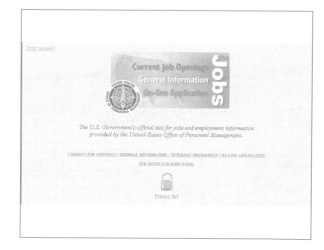

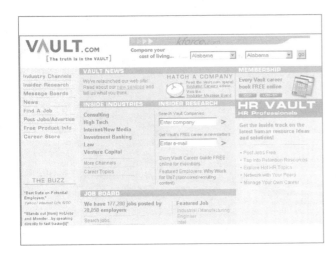

Vault.com

Web Address: *www.vault.com*
Number of Job Listings: More than 175,00
Industries Included: All
Location of Jobs: United States
Frequency of Updates: Daily
Search By: Date Posted; Experience Level; Job Category; Job Type; Location
Employer Profiles ☑

Summary: Vault.com is a very easy-to-navigate and user-friendly site that offers a number of job listings (from some big name companies) in an organized format. One great option they allow for is the ability to exclude recruiters and headhunters from your search results. Because Vault.com offers free job posting services to employers, you can often find as many as 30,000 companies or more posting job descriptions at any one time.

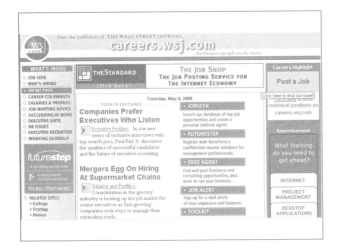

Wall Street Journal Interactive Edition

Web Address: *www.careers.wsj.com*
Industries Included: All
Location of Jobs: United States
Frequency of Updates: Two times per week
Search By: Company Name; Industry; Job Category; Keyword; Location
Employer Profiles ☑

Summary: Offers loads of career resources, including salary information, career columns, and links to executive recruiters. The *Wall Street Journal* Interactive Edition offers an e-mail service that notifies the job seeker of new opportunities and information. The site also links to a variety of career publications available through amazon.com. This informative site is backed by the reputation of the *Wall Street Journal*. The featured employers section is useful, but the multiple logos make it less appealing for users with slow Internet access.

Northeast/Mid-Atlantic

Boston.com

Web Address: *www.boston.com*
Number of Job Listings: More than 25,000
Industries Included: All
Location of Jobs: Greater Boston Area
Frequency of Updates: Daily
Search By: Job Category; Keyword; Location
Resume Database ☑
Employer Profiles ☑

Summary: This site is a service of the *Boston Globe*, and includes both print and online-only listings. While doing basic job browsing, there were a considerable number of listings which were entered multiple times, probably due to the ad running for multiple weeks in the *Globe*. Access to career articles, a schedule of career fairs/activities, a directory of Boston-area employment agencies and recruiters, and links to other career sites are all some of the added extras to be found on Boston.com. Boston.com also hosts the Web pages of several local area businesses, where you can find additional job listings for the Bay State.

Boston Job Bank

Web Address: *www.bostonjobs.com*
Industries Included: All
Location of Jobs: Greater Boston Area
Frequency of Updates: Daily
Search By: Job Category; Keyword
Resume Database ☑

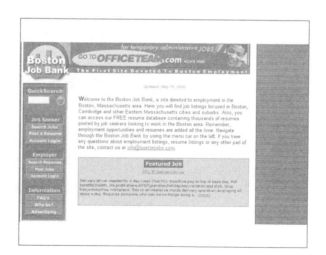

Summary: Boston Job Bank is a simple, no frills career site. Though there are a limited number of job and resume postings (compared with sites such as Monster.com), the site does provide current, thorough information. Boston Job Bank also lists a number of freelance positions. One drawback is the limitation on which job categories you can choose from (professional, computer, business, sales, general). All in all, a good site if you're looking to work in the greater Boston area.

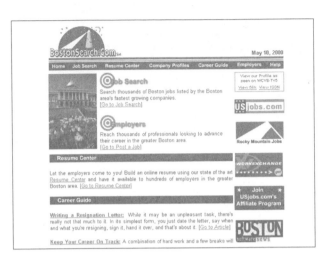

BostonSearch

Web Address: *www.bostonsearch.com*
Number of Job Listings: More than 1,000
Industries Included: All
Location of Jobs: Greater Boston Area
Frequency of Updates: Daily
Search By: Job Category; Keyword; Type of Job
Resume Database ☑
Employer Profiles ☑

Summary: One nice feature of this site is that most searches performed, whether it be for company profiles or jobs in marketing, will list all of the results on a single page, so there's no shifting back and forth between pages. The site offers additional information on general career advice, salary negotiations, resume writing, and interviewing. They list a number of "Hot Companies" too, and will link you directly to their company profile as well as their available job opportunities.

JobNet

Web Address: *www.jobnet.com*
Number of Job Listings: More than 1,000
Industries Included: All
Location of Jobs: Greater Philadelphia Area
Frequency of Updates: Daily
Search By: Job Category; Keyword; Location
Resume Database ☑
Employer Profiles ☑

Summary: This small, localized database is noteworthy for its partnerships with Web giants like CareerWeb and CareerMagazine. As a subscriber to JobNet, you can post to JobNet's Philadelphia-area database for free. Job seekers can also link to specific companies listed at the site, view their job openings, and submit a resume for free.

New Jersey Online

Web Address: *www.nj.com*
Number of Job Listings: More than 1,000
Industries Included: All
Location of Jobs: New Jersey
Frequency of Updates: Daily
Search By: Job Category; Job Title; Keyword; Newspaper
Resume Database ☑
Employer Profiles ☑

Summary: New Jersey Online offers all the typical information you'd find in a printed newspaper: information on news, local happenings, entertainment, business, and more is readily available on this site. They also offer forums, information on employment agencies and technical schools, career advice, and relocation tools.

Philadelphia Online

Web Address: *jobhunter.philly.com*
Industries Included: All
Location of Jobs: Greater Philadelphia Area
Frequency of Updates: Daily
Search By: Job Category; Keyword
Resume Database ☑
Employer Profiles ☑

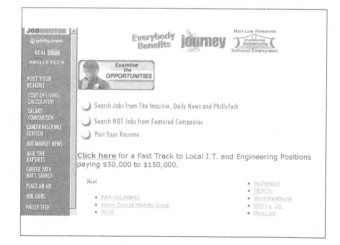

Summary: Philadelphia Online is a comprehensive site that provides information on job openings with some of the area's largest employers. They also offer some informative career advice and give you the opportunity to "Ask the Experts" if you still have a question about your job search. The site links to employment agencies, computer training services, and resume services as well.

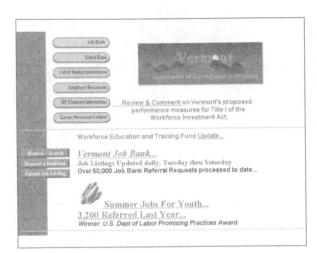

Vermont Department of Employment and Training

Web Address: *www.det.state.vt.us*
Number of Job Listings: More than 1,000
Industries Included: All
Location of Jobs: Vermont
Frequency of Updates: Daily
Search By: Date Posted; Education; Job Category; Keyword; Location; Skill Set; Job Type
Resume Database ☑

Summary: Job seekers registered with this site may request that a referral be sent from the Vermont Department of Employment and Training directly to an employer. One drawback of this site is that large-scope searches tend to take a while. However, because the lists generated usually include such useful information as experience requirements, salary, job title, and location, the waiting period is often merited. By getting this information up front, job seekers can quickly select the most appropriate jobs and get a more detailed description, which may actually save time in the long run. The site's Labor Market Information offers access to Vermont labor market information, unemployment rates, statewide wages, and employment statistics as well as a summer jobs section, access to federal and national job listings, and links to additional job listings and training programs.

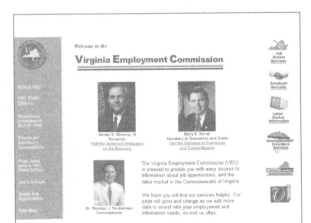

Virginia Employment Commission

Web Address: *www.vec.state.va.us*
Industries Included: All
Location of Jobs: Virginia
Search By: Job Category; Job Code; Keyword; Location; Military Occupation Code
Resume Database ☑

Summary: Some services at this site require registration, but all are free. As the site is powered by America's Job Bank, you know the listings are of a high-quality nature. The site makes information on occupational trends, wages, and geographic areas readily available, and links to many more useful career resources.

Southeast
CareeRGuide

Web Address: *www.careerguide.com*
Number of Job Listings: More than 1,000
Industries Included: All
Location of Jobs: Southeastern United States
Search By: Company Name; Job Category; Keyword; Location
Resume Database ☑
Employer Profiles ☑

Summary: CareeRGuide has a number of services for both the job seeker and the recruiter. ResuNet is a resume service for recruiters, listing the most appropriate resumes from its database that match a recruiter's criteria. CareeRGuide will then e-mail the list of applicants directly to the recruiter. e-Signal is an e-mail service for job seekers, notifying them of new listings matching their criteria. CareeRGuide also offers *The Bridge* newsletter, which serves both job seekers and employers. Look to the site's Virtual Job Fair for additional help in your job search.

Florida CareerLINK

Web Address: *www.floridacareerlink.com*
Industries Included: All
Location of Jobs: Florida
Frequency of Updates: Weekly
Search By: Company Name; Job Category; Job Type; Keyword; Location
Resume Database ☑
Employer Profiles ☑

Summary: Florida CareerLINK was voted Florida's number one employment site and it's easy to see why. They've got loads of information on statewide job openings, local career fairs, and relocation information. The site also provides even more help to the job seeker by linking to recruiters and other career sites. The job listings are current and fairly well-detailed.

Triangle Jobs

Web Address: *www.trianglejobs.com*
Industries Included: All
Location of Jobs: The Carolinas
Search By: Date Posted; Job Category; Job Title
Resume Database ☑
Employer Profiles ☑

Summary: This could very well be the best site out there for a job seeker wishing to relocate to the Carolinas. In addition to detailed job listings, Triangle Jobs provides job training and job fair information, an informative career advice column, and tips on job search topics such as writing a resume and negotiating an offer.

Midwest

CareerBoard.com

Web Address: *www.careerboard.com*
Industries Included: All
Location of Jobs: Akron, Cincinnati, Cleveland, Columbus, Milwaukee, and surrounding areas
Search By: Date Posted; Job Category; Job Type; Keyword
Resume Database ☑
Employer Profiles ☑

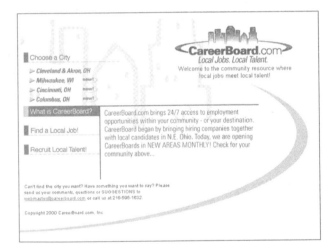

Summary: The slogan at CareerBoard pretty much says it all: "Local Jobs. Local Talent." It doesn't get much more clear-cut than that. CareerBoard is a straightforward job site where you choose the area you want to work, the field you want to work in, and *voila!* your list of possible employers magically appears. Most listings give a very detailed job description, company profile, and contact information, so you're not left wondering just what kind of company you're applying to.

Careerlink.org

Web Address: *www.careerlink.org*
Number of Job Listings: More than 1,000
Industries Included: All
Location of Jobs: Nebraska
Search By: Job Category; Job Title
Resume Database ☑
Employer Profiles ☑

Summary: Maintained by the Applied Information Management Institute (AIM), Careerlink.org is a mighty impressive site. It is one of the few sites you will find that is devoted solely to employment opportunities in the state of Nebraska. In addition to the many job postings, Careerlink.org offers information on volunteer and internship opportunities, local job fairs, Nebraska employment statistics, and careers in general. If you're just starting out and aren't really sure what it is you want to do, Careerlink.org provides brief descriptions of commonly filled positions in a variety of industries.

The Kansas Job Bank

Web Address: *www.kansasjobs.org*
Number of Job Listings: More than 20,000
Industries Included: All
Location of Jobs: Colorado, Kansas, Missouri, Nebraska, and Oklahoma
Search By: Job Category; Job Title; Job Type; Keyword; Location
Resume Database ☑
Employer Profiles ☑

Summary: The Kansas Job Bank covers more than just Kansas, and it does a pretty good job, too! Operated by the Kansas Department of Human Resources, the Kansas Job Bank lists opportunities in Colorado, Missouri, Nebraska, and Oklahoma, too. The site's Job Scout service notifies registered users via e-mail when a new opportunity has arisen that matches their needs. This resourceful site offers some solid search and resume capabilities.

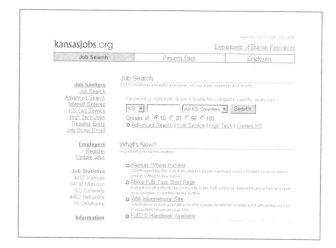

MinnesotaJobs.com

Web Address: *www.minnesotajobs.com*
Number of Job Listings: More than 1,000
Industries Included: All
Location of Jobs: Minnesota
Search By: Company Name; Job Category; Keyword; Location
Resume Database ☑
Employer Profiles ☑

Summary: This no-frills site allows you to search out employment by typing in your criteria or by linking to one of the many featured employers' profiles. The site lists up-to-date career information, like the dates and times of local career fairs, and also offers information on how you can best manage your career. A solid choice for people looking to work in the Twin Cities area.

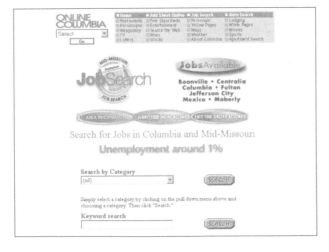

Online Columbia

Web Address: *www.onlinecolumbia.com/jobsearch*
Number of Job Listings: Fewer than 200
Industries Included: All
Location of Jobs: Mid-Missouri
Frequency of Updates: Daily
Search By: Job Category; Keyword
Resume Database ☑

Summary: While they may not offer an exorbitant amount of job listings or job information, this site does succeed in filling a niche and doing it nicely. For mid-Missouri and Columbia-area job seekers, this specialized site might be just the ticket to happy employment. The site also includes information on the area, which could definitely be useful to those looking to relocate.

West/Southwest

Alaska Jobs Center

Web Address: *www.ilovealaska.com/alaskajobs*
Number of Job Listings: Less than 250
Industries Included: All
Location of Jobs: Alaska

Summary: The fact that some of the ads that came up in my employment search referred to missing cats and Beanie Babies, leads me to warn you that you may have to edit the information you receive. Still, the site includes lots of related links as well as a plethora of tourist and commercial information on Alaska that could prove useful to someone planning a move or visit. Plus, since Alaska's limited job market makes every resource precious, this site is one that definitely warrants a visit if you currently live in or are looking to relocate to Alaska.

BAjobs.com

Web Address: *www.bajobs.com*
Number of Job Listings: More than 1,000
Industries Included: All
Location of Jobs: The San Francisco Bay Area
Frequency of Updates: Daily
Search By: Company Name; Industry; Keyword
Resume Database ☑
Employer Profiles ☑

Summary: This site is very well designed, clearly defining all its useful links no matter where you are in the site. It's user-friendliness and pleasant graphics, coupled with its large number of listings for this specific area make it one of the Bay Area's best sites. Featured employers' ads are also mentioned on KTVU/FOX2, a local television station.

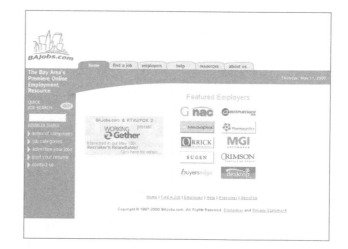

ColoradoJobs.com

Web Address: *www.coloradojobs.com*
Number of Job Listings: More than 250
Industries Included: All
Location of Jobs: Colorado
Search By: Keyword
Resume Database ☑
Employer Profiles ☑

Summary: Operated in partnership with KMGH-TV in Denver, this site allows you to browse through the entire job database with the listings sorted by city, job title, industry, or company. While it's not quite as useful as having search fields, it is certainly a step above a random list of jobs.

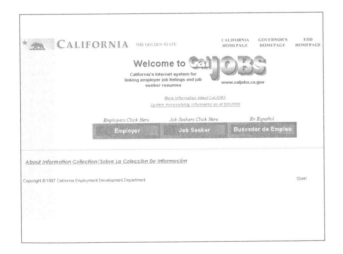

CalJobs

Web Address: *www.caljobs.ca.gov*
Number of Job Listings: More than 20,000
Industries Included: All
Location of Jobs: California
Search By: Location
Resume Database ☑

Summary: The most effective way to search jobs on this site is to register (for free) and fill out a resume profile. After this is done, you can match your profile to the site's job ads for each county or city. The matching process is a little broad, giving the average job seeker one good job lead to every two or three bad ones.

Oregon Employment Department

Web Address: *www.emp.state.or.us*
Number of Job Listings: More than 250
Industries Included: All
Location of Jobs: Oregon
Frequency of Updates: Daily
Search By: Job Category; Keyword; Location

Summary: Job seekers interested in a position must contact the employment office nearest them in order to apply for a position with this site. The Oregon Employment Department Web site includes links to state jobs; JOBS Plus, a program for needy families; and America's Job Bank. The online segment of the Oregon Career Network provides a wealth of information for both job seekers and employers, and instructs both on how to use its services to find good employer/employee matches.

The Silicon Valley Job Source

Web Address: *www.valleyjobs.com*
Number of Job Listings: More than 1,000
Industries Included: All
Location of Jobs: California
Search By: Date Posted; Job Category; Keyword; Location
Resume Database ☑
Employer Profiles ☑

Summary: Are you looking for a job with some of the best high-tech companies in the country? If so, check out this site, which has direct links to those companies. For the different areas of Silicon Valley, the site provides regional information, company links broken down by area, a government jobs section, links to venture capital firms, and links to news sources in the Bay Area, both print and online.

680careers.com

Web Address: *www.680careers.com*
Location of Jobs: California (Contra Costa and Alameda Counties)
Frequency of Updates: Monthly
Employer Profiles ☑

Summary: While there are no job listings to speak of on this site, job seekers can get help in their search with these links to major corporations in the 680 corridor of the above mentioned counties in California. While many of the companies found at this site were either high-tech/computer or communications related, there's a little bit of something for everyone. The site's Resubot e-mail service allows job seekers to select companies from an online list, and e-mail a cover letter and resume to those companies. 680careers.com also offers local information and resources, and news of upcoming career fairs. The site also contains links directly to the job opening section of nearly 150 area companies' Web sites.

Topjobs USA

Web Address: *www.topjobsusa.com*
Number of Job Listings: Less than 250
Industries Included: All
Location of Jobs: Utah
Frequency of Updates: Weekly
Search By: Company Name; Job Category; Keyword
Resume Database ☑
Employer Profiles ☑

Summary: While it is currently one of the only Utah-dedicated job sites out there, the success of this detailed site has led them to begin looking into other Western states in which they can employ the same job search resources. A definite visit for Beehive State natives and wannabes alike.

Washington Employment Web Pages

Web Address: *members.aol.com/gwattier/washjob.htm*
Location of Jobs: Washington State
Employer Profiles ☑

Summary: While you will not find actual job listings or resume banks on this site, you will find plenty of links to more than 1,500 employment sites! The Washington Employment Web Pages is a great starting point for people interested in working in Washington State. Links include connections to private employer Web pages, public employer Web pages, local employment agency Web sites, and other sites offering general information that would be valuable to job seekers looking in the Northwest.

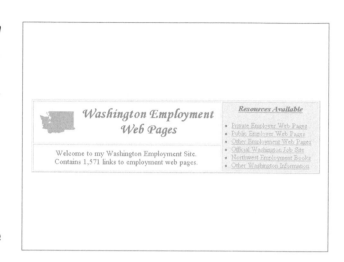

WorkSource Washington

Web Address: *www.wa.gov/esd/employment.html*
Number of Job Listings: More than 2,500
Industries Included: All
Location of Jobs: Washington State
Search By: Job Category; Keyword; Location
Resume Database ☑

Summary: This site, hosted by the Washington State Employment Security Department and in conjunction with America's Job Bank, links to over 30 Washington newspaper Web sites that contain job ads, and various employment and financial links. The site's "no thrills" text version allows faster access to the wealth of information this site has to offer.

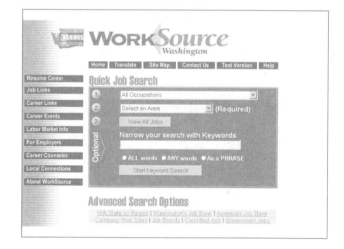

International Sites

Asia-Net

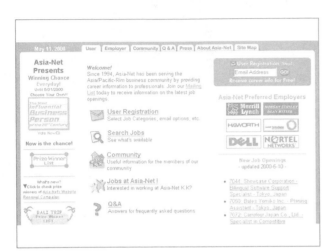

Web Address: *www.asia-net.com*
Number of Job Listings: More than 250
Industries Included: All
Location of Jobs: Asia/Pacific Rim, including Australia and New Zealand. Also includes some United States
Search By: Company Name; Job Category; Keyword; Language; Location

Summary: This comprehensive site is also available in Japanese, Chinese, and Korean.

Australian Job Search

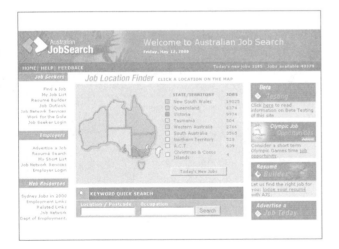

Web Address: *jobsearch.deetya.gov.au*
Number of Job Listings: More than 20,000
Industries Included: All
Location of Jobs: Australia
Search By: Industry; Job Category; Location
Resume Database ☑

Summary: This site, a service of the Australian government, is only open to Australian companies. The site's clean design and user-friendly links make it a must-see for anyone interested in employment in Australia. An automatic e-mail service alerts job seekers to newly posted jobs.

Byron Employment Australia

Web Address: *employment.byron.com.au*
Industries Included: All
Location of Jobs: Australia
Search By: Job Category; Keyword; Location

Summary: This site's big drawback is that the generated list of jobs that match your criteria are in the form of a list of links. The list only includes the job title and a short phrase that, in general, doesn't give you too much of a description of the job. Still, this is probably the most comprehensive job listing site focused on Australia, so (with a little patience) a job seeker should find all the information they are looking for here including links to other career resources. The site's JobMail e-mail service regularly e-mails subscribers jobs that match their registered criteria. Byron Employment Australia also offers insightful information for people interested in moving to Australia.

Canadian Jobs Catalogue

Web Address: *www.kenevacorp.mb.ca*
Industries Included: All
Location of Jobs: Canada
Search By: Keyword
Resume Database ☑

Summary: Canadian Jobs Catalogue provides job seekers access to approximately 100,000 job openings via more than 3,500 direct links. Again, this is one of those sites that does not list any specific job openings themselves, but they do provide a fantastic launching ground for someone looking to start a career in Canada.

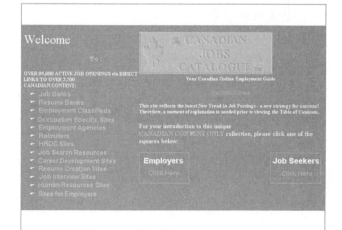

Career India

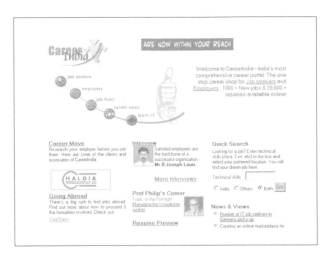

Web Address: *www.careerindia.com*
Number of Job Listings: More than 1,000
Industries Included: All
Location of Jobs: India
Frequency of Updates: Daily
Search By: Job Category
Resume Database ☑
Employer Profiles ☑

Summary: This site offers tips and news for job seekers and employers, links to India's colleges and universities, and resume assistance.

Cyber India Online

Web Address: *www.cioljobs.com*
Number of Job Listings: More than 2,500
Industries Included: Computers
Location of Jobs: India, United States, and Other International Locations
Frequency of Updates: Daily
Search By: Experience Level; Job Category; Location; Salary
Resume Database ☑
Employer Profiles ☑

Summary: In addition to a decent-sized job database, this site offers an assortment of message boards where employers, job seekers, and general IT professionals can share their thoughts and views. The site also offers a variety of IT-related e-newsletters that are quite informative and free of charge.

Indoscape

Web Address: *www.indoscape.com*
Industries Included: All
Location of Jobs: Indonesia
Search By: Company; Date Posted; Job Category; Location
Resume Database ☑
Employer Profiles ☑

Summary: IndoScape is an all-in-one site for news and information relating to Indonesia. The site offers multiple e-mail mailing lists relating to both employment and general interest.

The Irish Jobs Page

Web Address: *www.irishjobs.ie*
Number of Job Listings: More than 5,000
Industries Included: All
Location of Jobs: Ireland
Search By: Company Name; Job Category; Keyword; Top Companies/Agencies
Resume Database ☑

Summary: As the leading career site in Ireland, IrishJobs offers job seekers and employers alike a well-designed site with no shortage on resources. The My Jobs section of their Web page allows job seekers to create their own personal section on the site in which they can receive updates about new job openings. The site can also be broken into a Graduate section or an Executive section, allowing for a more narrow and specialized search, according to education and/or experience level.

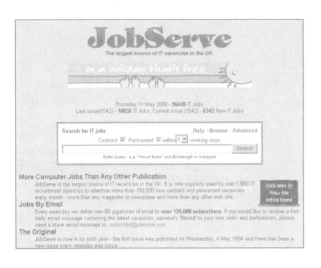

JobServe

Web Address: *www.jobserve.com*
Number of Job Listings: More than 50,000
Industries Included: Computers; Information Technology
Location of Jobs: United Kingdom
Frequency of Updates: Daily
Search By: Date Posted; Keyword; Job Type
Resume Database ☑
Employer Profiles ☑

Summary: Focusing on IT jobs in the U.K., JobServe has an impressive array of clever benefits for job seekers. "Instants" is a page on the site that features the newest job listings each day, and is automatically updated each time a position is posted online. That said, be sure to reload often! JobServe also offers several links to company Web pages, many of which are IT recruitment specialists; inclusion of your resume on a list sent to more than 1,000 IT recruitment specialists across the UK and Europe; several different options to have job listings e-mailed to you (they boast more than 120,000 subscribers); and a directory of recruiters that includes contact information and e-mail addresses.

Jobsite Group

Web Address: *www.jobsite.co.uk*
Number of Job Listings: Approximately 100,000
Industries Included: All
Location of Jobs: Europe
Frequency of Updates: Daily
Search By: Date Posted; Job Category; Job Title; Job Type; Keyword; Skill Set
Resume Database ☑
Employer Profiles ☑

Summary: There's no denying the enormity of this job site, with access to approximately 100,000 jobs at any given time. Jobsite Group's e-mail service lets job seekers know about new job postings. Just bear in mind that resumes are referred to as "curriculum vitae" or "CVs."

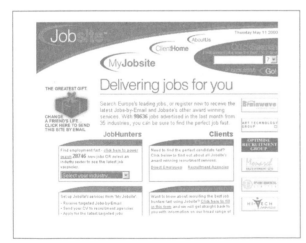

JobStreet.com

Web Address: *www.jobstreet.com*
Number of Job Listings: More than 20,000
Industries Included: All
Location of Jobs: Australia; Hong Kong; India; Indonesia; Malaysia; Philippines; Singapore; Thailand
Search By: Experience; Industry; Keyword; Location
Employer Profiles ☑

Summary: To fully benefit from all this site has to offer, you have to register. With more than 200,000 other registered users under their belt, maybe it's not such a bad idea! And hey, it's free. JobStreet.com claims to receive 10,000 new job listings each month. In addition to job listings, they offer plenty of advice on looking for a job as well as an e-mail notification system.

Jobs Unlimited

Web Address: *www.jobsunlimited.co.uk*
Number of Job Listings: More than 2,500
Industries Included: All
Location of Jobs: The United Kingdom
Frequency of Updates: Daily
Search By: Job Category; Keyword; Location; Salary
Employer Profiles ☑

Summary: In addition to several thousand job openings, Jobs Unlimited offers you the chance to purchase career-related books and other reference materials, and seek out information that is pertinent to your specific job search. The site's Career Manager allows each individual job seeker their own page where they can search out suitable employment and store the ads in one convenient and easy to access area.

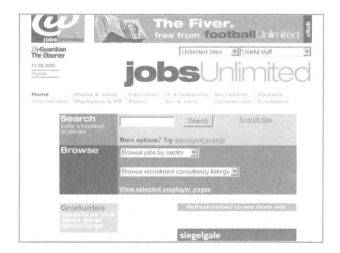

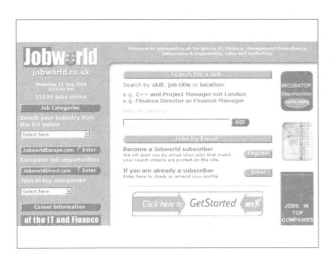

Jobworld UK

Web Address: *www.jobworld.co.uk*
Number of Job Listings: More than 25,000
Industries Included: All
Location of Jobs: United Kingdom
Frequency of Updates: Daily
Search By: Company Name; Industry; Keyword
Employer Profiles ☑

Summary: In addition to browsing through Jobworld's own 25,000+ job listings, job seekers can search jobs links to JobworldEurope.com and JobworldDirect.com. That said, there's a whole lot of information to be researched here. They also provide information on training and getting hired.

Overseas Jobs Express

Web Address: *www.overseasjobs.com*
Number of Job Listings: More than 250
Industries Included: All
Location of Jobs: International
Search By: Job Category
Resume Database ☑
Employer Profiles ☑

Summary: As part of the AboutJobs.com network of Web sites, OverseasJobs.com makes a great international addition. Besides the job listings, the Web site offers job seekers a list of resources that includes links to other related sites and FAQs, as well as a support page that encourages questions and tells you where you can send them.

StepStone

Web Address: *www.stepstone.co.uk*
Number of Job Listings: Approximately 100,000
Industries Included: All
Location of Jobs: Europe
Search By: Company; Job Category; Job Title; Job Type; Keyword; Location
Resume Database ☑

Summary: In addition to nearly 100,000 job listings across Europe, StepStone offers some insightful tips and advice that can help you in each and every step of your job search. Register with their e-mail service, and you will be alerted each time a new job that matches your profile is added to the site.

Top Jobs on the Net

Web Address: *www.topjobs.co.uk*
Industries Included: All
Location of Jobs: United Kingdom
Frequency of Updates: Daily
Search By: Company Name; Job Category; Location
Employer Profiles ☑

Summary: A top banana like you deserves a site like Top Jobs. At least that's what *they* say. Every day brings new jobs to the Top Jobs site, and it's likely that you won't want to miss out on them. Register with their e-mail service and you will be alerted every time a matching job is posted to the site. Top Jobs on the Net also offers links to private and public company Web sites. A nice feature for recent graduates is that they can select to see entry-level positions only.

Vacancies

Web Address: *www.vacancies.ac.uk*
Number of Job Listings: Fewer than 250
Industries Included: Higher Education
Location of Jobs: United Kingdom and Ireland
Search By: Keyword; Posting date; Job Type (temporary, contract, research); Subject

Summary: Operated by National Information Services and Systems (NISS), this site is very much dedicated to helping job seekers find suitable employment. Job listings are quite detailed, and often include such pertinent (and decision-making) information as salary.

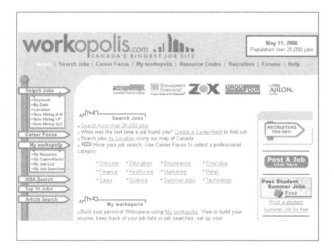

Workopolis.com

Web Address: *www.workopolis.com*
Number of Job Listings: More than 25,000
Industries Included: All
Location of Jobs: Canada
Frequency of Updates: Daily
Search By: Company Name; Job Category; Keyword
Resume Database ☑
Employer Profiles ☑

Summary: They refer to themselves as "Canada's Biggest Job Site," but they're also one of the Internet's most personal. More so than many other job sites, Workopolis.com is dedicated to helping job seekers find the job, salary, and company that is right for *them* by offering personalized services like an e-mail alert system and the option to save personalized job lists and job searches.

Accounting/Banking/Finance

Accounting.com

Web Address: *www.accounting.com*
Number of Job Listings: More than 250
Industries Included: Accounting
Location of Jobs: United States
Frequency of Updates: At least every three weeks
Search By: Company; Job Category; Keyword; Location
Resume Database ☑

Summary: Aside from offering several hundred job listings, accounting.com offers job seekers the opportunity to read about the industry's latest happenings, find additional resources, and join in a discussion group.

Bankjobs.com

Web Address: *www.bankjobs.com*
Number of Job Listings: More than 5,000
Industries Included: Banking; Financial Services
Location of Jobs: United States
Frequency of Updates: Twice Weekly
Search By: Keyword; Location
Resume Database ☑

Summary: In addition to hosting job listings for several well-known banking and finance firms (First Union, Wachovia), bankjobs.com offers job seekers the privacy they need and deserve. You can post your resume anonymously. The site claims that more than 60,000 hiring professionals browse through these resumes every month; if that's true, it may be a good idea to post your resume anonymously.

Bloomberg.com

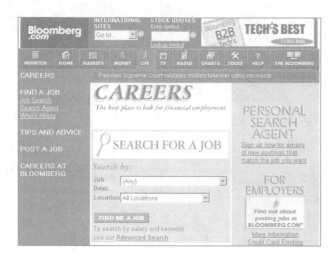

Web Address: *www.bloomberg.com/careers*
Number of Job Listings: Fewer than 250
Industries Included: Financial Services
Location of Jobs: United States; Some International
Frequency of Updates: Daily
Search By: Job Category; Keyword; Location; Salary

Summary: Bloomberg.com is an all-in-one financial services site with extensive information that should prove valuable to any professional in the financial services industry. A personal search agent e-mails job seekers when new openings arise that meet his or her criteria.

CFO's Featured Jobs

Web Address: *www.cfonet.com*
Number of Job Listings: Fewer than 250
Jobs Included: Chief Financial Officer; Senior **Financial Executive;** Treasurer
Location of Jobs: United States
Resume Database ☑

Summary: This is the online site for *CFO* magazine. Basically, job seekers should be of a very experienced level if they want to have any success with this site. While the quantity of jobs found here is not very plentiful, the positions are all executive-level jobs. Candidates can fill out a profile and have matching job listings e-mailed directly to them as they open. For the seasoned financial professional, the e-mail service is a great way to keep informed of current opportunities while you're not yet looking *too* hard.

Fincareer.com

Web Address: *www.fincareer.com*
Number of Job Listings: More than 1,000
Jobs Included: Advisory; Corporate; Financial Engineering; Investment Marketing; Marketing; Operations; Research; Risk Management; Sales; Trading; Underwriting
Location of Jobs: United States; Some International
Frequency of Updates: Daily
Search By: Experience Level; Job Category; Location
Resume Database ☑

Summary: Fincareer.com offers all sorts of positions—from entry-level to senior executive—in a variety of financial settings. The site highlights jobs at some of today's biggest financial institutions such as Merrill Lynch, J.P. Morgan, Chase Manhattan, and PaineWebber. Rather than having to post your entire resume (or have an employer riffle through several resumes), you can post a candidate profile for recruiters to look at.

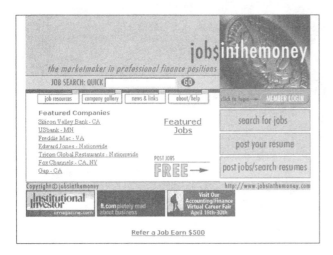

Job$inthemoney

Web Address: *www.jobsinthemoney.com*
Number of Job Listings: More than 1,000
Industries Included: Accounting; Banking;
Economics; Finance; Insurance;
Location of Jobs: United States; Some International
Frequency of updates: Daily
Search By: Industry and Subindustry; Location;
Keyword
Resume Database ☑
Employer Profiles ☑

Summary: Although this site allows companies to
post a job free of charge, there didn't seem to be
too many spam-like listings, hinting that the listings had been properly screened. The company
profiles are also to-the-point and informative and
include such information as contact data, a brief
position description, and a link to the company's
Web site. The site offers a privacy policy that
includes anonymous resumes and "Company
Hide," which allows job seekers to show their
resume only to approved companies. Similar privacy features are offered to companies posting job
openings. The site also includes and extensive list
of links offering a variety of information of value to
both financial professionals and job seekers.

Advertising/Marketing/Public Relations

Adweekonline Careernetwork

Web Address: *www.adweek.com*
Number of Job Listings: More than 200
Industries Included: Advertising; Marketing; Media; Publishing; TV/Radio; Production/Traffic; New Media/Information Technology
Location of Jobs: United States
Frequency of Updates: Weekly
Search By: Company Name; Job Category; Keyword; Location
Resume Database ☑

Summary: AdweekOnline is the online version of the weekly magazine filled with news of interest to advertising firms and professionals. The site also offers online access to the Adweek Directory, Brandweek Directory, Mediaweek Directory, and IQ Directory. Each of these directories provides extensive information on thousands of companies in each of their respective industries.

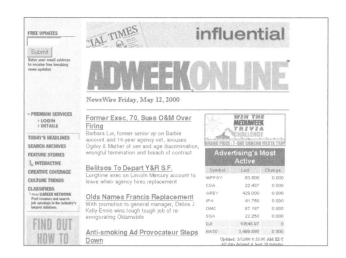

The DMA Interactive

Web Address: *www.the-dma.org*
Number of Job Listings: More than 250
Jobs Included: Direct Marketing Positions
Location of Jobs: United States; Some International
Search By: Experience; Job Category; Location; Salary
Resume Database ☑

Summary: In addition to various job listings, this site also offers a directory of various direct marketing service providers and an array of other information sources designed primarily for direct marketing companies.

MarketingJobs.com

Web Address: *www.marketingjobs.com*
Number of Job Listings: More than 5,000
Industries Included: Advertising; Marketing; Sales
Location of Jobs: United States
Search By: Company; Industry; Job Category; Keyword; Location
Resume Database ☑
Employer Profiles ☑

Summary: This site does a good job of telling you what it offers, how much of it is available, and all the costs involved. The number of listings for each job category is impressive and clearly defined. This site is highly recommended for anyone who might be interested in these fields.

Aerospace/Aviation

AviationEmployment.com

Web Address: *www.aviationemployment.com*
Number of Job Listings: More than 250
Industries Included: Aviation
Location of Jobs: United States
Search By: Company Name; Date Posted; Education; Job Category; Job Type; Location; Salary
Employer Profiles ☑

Summary: If you choose to select your own criteria, this site will really let you get down to the nitty gritty. Entering too much information (job category, job type, location, salary, etc.) may limit the jobs retrieved, but it will give you an inkling into your desired job market. If you're not too concerned about the minor details, jobs will appear in alphabetical order, making them a bit difficult to sift through.

Space Jobs

Web Address: *www.spacejobs.com*
Number of Job Listings: Less than 250
Industries Included: Aerospace
Location of Jobs: United States; Some International
Search By: Company Name; Keyword; Location
Employer Profiles ☑

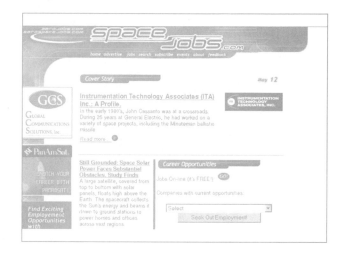

Summary: Space Jobs offers an e-mail notification service so job seekers can hear about possible opportunities as soon as they become available on the site. Space Jobs can also give you access to a schedule of related conferences. Go to their Events section for a list of worldwide events such as conventions and seminars relating to the aerospace industry. Finally, link to their List of All Organizations for links to aerospace companies worldwide.

Arts/Entertainment

The Internet Music Pages

Web Address: *www.musicpages.com*
Number of Job Listings: Less than 250
Industries Included: Music
Location of Jobs: United States; Some International

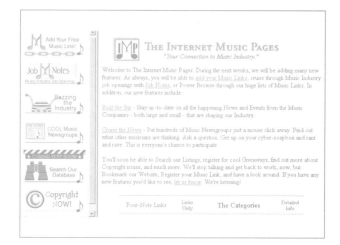

Summary: This site has a well-organized system of every music-related link imaginable from education to indie labels' Web sites. This site also provides links to music-related newsgroups. Job listings come from companies like Dolby, Microsoft, and Fender. The site allows other sites to get links for free, making this a good networking platform for both musicians and music professionals in the industry.

Showbizjobs.com

Web Address: *www.showbizjobs.com*
Number of Job Listings: More than 250
Industries Included: Film; Television; Recording; Multimedia; Theme Parks
Location of Jobs: United States
Frequency of Updates: Daily
Search By: Company; Date Posted; Job Category; Location
Resume Database ☑
Employer Profiles ☑

Summary: The job listings found here are basically for behind-the-scenes positions in a number of entertainment-related fields. Many of the search features on this site have recently been improved and it appears that the site's administrators are eager to cater to the needs of both its corporate clients and the job seekers who use their service. The site allows you to send a job to a friend or send resumes directly to employers from the site. Their e-mail notification system is another plus.

Biotechnology/Scientific

Bio Online

Web Address: *www.bio.com*
Number of Job Listings: More than 1,000
Industries Included: Life Sciences
Location of Jobs: United States; Some International
Frequency of Updates: Daily
Search By: Company Name; Job Category; Keyword; Location
Resume Database ☑
Employer Database ☑

Summary: Be aware that clicking on "search" puts you on a page that searches the entire Web site. Select "Jobs" from the advanced search menu to search for job postings. A big bonus of this site is the user-friendly forms used for entering resumes, posting a job, and applying for a job. The site also includes links to industry news and activities, and links to research and education sources. There is also an open forum discussion area for possible networking use.

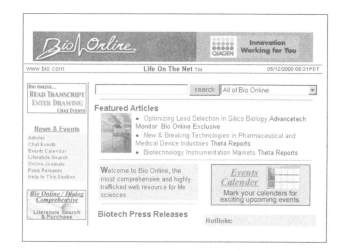

The Biospace Career Center

Web Address: *www.biospace.com*
Number of Job Listings: More than 250
Industries Included: Biotechnology
Location of Jobs: Worldwide
Search By: Company; Job Category; Keyword; Location
Employer Profiles ☑

Summary: The Biospace Career Center offers a ton of links and information on industry news, events, and resources. Check out the Career Center links on the left sidebar of the site's home page to get the search options other than by keyword. One gripe with this site is you cannot connect between job openings and company profiles or vice versa.

Science Professional Network

Web Address: *recruit.sciencemag.org*
Number of Job Listings: More than 1,000
Industries Included: Sciences
Location of Jobs: United States; Some International
Search By: Company; Date Posted; Job Category; Job Title; Keyword; Location
Resume Database ☑
Employer Profiles ☑

Summary: This site, which is connected to *Science* magazine, offers a very detailed search option, and has a decent number of job listings and company profiles for a relatively limited audience. Their e-mail service notifies job seekers of new job listings. The site also offers links to career fair information, related career sites, and news and educational programs.

Charities/Social Services

Community Career Center

Web Address: *www.nonprofitjobs.org*
Number of Job Listings: More than 250
Industries Included: Nonprofits
Location of Jobs: United States; Some International
Search By: Company Name; Job Category; Job Title; Job Type; Keyword; Location; Salary; Skill Set; Work Type
Resume Database ☑
Employer Profiles ☑

Summary: A very detailed job search page makes this a great choice for applicants who know exactly what they want. The Web site has a separate section for freelance projects, which is kind of a rare find when talking about nonprofits.

The *Nonprofit Times* Online

Web Address: *www.nptimes.com*
Industries Included: Charities; Social Services; Nonprofits
Location of Jobs: United States
Frequency of Updates: Monthly

Summary: Operated by the folks that bring you The *Nonprofit Times*, this site will give you a great base of knowledge in the nonprofit industry and provide you a directory that includes the names and contact information of a wide range of nonprofit organizations.

OpportunityNOCs

Web Address: *www.opportunitynocs.org*
Number of Job Listings: More than 250
Industries Included: Arts; Education; Health; Nonprofits; Social Services
Location of Jobs: United States
Frequency of Updates: Daily
Search By: Date Posted; Keyword; Location; Job Type; Job number

Summary: This site is brought to you by the same people who bring you *Opportunity NOCs*, the printed newsletter. The newsletter, with editions for Boston, New York, Philadelphia, and other metropolitan areas, details more than 1,000 new job listings each month to a subscriber base of more than 50,000. If you're a job seeker looking for a new job in the nonprofit arena, or you're a nonprofit looking for employees, this is a good place to start.

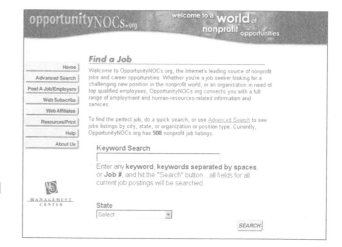

SocialService.com

Web Address: *www.socialservice.com*
Industries Included: Social Service
Location of Jobs: United States

Summary: SocialService.com is a good source for narrowing your search for social service jobs to a particular geographic area. An e-mail service notifies job seekers of new listings in their state. Along with job listings for each state, each state page includes an assortment of job links for that state including links to specific company/organization job lists and to employment agencies.

Computers

The Computer Jobs Store

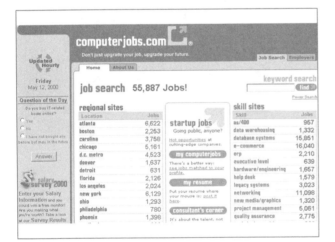

Web Address: *www.computerjobs.com*
Number of Job Listings: More than 20,000
Industries Included: Computer
Location of Jobs: United States
Frequency of Updates: Hourly
Search By: Job Category; Keyword; Location
Resume Database ☑
Employer Profiles ☑

Summary: Overall, this site is tops for its industry. The Consultant's Corner provides an effective venue for contract fulfillment. The site offers salary information and allows job seekers to save their job search results. This site is also broken down into over 20 regional sites, a site for start ups, and one for computer consultants. Job seekers can also have their resume matched to all available positions.

Computerwork.com

Web Address: *www.computerwork.com*
Number of Job Listings: More than 10,000
Industries Included: Computer
Location of Jobs: Canada; United States
Frequency of Updates: Daily
Search By: Date Posted; Job Category; Job Type;
Keyword; Location;
Resume Database ☑
Employer Profiles ☑

Summary: Computerwork.com links to related
sites and offers a Career Resources section that
offers information on computer training, career
fairs information, career news, reference articles,
and more. Check out the Other Sites section for
links to sites targeted at specific geographic and
professional areas.

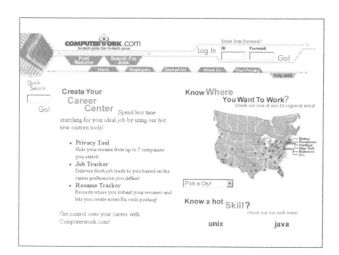

Dice.com

Web Address: *www.dice.com*
Number of Job Listings: Over 200,000
Types of Job Listings: High-Tech
Location of Jobs: United States
Search By: Area Code; Date Posted; Job Type;
Keyword; Location
Resume Database ☑
Employer Profiles ☑

Summary: The unlimited job postings feature on this
site makes the number of ads increase by the thousands day to day. The site offers an e-mail service
that notifies job seekers of new listings; relocation
information; and an Announce Availability feature
that job seekers fill out, and Dice.com then sends
via e-mail to member companies.

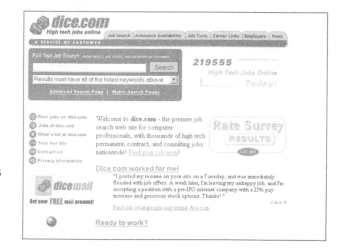

High Technology Careers Magazine

Web Address: *www.hightechcareers.com*
Number of Job Listings: More than 50,000
Industries Included: High-Tech
Location of Jobs: United States
Frequency of Updates: Daily
Search By: Keyword; Location
Resume Database ☑
Employer Profiles ☑

Summary: The site offers access to a half million articles and one of the most extensive databases of high-tech employer profiles around. The job listings are powered through Westech's Incpad.com. The site provides lots of career guidance and career fair information, and links to high-tech job sites

1-Jobs.com

Web Address: *www.1-jobs.com*
Number of Job Listings: More than 2,500
Industries Included: Computers; Engineering; Telecommunications
Location of Jobs: United States; Some International
Frequency of Updates: Hourly
Search By: Company Name; Date Posted; Job Category; Keyword; Location; Salary
Resume Database ☑
Employer Profiles ☑

Summary: 1-Jobs.com is a must-see for anybody interested in this particular field. The site offers a schedule of high-tech career fairs; links to tons of career sites (including city and state sites), association sites, newsgroups, online newspapers, and much more. Registered job seekers get a free subscription to *TechJobs* magazine; a free newsletter for registered employers; and a Job Search Agent, which matches a job seeker's resume to available positions.

IT Careers

Web Address: *www.ITcareers.com*
Number of Job Listings: More than 5,000
Industries Included: Information Technology
Location of Jobs: United States
Search By: Job Type; Keyword; Location

Summary: This straightforward site offers plenty of detailed job descriptions in an easy-to-read format. It also provides an IT career events list, electronic newsletters, and general recruiting information.

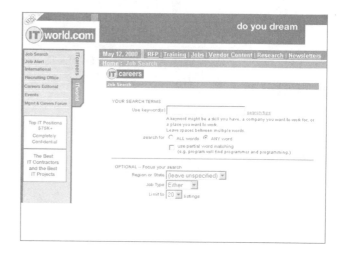

Jobs for Programmers

Web Address: *www.prgjobs.com*
Industries Included: Computer Programming
Location of Jobs: United States
Search By: Keyword; Location; Miscellaneous Qualifiers
Resume Database ☑

Summary: This is, by far, the largest and most detailed site dedicated to computer programmers. The very detailed job descriptions make it a good site for those in the profession.

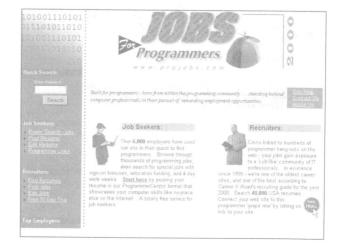

Jobs.Internet.com

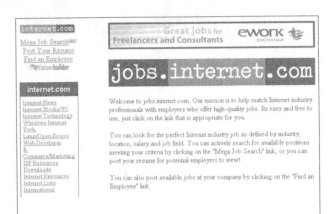

Web Address: *jobs.internet.com*
Industries Included: Computer
Location of Jobs: United States
Frequency of Updates: Daily
Search By: Job Category; Keyword; Location; Salary

Summary: This site enjoys a partnership with the CareerBuilder Network, which offers broad Web exposure and more efficient job search/employee search capabilities. It features a personal search agent that notifies job seekers of new listings matching their criteria; Job of the Week listing on their home page; links to various Internet resources, including a news section with articles on Internet careers; and links to sites under the heading "internet.commerce" (banking, e-commerce, and others).

Job Warehouse

Web Address: *www.jobwarehouse.com*
Number of Job Listings: More than 5,000
Industries Included: Computer; Information Technology
Location of Jobs: United States; Some International
Search By: Company Name; Date Posted; Keyword; Location; Job ID Number
Resume Database ☑
Employer Profiles ☑

Summary: Job seeker's must register their resume in order to view job openings; however, confidentiality can be maintained. Most of the jobs posted were multiple postings from a select few companies, often executive recruiters. The site offers links to helpful sites for job seekers, with topics ranging from salary information to tax rates; and an e-mail service which notifies job seekers of new opportunities, and notifies employers of newly listed resumes matching their requirements.

MacTalent

Web Address: *www.mactalent.com*
Number of Job Listings: Less than 250
Industries Included: Jobs involving Macintosh Computer Skills Including: Programming, Graphic Design, Web Design, and Desktop Publishing.
Location of Jobs: United States; Some International
Frequency of Updates: Daily
Resume Database ☑

Summary: This is the only site we know of designed specifically for the Mac-savvy professional. About a third of the jobs posted were in California. The site has a bookstore containing over 200 Mac-related titles and tips on dealing with recruiters.

SelectJOBS

Web Address: *www.selectjobs.com*
Number of Job Listings: More than 5,000
Industries Included: Computer; High-Tech
Location of Jobs: United States; Some International
Frequency of Updates: Daily
Search By: Company Name; Job Title; Job Category; Job Type; Location; Skill Set
Resume Database ☑
Employer Profiles ☑

Summary: An extensive site for the computer industry since 1996, SelectJOBS has teamed up with 14 other Internet career sites. The site won't send your resume to a company unless you've given your approval to do so. If you plan on using this site, be prepared to deal with employment agencies, which make up a big chunk of the job listings. Automatic e-mail notification of job matches and links to other career resource sites are some of their additional services.

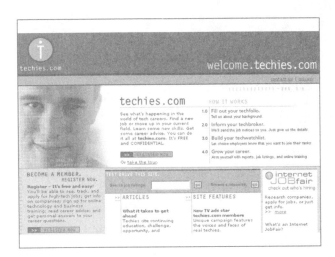

Techies.com

Web Address: *www.techies.com*
Number of Job Listings: More than 5,000
Industries Included: High-Tech; Information Technology
Location of Jobs: United States
Search By: Company Name; Job Category; Job Title; Location
Resume Database ☑
Employer Profiles ☑

Summary: Techies.com has been aggressively promoting their site for some time now, and with good reason. The sharp design and high-profile clientele have made this one of the fastest growing sites on the Net.

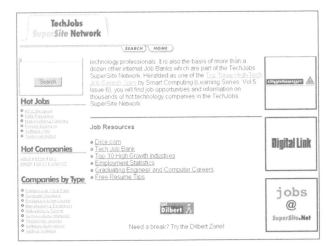

Techjobs Supersite Network

Web Address: *techjobs.supersites.net*
Number of Job Listings: More than 2,500
Industries Included: High-Tech
Location of Jobs: United States
Frequency of Updates: Daily
Search By: Company Name; Keyword

Summary: This site offers more than a dozen other high-tech job sites on the Web. That said, it is undoubtedly one of the better sites out there for high-tech professionals on the prowl for new employment. In addition to job listings, the site will provide you with tips for writing an attention-getting resume, employment statistics, and other information that may be relevant to you and the future of your career.

Education

Academic360.com

Web Address: *www.academic360.com*
Industries Included: Academic
Location of Jobs: Australia; Canada; United Kingdom; United States
Search By: Company Name; Job Category; Location
Employer Profiles ☑

Summary: This is not a job search site, per se. Rather, Academic360.com is a superb collection of links that can allow job seekers to quickly navigate their way into a new job. Links include topical or geographic sites, access to related newsgroups, and a listing of relevant associations.

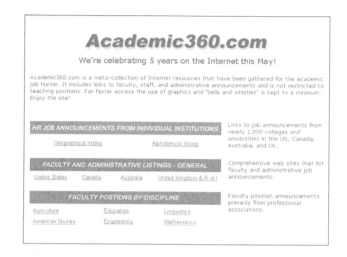

Academic Employment Network

Web Address: *www.academploy.com*
Number of Job Listings: Fewer than 250
Industries Included: Academic; Teaching
Location of Jobs: United States; Some International
Search By: Job Title; Location
Resume Database ☑

Summary: This fairly small site is easy to navigate and offers a good deal of useful information for the job seeker focused on academics. The site links to education-related Web sites, relocation services, certification and development resources, as well as its own forum.

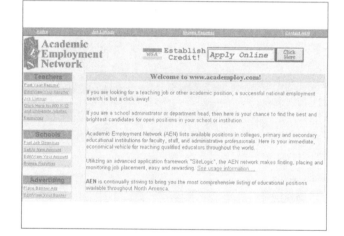

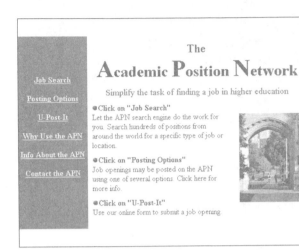

Academic Position Network

Web Address: *www.apnjobs.com*
Number of Job Listings: Less than 250
Industries Included: Education
Location of Jobs: United States; Some International
Frequency of Updates: Daily
Search By: Field of Interest; Institution Type; Job Type

Summary: This site is pretty lean on the frills, which makes it easy for those eager to get down to business.

The *Chronicle of Higher Education's* Career Network

Web Address: *chronicle.com/jobs*
Number of Job Listings: More than 1,000
Industries Included: Academic
Location of Jobs: United States; Some International
Frequency of Updates: Weekly
Search By: Job Category; Keyword; Region

Summary: The Career Network contains hundreds of listings for faculty, administrative, and executive positions at prestigious U.S. colleges. The job database includes listings for related positions outside of academe, in organizations such as art galleries, government agencies, museums, and other nonprofit organizations. Subscribers can see the full text of The *Chronicle of Higher Education*, the trade newspaper for academics.

HigherEdJobs.com

Web Address: *www.higheredjobs.com*
Number of Job Listings: More than 1,000
Industries Included: Higher Education
Location of Jobs: United States
Search By: Company Name; Job Category; Job Title; Keyword; Location

Summary: As the name suggests, this site lists information for institutions of higher education only. Job seekers can search for staff or faculty positions, or by state or institution. A free subscription to Higher Ed Jobs Online, offered to educational institutions (restrictions apply), and an e-mail service that sends occasional updates to registered job seekers, detailing information on newly listed educational institutions, are just a few of the extras you'll find here.

Engineering

EngineerJobs.Com

Web Address: *www.engineerjobs.com*
Number of Job Listings: More than 250
Industries Included: Engineering
Location of Jobs: United States
Search By: Date Posted; Keyword; Location
Resume Database ☑

Summary: This is one of the more popular and resourceful sites related to engineering jobs, and they are working to expand their services nationwide. Extras include an e-mail service for job seekers, very detailed job descriptions, and links to other engineering and technical sites.

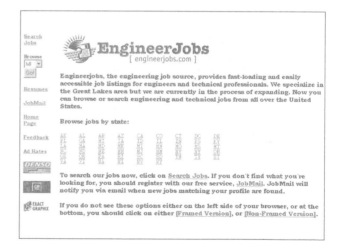

Government

Corporate Gray Online

Web Address: *www.bluetogray.com*
Number of Job Listings: More than 5,000
Industries Included: All
Resume Database ☑
Employer Profiles ☑

Summary: This site is offered as a career resource to military personnel leaving the service. Powered by CareerWeb, it links to several career resources specifically for people leaving the military; a topic you might have trouble finding on your own.

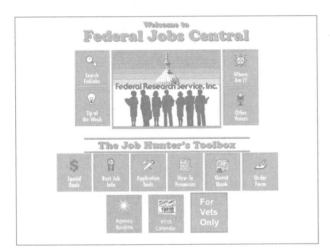

Federal Jobs Central

Web Address: *www.fedjobs.com*
Number of Job Listings: More than 5,000
Industries Included: Federal Government
Location of Jobs: United States
Frequency of Updates: Daily
Search By: Industry; Job Category; Job Title; Keyword; Location; Salary; Skill Set

Summary: This site gathers its job openings through its own research. Even with meticulous tending, such a large database would tend to have outdated information. Considering its size, the price (there is a cost) may be worth it to job seekers serious about working for the federal government. Those who are unsure, can sample the listing without the full details for free. Includes a calendar of events, career tips, information on federal agencies, and more.

Federal Jobs Digest

Web Address: *www.jobsfed.com*
Number of Job Listings: More than 5,000
Industries Included: Government
Location of Jobs: United States
Frequency of Updates: Daily
Search By: Job Category; Job Title; Location
Resume Database ☑

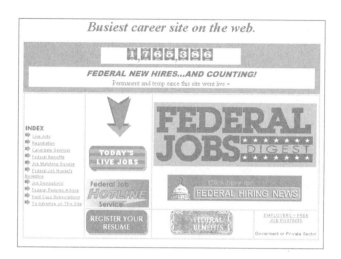

Summary: Government and private sector employers can place job listings here, free of charge. That said, job descriptions tend to be more detailed, as money and space are not a concern. A detailed resume posting area, a listing of the most recent job postings, a jobs bulletin board, a listing of hotlines, a job matching service, and information on federal benefits are a few of the site's added perks.

Health Care

America's Health Care Source

Web Address: *www.healthcaresource.com*
Number of Job Listings: More than 1,000
Industries Included: Health Care
Location of Jobs: United States
Search By: Industry; Job Category; Job Title; Location
Resume Database ☑

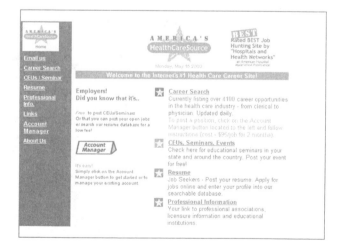

Summary: This site was rated the best job-hunting site by *Hospitals and Health Networks*, a publication of the American Hospital Association. It links to health care industry sites, career resources, and professional associations for added help in your job search.

A Great Place to Advertise Jobs . . .
and Find Outstanding Candidates

"Just a quick note to let you know that I posted my resume on Wednesday night, had a phone interview Friday and an in-person interview the next Wednesday, and was hired at my dream job that Friday. Thanks so very much. . . A. Kennedy"

More Comments

The new **chemistry** of matching the right job and the right candidate.
Exclusively Biotechnology, Pharmaceuticals, Science, Medicine and Healthcare since 1994.
3880 Jobs Online Today, 5/15/2000.

Medzilla

Web Address: *www.medzilla.com*
Number of Job Listings: More than 2,500
Industries Included: Biotechnology; Health Care; Science
Location of Jobs: United States
Search By: Keyword
Resume Database ☑
Employer Profiles ☑

Summary: This site is a good resource for job seekers in health care and related fields. Some listings include extensive employer descriptions and an area set up to automatically e-mail the employee. The site links to employer Web sites, and articles on job searching, as well as information on the health care industry in general.

Nursing Spectrum Career Fitness Online

Web Address: *www.nursingspectrum.com*
Number of Job Listings: More than 1,000
Industries Included: Nursing
Location of Jobs: United States
Search By: Job Category; Keyword; Location
Employer Profiles ☑

Summary: Check this site out if you have any interest in nursing—whether you're looking for a new job, looking for a new employee, or you're simply interested in staying informed or learning more about the nursing profession. The site includes a schedule of nationwide nursing events, a chat area, a nursing forum, and other resources including nursing books, health care policy information, educational resources, and an e-mail agent that notifies job seekers of newly posted jobs.

Physicians Employment

Web Address: *www.physemp.com*
Number of Job Listings: More than 5,000
Industries Included: Health Care
Location of Jobs: United States
Search By: Job Category; Location

Summary: This is one of the Web's largest and oldest job sites devoted to health care. Before being able to view just about any information the site asks for basic profile information. By clicking "send information" with all the fields left blank, you can access the job listings.

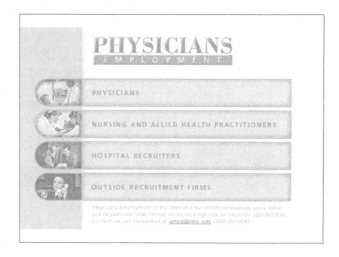

Hotels/Restaurant

StarChefs

Web Address: *www.starchefs.com*
Number of Job Listings: More than 250
Industries Included: Hotel & Restaurant
Location of Jobs: United States; Some International
Frequency of Updates: Daily
Search By: Job Title; Keyword; Location
Resume Database ☑
Employer Profiles ☑

Summary: This site could use more listings, especially since most highly specialized positions are only offered in one or two places in the country. But, if you are looking to find a job as a sous chef, you're in luck! Job categories can be narrowed down to such precise positions as "pasta cook" and "wine service." The site also offers information on various culinary careers and tons of info for chefs including hot recipes, discussion groups, and topics of interest.

Human Resources/Recruiting

HR World

Web Address: *www.hrworld.com*
Industries Included: Human Resources
Location of Jobs: United States
Search By: Job Title; Location

Summary: Much of the info is only accessible to registered users but, since registration is free, there's no reason not to do it. HR World is a must for all HR professionals to check out, whether you're seeking employment or seeking employees. The site includes discussion forums, information on human resources products and services, access to human resources articles and publications, and links to worldwide human resources sites.

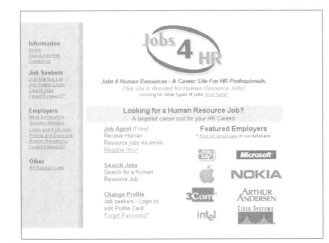

Jobs 4 HR

Web Address: *www.jobs4hr.com*
Industries Included: Human Resources
Location of Jobs: United States
Search By: Company Name; Job Category; Keyword; Location

Summary: Employers that use this site include Microsoft and Manpower, among others. Isn't it time you play with the big guys? Jobs 4 HR is operated by Recruiter's Network. The site offers a free e-mail job agent, a mailing list connecting job seekers and employers, and links to other HR sites.

Society for Human Resource Management

Web Address: *www.shrm.org/jobs*
Number of Job Listings: More than 1,000
Industries Included: Human Resources
Location of Jobs: United States; Some International
Frequency of Updates: Daily
Search By: Date Posted; Job Title; Keyword; Location by state

Summary: Since it's often the job of the HR professional to find employees, you can imagine what a site dedicated to recruiting HR professionals would look like. This site is detailed, organized, and—above all—chock full of employment listings that can be organized in multiple convenient lists for the job seeker's browsing pleasure. Many of the site's features are only available to SHRM members. Openings are organized as a list of job titles linking to the full, written description of the position.

Legal

Law Jobs

Web Address: *www.lawjobs.com*
Number of Job Listings: More than 250
Industries Included: Legal
Location of Jobs: United States
Search By: Job Category; Location

Summary: This site is a service of American Lawyer Media, which prints newspapers and journals. In addition to a decent amount of job listings, they also include a list of recruiters; an e-mail service that allows you to send a listing to a friend; and links to temporary agencies, regional classified ads, and related news.

The Legal Employment Search Site

Web Address: *www.legalemploy.com*
Industries Included: Legal
Location of Jobs: United States

Summary: This site is one massive list of links to sites covering legal-related employment, law school career services offices, general employment, online resume posting, and other general sites that may be of value to job seekers in the legal field.

Mining/Gas/Petroleum

Oil-Link

Web Address: *www.oillink.com*
Industries Included: Mining/Gas/Petroleum/ Energy Related
Location of Jobs: United States
Search By: Company Name; Job Title; Keyword
Resume Database ☑
Employer Profiles ☑

Summary: For oil and gas jobs, this is a big site. The site reports 120,000 visits per month, by 38,000 unique users. Companies that post listings include: Texaco, Schlumberger, Hunt Oil Company, and many more. The site details lots of industry information including news, surveys, stats, books, a salary calculator, resume assistance, and more. It provides links to all sorts of Web resources—newsgroups, government sites, events schedules, educational information, associations, and listings for different oil and gas categories. Sign up to receive "Inbox Direct," a free, daily newsletter sent to you via e-mail, that details current news and offers new job listings.

Retail

Retail Jobnet

Web Address: *www.retailjobnet.com*
Number of Job Listings: More than 250
Industries Included: Retail
Location of Jobs: United States
Frequency of Updates: Weekly
Search By: Location; Job Category; Job Title
Resume Database ☑
Employer Profiles ☑

Summary: This site is focused exclusively on positions in the retail industry, and continues to work diligently to add listings and sponsors. Nearly 500 of the sites' posted jobs were for store managers. An added bonus is their many links to other retail sites.

Transportation

1-800-Drivers

Web Address: *www.1800drivers.com*
Industries Included: Trucking
Location of Jobs: United States; Some International
Search By: Experience Level; Job Title; Location; Skills; Trailer Type
Employer Profiles ☑

Summary: Whether looking for the long hauls or local delivery, truckers should check out this stop for their future employment needs. The site offers information on road conditions, construction notices, and trucking regulations for most major highways in the United States. The site also has online application forms and links to the employers' Web sites as well as a myriad of other links in the industry.

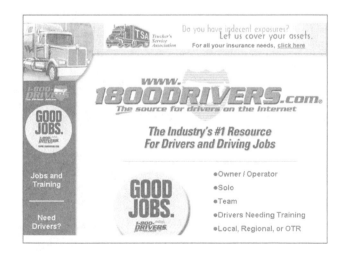

Newspapers Online

The saying goes that "the more things change, the more they stay the same." In the case of the Internet, this is definitely true. Even with all the new dot.com companies that have come into being, people—Internet users, specifically—still enjoy such traditions as reading the daily newspaper. Sure, any search engine or commercial online service home page will give you up-to-the-second information on the latest happenings in the world, but there's still something comforting about being able to read *Hometown News* and know that the world hasn't changed too much!

Newspapers are a prime source of employment news (come on, we've all been known to circle a help wanted ad or two), and most of the country's big newspapers have gone online. In the process of this change, they have even made it easier for you to search through the help wanted section when doing so online. Instead of skimming through the pages, looking for the skills, location, and salary that meet your needs, many online newspapers will allow you to enter a set of criteria and search out those specific openings. This is also great for the individual looking to relocate. Rather than trekking to the local library for a glimpse of the newspapers in other areas or instead of calling up the newspaper and ordering your own subscription, the Internet makes it possible for you to view these papers (and their employment sections) right from your computer. Once you find the perfect job, you can also use these same newspapers to find an apartment, home, or any other information you think may be pertinent. Is your favorite newspaper online? Browse through the following list and see.

Alabama

Birmingham News
www.al.com/birmingham

Birmingham Post-Herald
www.postherald.com

Huntsville Times
www.al.com/huntsville

Mobile Register
www.al.com/mobile

Montgomery Advertiser
www.montgomerycareerpath.com

Troy Messenger
www.troymessenger.com

Alaska

Anchorage Daily News
www.adn.com

The Anchorage Press
www.anchoragepress.com

Fairbanks Daily News-Miner
www.newsminer.com

Frontiersman
www.frontiersman.com

Juneau Empire
www.juneauempire.com

Arizona

Arizona Daily Star
www.azstarnet.com

Arizona Daily Sun
www.azdailysun.com

Arizona Republic
www.arizonarepublic.com

The Daily Courier
www.prescottaz.com

Today's News-Herald
www.havasunews.com

Tucson Citizen
www.tucsoncitizen.com

The Yuma Daily Sun
www.yumasun.com

Arkansas

Arkansas Democrat-Gazette
www.ardemgaz.com

The Daily Citizen
www.thedailycitizen.com

East Arkansas News Leader
www.earknewsleader.com

The Morning News of Northwest Arkansas
www.nwamorningnews.com

Northwest Arkansas Times
www.nwarktimes.com

Southwest Times Record
www.swtimes.com

California

The Californian
www.thedailycalifornian.com

Contra Costa Times
www.hotcoco.com

Daily News Los Angeles
www.dailynews.com

The Davis Enterprise
www.davisenterprise.com

Fresno Bee
www.fresnobee.com

Los Angeles Times
www.latimes.com

Modesto Bee
www.modbee.com

Orange County Register
www.ocregister.com

Sacramento Bee
www.sacbee.com

San Diego Union-Tribune
www.uniontrib.com

San Francisco Chronicle
www.sfgate.com/chronicle

San Francisco Examiner
www.examiner.com

San Jose Mercury News
www.mercurycenter.com

Colorado

Aspen Daily News
www.aspendailynews.com

Boulder Daily Camera
www.thedailycamera.com

Denver Post
www.denverpost.com

Durango Herald
www.durangoherald.com

The Gazette
www.gazette.com

The Greeley Daily Tribune
www.greeleytrib.com

Rocky Mountain News
www.insidedenver.com

Telluride Daily Planet
www.telluridegateway.com

Vail Daily
www.vaildaily.com

Connecticut

Connecticut Post
www.connpost.com

Greenwich Time
www.greenwichtime.com

Hartford Advocate
www.hartfordadvocate.com

Hartford Courant
www.hartfordcourant.com

New Haven Advocate
www.newhavenadvocate.com

Stamford Advocate
www.stamfordadvocate.com

Delaware

Cape Gazette
www.capegazette.com

Delaware Coast Press
www.shore-source.com/dcp

Dover Post
www.doverpost.com

The Newark Post
www.ncbl.com/post

The News Journal
www.delawareonline.com

District of Columbia

The Common Denominator
www.thecommondenominator.com

Roll Call
www.rollcall.com

Washington City Paper
www.washingtoncitypaper.com

Washington Post
www.washingtonpost.com

The Washington Times
www.washtimes.com

Florida

The Florida Times-Union
jacksonville.com

Florida Today
www.flatoday.com

Herald-Tribune Newscoast
www.newscoast.com

The Miami Herald
www.herald.com

Naples Daily News
www.naplesnews.com

The News Herald
www.newsherald.com

The News-Press
www.news-press.com

Northwest Florida Daily News
www.nwfdailynews.com

Orlando Sentinel
www.orlandosentinel.com

Pensacola News Journal
www.pensacolanewsjournal.com

The Sun-Sentinel
www.sun-sentinel.com

Tallahassee Democrat
www.tdo.com

Tampa Tribune
www.tampatrib.com

Georgia

Athens Daily News
www.onlineathens.com

The Atlanta Journal-Constitution
www.ajc.com

The Augusta Chronicle
www.augustachronicle.com

The Courier-Herald
www.courier-herald.com

Macon Telegraph
www.macontel.com

Savannah Morning News
www.savannahnow.com

Hawaii

The Garden Island
www.kauaiworld.com

Hawaii Tribune-Herald
www.hilohawaiitribune.com

Honolulu Star-Bulletin
www.starbulletin.com

Lahaina News
www.westmaui.com

Maui News
www.mauinews.com

West Hawaii Today
www.westhawaiitoday.com

Idaho

The Boise Weekly
www.boiseweekly.com

The Coeur d'Alene Press
www.cdapress.com

Idaho Mountain Expres
www.mtexpress.com

The Idaho Press-Tribune
www.idahopress.com

Idaho State Journal
www.journalnet.com

Idaho Statesman
www.idahostatesman.com

Mountain Home News
www.mountainhomenews.com

South Idaho Press
www.southidahopress.com

Illinois

Chicago Sun-Times
www.suntimes.com

Chicago Tribune
www.chicagotribune.com

The Daily Clay County Advocate-Press
www.advocatepress.com

Daily Herald
www.dailyherald.com

Daily Southtown
www.dailysouthtown.com

The Dispatch
www.qconline.com

Herald & Review
www.herald-review.com

The Morning Sentinel
www.morningsentinel.com

The News-Gazette
www.news-gazette.com

Northwest Herald
www.nwherald.com

Peoria Journal Star
www.pjstar.com

The Rockford Register Star
www.rrstar.com

Southern Illinoisian
www.southernillinoisan.com

The State Journal-Register
www.sj-r.com

The Telegraph
www.thetelegraph.com

Indiana

The Bloomington Independent
www.indepen.com

Evansville Courier & Press
www.courierpress.com

Fort Wayne News Sentinel
www.news-sentinel.com

The Herald Times
www.hoosiertimes.com

The Indianapolis Star
www.starnews.com

The Journal Gazette
www.jg.net

The Post-Tribune
www.post-trib.com

South Bend Tribune
www.southbendtribune.com

The Star Press
www.thestarpress.com

The Tribune-Star
www.tribstar.com

Iowa

The Des Moines Register
www.dmregister.com

The Gazette
www.gazetteonline.com

The Iowa City Press-Citizen
www.press-citizen.com

The Sioux City Journal
www.siouxcityjournal.com

The Telegraph Herald
www.thonline.com

The Tribune
www.amestrib.com

Kansas

Kansas City Kansan
www.kansascitykansan.com

Lawrence Journal-World
www.ljworld.com

The Salina Journal
www.saljournal.com

The Topeka Captial-Journal
www.cjonline.com

The Witchita Eagle
www.wichitaeagle.com

Kentucky

The Courier-Journal
www.courier-journal.com

The Daily News
www.bgdailynews.com

The Kentucky Post
www.kypost.com

The Messenger-Inquirer
www.messenger-inquirer.com

The Paducah Sun
www.sunsix.com

The Voice-Tribune
www.louisville.com/voice.html

Louisiana

The Advocate
www.theadvocate.com

New Orleans City Business
citybusiness.neworleans.com

The Times
www.nwlouisiana.com

Times-Picayune
www.nola.com

The Town Talk
www.thetowntalk.com

Maine

Bangor Daily News
www.bangornews.com

Kennebec Journal
www.kjonline.com

Lewiston Sun Journal
www.sunjournal.com

Portland Press Herald
www.portland.com

Maryland

The Baltimore Sun
www.sunspot.net

The Capital
www.hometownannapolis.com

The Daily Record
www.mddailyrecord.com

The Frederick News-Post
www.fredericknewspost.com

The Herald-Mail
www.herald-mail.com

Massachusetts

The Boston Globe
www.boston.com

The Boston Herald
www.bostonherald.com

The Boston Phoenix
www.bostonphoenix.com

The Eagle-Tribune
www.eagletribune.com

The Herald News
www.heraldnews.com

The Springfield Union News
www.masslive.com

Worcester Telegram & Gazette
www.telegram.com

Michigan

The Ann Arbor News
aa.mlive.com

The Detroit Free Press
www.freep.com

The Detroit News
www.detnews.com

The Flint Journal
fl.mlive.com

The Grand Rapids Press
gr.mlive.com

The Kalamazoo Gazette
kz.mlive.com

Lansing State Journal
www.lansingstatejournal.com

Metro Times
www.metrotimes.com

Minnesota

Duluth News Tribune
www.duluthnews.com

The Independent
www.oweb.com/independent

St. Paul Pioneer Press
www.pioneerplanet.com

Star Tribune
www.startribune.com

Thisweek Newspapers
www.thisweek-online.com

Mississippi

The Clarion Ledger
www.clarionledger.com

The Natchez Democrat
www.natchezdemocrat.com

Northeast Mississippi Daily Journal
www.djournal.com

The Oxford Eagle
www.oxfordeagle.com

The Sun Herald
www.sunherald.com

Missouri

Columbia Missourian
www.digmo.org

The Examiner
www.examiner.net

The Kansas City Star
www.kcstar.com

St. Louis Post-Dispatch
www.postnet.com

The St. Louis Suburban Journals
www.yourjournal.com

The Springfield News-Leader
www.springfieldnews-leader.com

Montana

Billings Gazette
www.billingsgazette.com

Bozeman Daily Chronicle
www.gomontana.com

Helena Independent Record
www.helenair.com

The Missoulian
www.missoulian.com

The Montana Standard
www.mtstandard.com

Sidney Herald-Leader
www.sidneyherald.com

Nebraska

The Grand Island Independent
www.theindependent.com

Lincoln Journal Star
www.journalstar.com

Omaha World Herald
www.omaha.com

The North Platte Telegraph
www.nptelegraph.com

Scottsbluff Star-Herald
www.starherald.com

Nevada

Las Vegas Review-Journal
www.lvrj.com

Las Vegas Sun
www.lasvegassun.com

Nevada Appeal
www.tahoe.com/appeal

Reno Gazette-Journal
www.rgj.com

New Hampshire

Concord Monitor
www.cmonitor.com

Foster's Daily Democrat
www.fosters.com

Nashua Telegraph
www.nashuatelegraph.com

Portsmouth Herald
www.seacoastonline.com

The Union Leader
www.theunionleader.com

New Jersey

Ashbury Park Press
www.injersey.com

Courier-Post
www.courierpostonline.com

Daily Record
www.dailyrecord.com

Home News Tribune
www.thnt.com

The Press of Atlantic City
www.pressplus.com

The Record
www.bergen.com

The Star Ledger
www.nj.com

The Times
www.nj.com/times

New Mexico

Albuquerque Journal
www.abqjournal.com

The Albuquerque Tribune
www.abqtrib.com

The Daily Times
www.daily-times.com

Roswell Daily Record
www.roswell-record.com

The Santa Fe New Mexican
www.sfnewmexican.com

New York

The Buffalo News
www.buffalonews.com

The Journal News
www.nyjournalnews.com

Long Island Newsday
www.newsday.com

New York Daily News
www.nydailynews.com

New York Post
www.nypostonline.com

The New York Times
www.nytimes.com

Observer-Dispatch
www.uticaod.com

Rochester Democrat & Chronicle
www.rochesternews.com

Syracuse Herald-Journal
www.syracuse.com

Times Union
www.timesunion.com

North Carolina

Asheville Citizen-Times
www.citizen-times.com

The Charlotte Observer
www.charlotte.com

Fayetteville Observer
www.fayettevillenc.com

The Herald-Sun
www.herald-sun.com

The News & Observer
www.news-observer.com

The News & Record
www.thedepot.com

The Winston-Salem Journal
www.journalnow.com

North Dakota

Bismark Tribune
www.bismarcktribune.com

The Forum
www.in-forum.com

Grand Forks Herald
www.gfherald.com

Minot Daily News
www.ndweb.com/mdnonline

Williston Daily Herald
www.willistonherald.com

Ohio

The Beacon Journal
www.ohio.com/bj

The Blade
www.toledoblade.com

The Cincinnati Enquirer
www.enquirer.com

The Cincinnati Post
www.cincypost.com

The Columbus Dispatch
www.dispatch.com

The Plain Dealer
www.cleveland.com

Sandusky Register
www.sanduskyregister.com

Oklahoma

The Daily Ardmoireite
www.ardmoreite.com

The Edmond Sun
www.edmondsun.com

Enid News & Eagle
www.enidnews.com

The Lawton Constitution
www.lawton-constitution.com

The News Press
www.stwnewspress.com

The Oklahoman
www.oklahoman.com

Tulsa World
www.tulsaworld.com

Oregon

The Bulletin
www.bendbulletin.com

The Daily Astorian
www.dailyastorian.com

Herald and News
www.heraldandnews.com

The Oregonian
www.oregonlive.com

The Register-Guard
www.registerguard.com

Statesman Journal
news.statesmanjournal.com

Pennsylvania

The Citizens' Voice
www.citizensvoice.com

The Inquirer
www.philly.com

Intelligencer Journal
www.lancnews.com

Philadelphia Daily News
www.philly.com

Pittsburgh Post-Gazette
www.post-gazette.com

The Scranton Times
www.scrantontimes.com

The Tribune-Review
www.tribune-review.com

Rhode Island

Bristol Phoenix
www.bristolri.com

The Call
www.woonsocketcall.com

The Pawtucket Times
www.pawtuckettimes.com

The Providence Journal
www.projo.com

The Providence Phoenix
www.providencephoenix.com

South Carolina

The Greenville News
www.greenvilleonline.com

The Post and Courier
www.charleston.net

The Spartanburg Herald-Journal
www.goupstate.com

The State
www.thestate.com

The Sun News
www.myrtlebeachaccess.com

South Dakota

Aberdeen American News
www.aberdeennews.com

Argus Leader
www.argusleader.com

Huron Plainsman
www.plainsman.com

Pierre Capital Journal
www.capjournal.com

Tennessee

Chattanooga Times & Free Press
www.timesfreepress.com

The Commercial Appeal
www.gomemphis.com

The Jackson Sun
www.jacksonsun.com

The Knoxville News-Sentinel
www.knoxnews.com

The Tennessean
www.tennessean.com

Texas

Abilene Reporter-News
www.reporternews.com

Austin American-Statesman
www.austin360.com

Beaumont Enterprise
www.ent-net.com

Corpus Christi Caller-Times
www.caller.com

The Dallas Morning News
www.dallasnews.com

El Paso Times
www.elpasotimes.com

Galveston County Daily News
www.galvnews.com

Houston Chronicle
www.chron.com

Lubbock Avalanche-Journal
www.lubbockonline.com

Midland Reporter-Telegram
www.mrt.com

San Antonio Express-News
www.mysanantonio.com

Star-Telegram
www.star-telegram.com

Utah

The Daily Herald
www.daily-herald.com

Deseret News
www.desnews.com

The Herald Journal
www.hjnews.com

The Orem Daily Journal
www.ucjournal.com

The Salt Lake Tribune
www.sltrib.com

Standard-Examiner
www.standard.net

Vermont

The Burlington Free Press
www.burlingtonfreepress.com

The Caledonian-Record
www.caledonian-record.com

The Rutland Herald
www.rutlandherald.com

Times Argus
www.timesargus.com

Valley News
www.vnews.com

Virginia

The Alexandria Journal
www.jrnl.com

The Arlington Journal
www.jrnl.com

The Daily Press
www.dailypress.com

The Fairfax Journal
www.jrnl.com

The Montgomery Journal
www.jrnl.com

The Roanoke Times
www.roanoke.com

Virginian-Pilot
www.pilotonline.com

Richmond Times-Dispatch
www.gatewayva.com

Washington

The Bellingham Herald
www.bellinghamherald.com

Eastside Journal
www.eastsidejournal.com

The News Tribune
www.tribnet.com

The Olympian
news.theolympian.com

Seattle Post-Intelligencer
www.seattle-pi.com

The Seattle Times
www.seattletimes.com

The Spokesman-Review
www.spokane.net

Yakima Herald-Republic
www.yakima-herald.com

West Virginia

Charleston Daily Mail
www.dailymail.com

The Charleston Gazette
www.wvgazette.com

The Herald-Dispatch
www.hdonline.com

The Intelligencer
www.theintelligencer.net

Going Once, Going Twice . . .

It's probably no news to you that Web sites like eBay and uBid are making a fortune off of the idea that one person's garbage is another person's treasure. Rather than spending the weekends scrambling through the streets, looking for the nearest garage sale or flea market, those with Internet access can simply haggle online at one of the many auction sites. And they can really buy anything . . . including employees!

That's right, even jobs and employees are being auctioned off on the Internet. The most popular of the auction sites is probably Bid4Geeks (*www.bid4geeks.com*). Here, self-proclaimed "geeks" post a brief description of their skills, what they're looking to do, and the minimum salary they are willing to accept. Employers can then decide whether or not they are willing to take a chance, and place a bid on this person. Likewise, employers can post descriptions of the positions they are looking to fill (usually contract), the type of employee they are looking for, and what they are willing to pay. Interested candidates can contact the hiring manager via e-mail and let the bargaining begin.

While it's a bit too early to determine whether or not this idea will really work out in the long run, it sure can be fun to browse through these sites. Even the more popular of the traditional job sites, like Monster.com, for example, are trying out the auctioning thing. Visit their talent market at *talentmarket.monster.com* and put your skills (technical and bartering) to work.

Wheeling News-Register
www.theintelligencer.net

Wisconsin

The Capital Times
www.madison.com

The Green Bay News-Chronicle
www.greenbaynewschron.com

Green Bay Press-Gazette
www.greenbaypressgazette.com

The Journal Times
www.racinecounty.com

Kenosha News
www.kenoshacounty.com

Milwaukee Journal Sentinel
www.jsonline.com

The Northwestern
www.thenorthwestern.com

Wisconsin State Journal
www.madison.com

Wyoming

Casper Star-Tribune
www.trib.com

Cody Enterprise
www.codyenterprise.com

Jackson Hole News
www.jacksonholenet.com

Wyoming Tribune-Eagle
www.wyomingnews.com

Chapter 10
Networking

To think that top executives, experienced professionals, and industry insiders are the only ones who can use a bit of networking to their advantage is completely false. In fact, many recruiters, outplacement specialists, and human resources professionals claim that networking is probably the best way to find employment. Think about it, wouldn't a cover letter sound better if you could start off with something like "Dear Sir: Maya Fairs suggested I contact you regarding possible employment within your agency." Being a "friend of a friend" or any such relation to a potential employer immediately establishes a bit of credence on your behalf. Assuming that the person who refers you is a person of integrity, an employer is likely to trust that you are worth a shot.

If you're looking to break into a particular industry or are even looking to change jobs within an industry, one of the best first steps you can take is to get the word out and let your network of contacts know that you are on the prowl for new employment. This does not mean that you have to be desperate and obvious in the way you say so; a simple "I've been thinking of possibly looking around for other options within the industry" or "I've been thinking about possibly taking my skills and applying them to a career in marketing instead" is a tactful way of asking a contact for help. Yet, even if you don't know a soul in your desired industry or *any* industry for that matter, one surefire way to begin making some contacts is through the Internet.

The Internet has made it easy to get in contact with other people who share your interests, hobbies, goals, and just about anything else that defines you as a person. No matter what your interest or career, chances are there is an online discussion group going on right now that could help you in your quest for employment. Three of the most popular ways Internet surfers begin engaging in these discussions is through mailing lists, special interest groups (also known as SIGs) through commercial online services, and Usenet newsgroups. Another good way to keep abreast of the latest happenings and possibly establish some contacts within an industry is to visit the Web site of specific industry associations. While most of these Web sites will not offer you the option of posting and/or viewing messages, they will afford you the opportunity to learn more about an industry and hear about upcoming industry-related events in your area (chapter meetings, etc. are a great way for you to start meeting people).

Just like in real life, opportunities won't be made available to you overnight. Just because you and another industry professional log onto the same newsgroup or discussion group won't automatically make you the best of friends. You must work at building and maintaining relationships with the people you meet over the Internet. For this reason, it is important that you maintain a continual presence in pertinent discussion groups, even when you are happily employed.

Mailing Lists

Mailing lists, also known as list serves or e-mail discussion groups, allow users to post and read messages that contain threads of discussions on various topics. What makes a mailing list different from a newsgroup or special interest group is that, instead of viewing and posting messages online, subscribers receive new messages and post their own comments to the group via e-mail. Many people like to use mailing lists because monitoring a group can be accomplished simply by checking your e-mail. Another benefit to mailing lists is that there is a discussion administrator who can moderate the discussion content.

The tens of thousands of mailing lists that are currently in existence cover all sorts of topics, from art to religion and everything in between. Though each mailing list has its own set of rules and regulations, the way it usually works is that, should you decide to join a mailing list, you send a message to the mailing list's system administrator. The administrator, in turn, reviews your request and adds you to the list of recipients. There are several online directories that will allow you to find the mailing list that best suits your needs.

Online Mailing List Directories

Liszt: The Mailing List Directory
www.liszt.com

eGroups
www.findmail.com

Publicly Accessible Mailing Lists
www.neosoft.com/internet/paml

Liszt: The Mailing List Directory
www.liszt.com

Publicly Accessible Mailing Lists
www.neosoft.com/internet/paml

eGroups
www.findmail.com

Special Interest Groups

Special interest groups can be found on commercial online services like America Online, Microsoft Network, CompuServe, and Prodigy. Though they're known by different names on each service—forums, bulletin boards, and roundtables are just a few of the other names you'll hear thrown around—collectively, they are referred to as special interest groups or SIGs.

Because the number of people that subscribe to commercial online services is less than the number of people who have Internet access, the number of people that engage in special interest group discussions is smaller still. One of the benefits of special interest groups is that most have system operators, also known as "sysops," who monitor the discussions that take place to be sure that posted messages are relevant to the group topic. System operators also help to make sure that discussions do not get out of hand, which has been known to happen, despite the usual attempt to uphold netiquette standards. In many special interest groups, general topics are broken down into several smaller subcategories, making it easier for you to isolate the topic you are interested in. Several of the better special interest groups within particular commercial online services are listed below.

America Online

In addition to its fantastic career resources, AOL has a number of discussion forums that will allow you to network with other professionals in your industry. For a complete list of AOL discussion groups, search for the keywords "clubs" or "forums" in the Directory of Services.

Health Professionals Network
Keyword: HRS or Better Health

The Teacher's Lounge
Keyword: Teacher's Lounge

Legal Information Network
Keyword: LIN

The Writers Club
Keyword: Writers

CompuServe

Of all the commercial online services, CompuServe has the most discussion groups for professionals, with forums in a wide range of fields. Best of all, CompuServe is well known for the quality of its forums and the participants who take part in them. CompuServe forums have three basic parts: the message section, where users can read and post messages; the conference area, where users can engage in real-time chats, scheduled meetings, and conferences with other participants; and libraries, where users can search for archived information. To find your specific topic, select "Find" from the "Services" menu, or click on the "Index" icon and type in your search word(s). The following forums represent some of the best that CompuServe has to offer.

Architecture & Building Forum
Go: ArchBldg

Health Professionals Forum
Go: MedSIG

Broadcast Professionals Forum
Go: BPForum

Journalism Forum
Go: Jforum

Computer Consultants
Go: Consult

Photo Professionals
Go: Photopro

Court Reporters Forum
Go: Crforum

ProPublishing Forum
Go: Propub

Desktop Publishing Forum
Go: DTP

Public Relations Forum
Go: Prsig

Education Forum
Go: Edforum

Writers Forum
Go: Writers

Newsgroups

Newsgroups are a marvelous place to network, as you're likely to find a discussion group to suit even the most unique of interests. Hence, Usenet newsgroups are probably one of the most popular ways to network online. However, because those who engage in newsgroup discussions tend to be more technologically savvy than those who simply know how to surf the Web, it is imperative to know and uphold proper netiquette at all times. Yet, while newsgroup participants are likely to be more sensitive to the rules of netiquette and those who embrace them, they are also usually very accommodating to those who have taken the time to learn the rules.

Usenet newsgroups are one of the Internet's oldest and most misunderstood areas. What was once the exclusive territory of this country's brain trust—academics, scientists, top government officials, and the like—has developed into the one of the most popular ways of exchanging information online. While many users are intimidated by what they perceive as an unapproachable Usenet culture, it can't be denied that newsgroups are one of the best ways to network online. By failing to engage in Usenet discussion groups, job seekers are missing out on what could potentially turn into hundreds of potential employment opportunities.

How newsgroups work is like this: if you have an Internet connection or use a commercial online service, you can join in a newsgroup. Anyone with access can post messages. In some cases, the message will be sent to a moderator, who will approve the message before it is posted. In other newsgroups, messages are generally unmonitored and left uncensored. Because the purpose of Usenet newsgroups is to allow the millions of Internet users around the world to engage in a single discussion, you're likely to find newsgroup discussions on just about any topic you can imagine (and probably those you don't want to imagine). Because newsgroups cover such a wide variety of topics, they are broken down by hierarchies, or general categories, that enable you to find the topics you want more easily. The main hierarchies are as follows:

alt.	alternative
comp.	computers

humanities	humanities such as arts and literature
misc.	miscellaneous
news.	news for Usenet users
rec.	recreation
sci.	science
soc.	social issues
talk.	serious discussions about often controversial topics

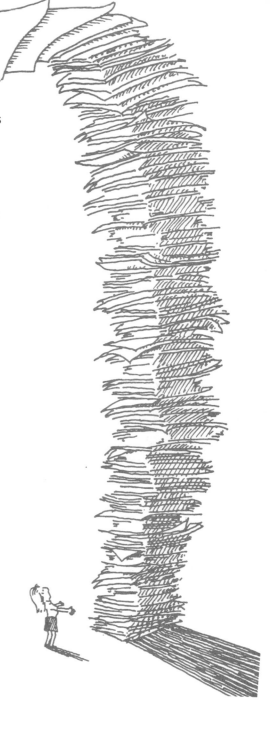

There are dozens of local hierarchies in existence as well—atl. (Atlanta), il. (Illinois), and swnet. (Sweden) for example—that don't fall into the hierarchies listed above. These local newsgroups offer information on city politics, online classifieds, and other information that would concern the local population.

Newsgroups can be broken down even further, according to subject. For example, alt.backrubs is the alternative hierarchy under the subject "backrubs." Newsgroups can get even more specialized: alt.movies.hitchcock and alt.movies.monsters are discussions of Alfred Hitchcock and monster movies (respectively) under the general subject of "movies" in the alternative hierarchy.

Finally, the last thing you need to know about newsgroups are the "threads" that hold them together. Basically, a thread is a group of messages that pertain to the same topic. Each time a new topic is broached within a newsgroup, a new thread is started.

Ironically, it is the regimented organization and hierarchical structure that puts far too many people off of newsgroups. Seeing newsgroups with directories and subdirectories can seem a bit like information overload; the sheer enormity is often enough to intimidate people not to even try. Unfortunately, people don't realize what they're missing out on with newsgroups. Taking the time to learn more about newsgroups, master the rules of netiquette, and engage in intelligent discussions with other professionals online can give your career an enormous boost.

How to Get Started in Newsgroups

Getting started on the road to newsgroup networking is easy! If you have a regular Internet connection, you will need the help of a newsreader. The job of the newsreader is to organize the thousands

of available newsgroups and allow you to post a message. Most Web browsers, like Netscape Navigator for example, have built-in news-readers. If you can't find a newsreader on your system, all you need to do is call your Internet provider and ask where you can find one.

Before you start posting messages, it is a good idea to check out some of the most commonly asked questions by new users. Visit *news.newusers.questions* or *news.announce.newusers* and read some of the messages. If, after reading the many messages, you still have a question, feel free to post your own message. Other useful information that you can find in these newsgroups include the history of the Internet, rules for posting messages, and hints about the Usenet writing style.

Once you have figured out how to post a message (or, at least when you think you've figured out how to post a message), test yourself. Visit either *alt.test* or *misc.test* and try posting a message to figure out whether or not your newsreader is configured properly. If you are having trouble posting a message, ask your Internet service provider or commercial online service for assistance.

Why Use Newsgroups

At current count, Usenet has over 200 newsgroups dedicated to job postings, each containing dozens (or possibly hundreds) of job listings. Some newsgroups that offer information for a nationwide audience can contain thousands of job listings. No matter what type of work you are looking for—temporary, permanent, full-time, part-time, freelance, consulting—chances are there is a newsgroup waiting for you.

As newsgroups can often intimidate those who are not com-pletely comfortable in their technical abilities, it makes sense that a majority of the job-related newsgroups out there are geared toward those who work in the computer or information technology fields. Still, even if you're not in a computer-related position, newsgroups are a wonderful way to corner the hidden job market; you just may need to look a little further to find an appropriate group.

For the most part, newsgroups are local; they tend to target specific geographical areas. That said, newgroups are a terrific way to begin networking in a new area. They are also a great place to get information on cost of living, employment statistics, and other relevant information if you are looking to relocate.

One of the main reasons why newsgroups are such a great place to find job listings is because of their comprehensiveness. Employers are not paying anything to post a job on a newsgroup; therefore, to avoid a large influx of unqualified applicants or applicants who do not fully understand the job, employers are more likely to spell out the entire job.

If you're not having much luck finding appropriate newsgroups on your own, there are several bigger job sites on the World Wide Web that will search these listings out for you. CareerMosaic (*www.careermosaic.com*), for example, has the ability to search more than 100 newsgroups for job openings. JobHunt (*www.job-hunt.org*) is another site that will allow you to search for newsgroup job postings.

Some Major Newsgroups to Check Out

While the following list of newsgroups represents Usenet's most popular when it comes to job postings, you should also check out the mainly discussion-oriented newsgroups that concern your occupation or field, as they too can yield an opportunity or two from time to time. If you're a veterinarian, for instance, you might very likely find a job opening by visiting the *alt.med.veterinary* newsgroup.

One final thing that you should be aware of: as with newspapers, job sites, or any other place where scams may lurk, be careful of postings that sound too good to be true or help wanted ads that are asking you for 1) impertinent information or 2) money! Since it can be very difficult to monitor the messages that get posted, you're likely to come across your fair share of unscrupulous characters.

The following list of newsgroups is designed to help you find job openings in your particular field or area. Be sure to explore Usenet on your own, as not every useful newsgroup is listed and new ones are popping up all the time. Also, please be aware that not every newsgroup will be available to every person as individual ISPs and commercial online services may restrict Usenet access.

Name That Tone

When posting a message to a newsgroup, the tone of the discussion can often vary between newsgroups and hierarchies. For example, alt. newsgroups tend to lean toward the casual side while comp. and sci. newsgroups are geared toward the factual. Both the tone and the subject matter of talk. newsgroups are usually pretty serious. Visiting several newsgroups and hierarchies in order to get a feel for the tone and subject matter is all part of good netiquette. For more information on proper netiquette, see Chapter 5.

Nationwide—United States

alt.bestjobsusa
Jobs opportunities across the U.S.A

misc.jobs.contract
Discussion of both short- and long-term
contract labor

misc.jobs.misc
General issues of employment and careers
are discussed here

misc.jobs.offered
Job opportunities available nationwide

misc.jobs.offered.entry
Entry-level jobs available nationwide

misc.jobs.resumes
Resumes for jobs across the U.S.

us.jobs
Jobs available in the U.S.

us.jobs.contract
Contract labor jobs in the U.S.

us.jobs.misc
Nationwide employment opportunities

us.jobs.offered
Nationwide employment opportunities

us.jobs.resumes
Resumes for nationwide jobs

Northeast/Mid-Atlantic

balt.jobs
Jobs available in Baltimore, Maryland

conn.jobs.offered
Jobs available in Connecticut

ct.jobs
Jobs available in Connecticut

dc.jobs
Jobs available in Washington, DC

ithaca.jobs
Job available in the Ithaca, New York, area

li.jobs
Jobs available on Long Island, New York

md.jobs
Jobs available in Maryland and
Washington, DC

me.jobs
Jobs available in Maine

ne.jobs
Jobs available in New England

ne.jobs.contract
Contract labor jobs in New England

nh.jobs
Jobs available in New Hampshire

niagara.jobs
Jobs available in the Niagara region of New York

nj.jobs
Jobs available in New Jersey

nyc.jobs
Employment opportunities in New York City

nyc.jobs.contract
Contract labor and consulting jobs in
New York City

nyc.jobs.misc
Discussion of the New York City job market

nyc.jobs.offered
More jobs available in New York City

nyc.jobs.wanted
Positions wanted in New York City

ny.jobs
Jobs in the state of New York

pa.jobs.offered
Jobs in Pennsylvania

pgh.jobs.offered
Jobs available in the Pittsburgh area

pgh.jobs.wanted
Positions wanted in the Pittsburgh area

phl.jobs.offered
Job opportunities in Philadelphia, Pennsylvania

phl.jobs.wanted
Jobs wanted in Philadelphia, Pennsylvania

Southeast

alabama.birmingham.jobs
Jobs in the Birmingham, Alabama, area

alabama.jobs
Jobs in Alabama

alt.jobs.nw-arkansas
Jobs in northwest Arkansas

atl.jobs
Jobs in and around Atlanta, Georgia

atl.resumes
Resumes for the Atlanta job market

fl.jobs
Job opportunities in Florida

hsv.jobs
Jobs available in Huntsville, Alabama

lou.lft.jobs
Jobs available in the Lafayette, Louisiana, area

memphis.employment
Jobs available in the Memphis, Tennessee, area

tnn.jobs
Professional job opportunities in Tennessee

us.sc.columbia.employment
Jobs available in Columbia, South Carolina

va.jobs
Job opportunities in Virginia

Midwest

akr.jobs
Jobs available in the Akron, Ohio, area

chi.jobs
Jobs available in Chicago, Illinois

chi.jobs.offered
Jobs in Chicago, Illinois

cle.jobs
Jobs in the Cleveland, Ohio, area

cmh.jobs
Job opportunities in Columbus, Ohio

ia.jobs
Jobs available in Iowa

il.jobs.misc
Discussion of the Illinois job market

il.jobs.offered
Employment opportunities in Illinois

il.jobs.resumes
Resumes for employment in Illinois

in.jobs
Job opportunities in Indianapolis, Indiana

kc.jobs
Jobs in the Kansas City, Missouri, area

mi.jobs
Jobs available in Michigan

milw.job
Jobs in the Milwaukee, Wisconsin, area

mn.jobs
Employment opportunities in Minnesota

nebr.jobs
Jobs in Nebraska

oh.jobs
Jobs available and wanted in Ohio

stl.jobs
Jobs available in St. Louis, Missouri

stl.jobs.resumes
Resumes for St. Louis, Missouri, jobs

West/Southwest

austin.jobs
Jobs available in Austin, Texas

az.jobs
Jobs available in Arizona

ba.jobs
Jobs in the San Francisco Bay area

ba.jobs.resumes
Resumes for the San Francisco Bay area

co.jobs
Jobs available in Colorado

houston.jobs
Jobs in the Houston, Texas, area

houston.jobs.offered
Jobs available in Houston, Texas

houston.jobs.wanted
Jobs wanted in Houston, Texas

la.jobs
Jobs available in the Los Angeles, California, area

nm.jobs
Jobs available in New Mexico

nv.jobs
Job opportunities in Nevada

pdaxs.jobs.computers
Computer jobs in Portland, Oregon

pdaxs.jobs.engineering
Engineering and technical jobs in Portland, Oregon

pdaxs.jobs.management
Management opportunities in Portland, Oregon

pdaxs.jobs.retail
Retail job opportunities in Portland, Oregon

pdaxs.jobs.sales
Sales opportunities in Portland, Oregon

sac.jobs
Jobs in the Sacramento, California, area

sat.jobs
Employment opportunities in the San Antonio, Texas, area

sdnet.jobs
Jobs available in San Diego, California

seattle.jobs
Job opportunities in the Seattle, Washington, area

seattle.jobs.offered
Job opportunities in the Seattle, Washington, area

seattle.jobs.wanted
Jobs wanted in Seattle, Washington

tx.jobs
Jobs available in Texas

ut.jobs
Jobs in Utah

utah.jobs
Jobs in Utah

vegas.jobs
Jobs available in Las Vegas, Nevada

wyo.jobs
Employment opportunities in Wyoming

International

ab.jobs
Job opportunities in Alberta, Canada

alt.jobs.overseas
Jobs all over the world

aus.ads.jobs
Jobs available in Australia

bc.jobs
Job opportunities in British Columbia,
Canada

bermuda.jobs.offered
Jobs available in Bermuda

can.jobs
Jobs available in Canada

eunet.jobs
Job opportunities in Europe

euro.jobs
More job opportunities in Europe

ie.jobs
Jobs available in Ireland

iijnet.jobs
Job opportunities in Israel

kw.jobs
Jobs in Kitchener-Waterloo, Canada

ont.jobs
Jobs available in Ontario, Canada

ott.jobs
Job opportunities in Ottawa, Ontario

qc.jobs
Jobs available in Quebec, Canada

swnet.jobs
Employment opportunities in Sweden

tor.jobs
Jobs available in Toronto, Ontario

uk.jobs
Job opportunities in the United Kingdom

za.ads.jobs
Employment opportunities in South Africa

Industry-Specific

Business Services
misc.business.consulting
Discusses the consulting business

Communications
alt.journalism.moderated
Moderated discussion group for journalists

misc.writing
A discussion group for writers of all types

Computers

cit.jobs
Computer-related employment opportunities

prg.jobs
Computer programming job opportunities

Education

k12.chat.teacher
Discussion group for teachers of all grades

misc.education
General discussion of the educational system

Government

dod.jobs
Jobs within the U.S. Department of Defense

Legal

misc.legal
Discussion group for legal professionals

Scientific/Medical

alt.medical.sales.jobs.resumes
U.S. medical sales positions

bionet.jobs
Job opportunities in biological science

bionet.women-in-bio
Discusses issues relevant to women in biology

bionet.microbiology
Discussion of issues related to microbiology

hepnet.jobs
Discussion relating to high-energy nuclear physics

sci.med
Discussion group for those in science and medicine

sci.med.pharmacy
Discusses the pharmaceutical field

sci.research.careers
Discusses various scientific research careers

sci.research.postdoc
Job opportunities in postdoctoral scientific research

Chapter 11

Getting the Interview

After spending countless hours preparing your resume and cover letter, posting your resume on every site from here to Timbuktu, contacting every person you've ever met since birth, and surfing the Internet looking for suitable employment, all your hard work is beginning to pay off: employers have begun calling and looking to set up interviews. While mentally preparing for the interview (thinking about what you'll say, conducting mock interviews with your friends and/or favorite stuffed animal, etc.) is definitely part of what will help you shine, this is really only half of the game. There's a lot of research and other preparation that must go into this meeting, and it's something that can all be done via the Internet.

Research the Company

As the most important part of the interview preparation process, researching the company should be first on your list of things to do. The most significant way you can set yourself apart from the rest of the candidate pack is to make a positive impression. One of the easiest ways to do this is to know the company you're inter- viewing with, inside and out. If you know the name of the person who is interviewing you, you can even go so far as to get a little background information on him or her (not to the degree that a stalker might, but just enough info to keep you talking). Researching each company you apply to before you're called in for an interview would be a waste of time (after all, not every company you apply to will call you in to an interview), so now is the time to begin.

What kind of information should you know? Everything! Pretend that you are being asked to make a 10-minute presentation on the company and learn as many facts as you can that would allow you to speak (intelligently) about the company for that span of time. You need to know the types of products and/or services the company offers, the types of customers they most often deal with, the name and business of the parent company, and the names and businesses of any subsidiaries. You should try and learn about the company's rank in industry, sales and profit trends, type of ownership, size, and anything else you deem important. You should make yourself familiar with the company's biggest competitors and the direction in which the industry, as a whole, is headed. If you don't know much of the industry jargon already, learn it. Pick up a trade paper, join in online discussion groups, visit industry organization meetings and Web sites. Believe me, research time is all time well spent.

Discover every resource you can that relates to the specific company you're applying to and their business in general. If the company has a Web site, memorize the information that it contains. Look into the current job openings to get an idea for the types of employees they are looking for. If the company doesn't have a Web site, execute a search for them on a search engine (do this even if the company does have a Web site). The more time you spend researching, the better off you will be in the interview. Even if you are set to interview tomorrow, don't step through that door without having spent at least an hour acquainting yourself with the company and their product line.

As you might expect, there are plenty of resources (besides individual company Web sites) that can help you research a company further when preparing for an interview. There are also plenty of sites that will help you learn a bit more about an industry and/or a specific occupation that you are looking to get into. Several of these sites are profiled below.

CareerCity.com

www.careercity.com

If you've ever used one of the many *JobBank* books in your job search, you know how helpful their detailed information on the nation's top employers can be. CareerCity.com takes much of this information and makes it available online. All you need to do is type in your criteria and, if the company is part of the *JobBank* family of employers (there are more than 25,000), you will be presented with some of their vital statistics. The site also provides links to companies that have registered their Web sites. Even if your interview is with an employment agency rather than an actual employer, CareerCity.com provides links to more than 7,000 American employment agencies and offers the same detailed information.

CompaniesOnline

www.companiesonline.com

Run by the Lycos Network, CompaniesOnline offers Webgoers information on more than 900,000 public and private companies. When you execute a search, the link will display such basic information as phone number, address, employee size, annual sales. By clicking on the link, you will be allowed more in-depth information including the big cheese's name and title, company DUNS number, SIC codes, and all the company's Web addresses (this is a good way to find out about the company's parent or any subsidiaries that might exist).

Hoover's Online: The Business Network

www.hoovers.com

Geared toward the businessperson, Hoover's Online makes company information (general summary, key players, recent news headlines) available to you, the job seeker, as well. The site is well organized and provides a variety of links, including links to current opportunities that exist at each company. While you're probably not interested in the positions they have available (you have, after all, been called in for an interview), you may be interested to read the listings to get a better sense of the type of employee they are looking for.

Jobfind.com

www.jobfind.com

In addition to providing tons of job postings, Jobfind.com offers job seekers the chance to research these companies further. They offer several hundred company profiles with links to current openings. While the company profiles are limited to the companies that are currently posting jobs, there are enough big and recognizable companies listed to make it worth your while to run a quick search.

My Job Search

www.myjobsearch.com

Here's another all-in-one site that can help you find a job, prepare for the interview, research a company, and negotiate a fair salary . . . all with one visit! This site is an invaluable source for job search information, no matter what phase of the game you are in. As much of the information is in the form of links to other sites, My Job Search can offer you access to a lot more information that your typical job site that tries to do it all on its own.

WetFeet.com

www.wetfeet.com

This completely comprehensive site will give you the lowdown on a particular career, industry, or company, all with the click of a mouse. The site will also allow you to type in your industry, zip code, and state and learn about what the average person in your position (or desired position) is making nowadays. The site offers specific advice to those who are just starting out, those who are changing careers, and students and MBAs. While the companies they offer research on are some of the bigger name companies within each industry, this can help you if you're looking to research the competition for a small start-up. Whether you're looking to get your feet wet or dive right in, WetFeet.com can answer just about any question you may want to ask.

Practice, Practice, Practice

You know that old saying that practice makes perfect? It's true. The more you interview (or at least practice interviewing), the more likely you are to master the art of it. There are plenty of books and Web sites around that will help you out when it comes to preparing for an interview. Be aware of the questions you are most likely to be asked ("What made you decide to work in this industry?" "What are your strengths?" "What are your weaknesses?" "Why should we hire you?") and come up with a good answer. Why should a company hire you? If you think about the answer carefully enough and practice through a mock interview with a friend or family member, you are more likely to answer the interviewer in a confident manner.

If you're just starting out in the world or have not interviewed in quite some time, don't be alarmed if the first interview goes off with some definite hitches. This is definitely the most difficult one

Accept All Interviews

If you're new to the job market or have not interviewed in a while, it can help to accept interviews for positions that you're not too enthusiastic about (assuming you have the time to do so). While you definitely don't have to accept an offer (not even for the sake of practice), it will help you to interview in front of a person who is not your mom or dad. Just remember, even if your intentions for accepting the interview are simply so that you can become an interviewee, you should take all the necessary steps to prepare (research, etc.) and make sure that you treat the employer with as much enthusiasm and respect as you would any other.

Industry Associations

One of the best ways to research an industry is to meet (in person or virtually) with the members of an industry association. As many of these associations maintain home pages on the Web, it might be worth your while to check them out. Read the information contained to get a better idea of the terminology used within the industry; find out about upcoming events that are taking place in your area; learn about industry professionals who may be willing to speak with you. Visiting an industry association is just a networking opportunity waiting to happen.

Advertising Research Foundation
www.arfsite.org

Air Transport Association of America
www.air-transport.org

Air & Waste Management Association
www.awma.org

Alliance for Children and Families
www.fsanet.org

Aluminum Association
www.aluminum.org

American Academy of Nurse Practitioners
www.aanp.org

American Accounting Association
www.aaa-edu.org

American Apparel Manufacturers
www.americanapparel.org

American Association of Advertising Agencies
www.aaaa.org

American Association of Engineering Societies
www.aaes.org

American Association of Health Care Consultants
www.aahc.net

American Association for Higher Education
www.aahe.org

American Association of Pharmaceutical Scientists
www.aaps.org

American Astronautical Society
www.astronautical.org

American Automobile Manufacturers
www.aama.com

American Bankers Association
www.aba.org

American Bar Association
www.abanet.org

American Booksellers Association
www.bookweb.org

American Design Drafting Association
www.adda.org

American Film Institute
www.afionline.org

American Frozen Food Institute
www.affi.com

American Hospital Association
www.aha.org

American Institute of Architects
www.aicnet.org

American Institute of CPAs
www.aicpa.org

American Institute of Chemical Engineers
www.aiche.org

American Institute of Contractors
www.aicnet.org

American Internet Association
www.amernet.org

American Iron and Steel Institute
www.steel.org

American Marketing Association
www.ama.org

American Nuclear Society
www.ans.org

American Society of Civil Engineers
www.asce.org

American Society for Clinical Laboratory Science
www.ascls.org

American Society of Composers, Authors & Publishers
www.ascap.com

American Society of Landscape Architects
www.asla.org

American Society of Mechanical Engineers
www.asme.org

American Society of Travel Agents
www.astanet.com

American Textile Manufacturers
www.atmi.org

American Trucking Association
www.trucking.org

American Women in Radio & Television
www.awrt.org

Americans for the Arts
artusa.org

Associated Builders & Contractors
www.abc.org

Association of American Publishers
www.publishers.org

Association for Clinical Chemistry
www.aacc.org

Association for Computing Machinery
www.acm.org

Association of Management Consulting Firms
www.amcf.org

Association for Manufacturing Excellence
www.asme.org

Association for Manufacturing Technology
www.mfgtech.org

Automotive Service Association
www.asashop.org

Biotechnology Industry Organization
www.bio.org

Catholic Charities USA
www.catholiccharities.org

Center for Software Development
www.center.org

Center for the Study of Sport in Society
www.sportinsociety.org

College & University Personnel Association
www.cupa.org

Competitive Telecommunications Association
www.comptel.org

Electrochemical Society
www.electrochem.org

Electronic Publishing Association
www.epaonline.com

Engineering Center
www.engineers.org

Equipment Leasing Association of America
www.elaonline.com

Fashion Group International
www.fgi.org

HTML Writers Guild
www.hwg.org

Institute of Clean Air Companies
www.icac.com

Insurance Information Institute
www.iii.org

International Advertising Association
www.iaaglobal.org

International Association of Food Industry
Suppliers
www.iafis.org

Marketing Research Association
www.mra-net.org

National Aeronautic Association
www.naa.ycg.org

National Association of Broadcasters
www.nab.org

National Association of Credit Management
www.nacm.org

National Association of Home Builders
www.nahb.com

National Association of Manufacturers
www.nam.org

National Association of Personnel Services
www.napsweb.org

National Association of Realtors
www.realtor.com

National Association of Social Workers
www.naswdc.org

National Association of Tax Practitioners
www.natpax.com

National Glass Association
www.glass.org

National Medical Association
www.nmanet.org

National Paralegal Association
www.nationalparalegal.org

National Recreation & Park Association
www.nrpa.org

National Restaurant Association
www.restaurant.org

National Retail Federation
www.nrf.com

National Society of Accountants
www.nsacct.org

National Society of Professional Engineers
www.nspe.org

Printing Industries of America
www.printing.org

Professional Aviation Maintenance Association
www.pama.org

Public Relations Society of America
www.prsa.org

Securities Industry Association
www.sia.com

Society for Information Management
www.simnet.org

Society for Mining, Metallurgy & Exploration
www.smenet.org

Technical Association of the
Pulp & Paper Industry
www.tappi.org

to get through. That said, try and get one or two interviews under your belt before you decide to meet with the hiring manager of the company of your dreams. If that's not possible, make sure you practice until you've got it nearly perfect, as you've only got one shot to impress them.

Appearance

As shallow as it sounds, employers will learn a lot about you from your appearance alone. This does not mean that just because you're not wearing the latest fashion, you won't get the job. By appearing in an appropriate ensemble and being well-groomed for the interview, you are telling an employer that you care about this job and that you should be taken seriously. While donning a sharp new suit won't secure your position as a public relations executive, failing to shower and/or brush your hair can certainly guarantee that you won't be getting the job.

If you're a man interviewing for a professional position, you should always wear a suit! A shirt and tie might cut it for tonight's dinner reservations, but it certainly won't score you any points with an employer. Conservative colors—colors like navy blue or charcoal gray—are your best bet. Not only do they look more professional, but it's easy to change the entire look of the suit by switching the accompanying shirt and tie (translation: if you have more than one interview at a particular company, you can wear the same suit).

Though the rules in the workplace are changing, professionalism still dictates that women wear a skirt to an interview. Again, regardless of what the dress code is in the workplace, women should also wear a suit . . . no exceptions! Colors should be conservative for women's attire too—a black or navy blue suit is the best way to go.

In addition to attire, personal grooming is also something you should pay close attention to. Careful grooming indicates both a sense of thoroughness and self-confidence. Women should not wear excessive makeup or jewelry. If you have painted nails, make sure they are of a conservative color (the latest Urban Decay color may look cool while you're clubbing, but it won't leave such a positive

Buying Your Attire Online

Just when you thought you were on your own (with buying an interview appropriate power suit, that is), the Internet comes to your rescue once again. No matter what time of day or night (even on major holidays), you can virtually visit some of your favorite stores and pick out just the right outfit for the big day. Whether you prefer to shop discount or designer, specialty store or department store, you can find all kinds of cyberspace shopping outlets. Since buying a suit can be expensive (for men and women), check out some of these online stores for the best selection at the best prices.

Bargain Clothing
www.bargainclothing.com

Bluefly.com
www.bluefly.com

DesignerSuits.com
www.designersuits.com

Discount Designer Menswear
www.menswear-discounts.com

Hugestore.com
www.hugestore.com

Savi
www.savishopper.com

impression on an interviewer). Both men and women should refrain from wearing perfume or cologne, as it only takes a small spritz to lead an allergic interviewer to a serious sneezing fit. Even if the interview is later in the day, men should be sure that they are clean shaven.

Essentials

Walking into an interview empty-handed is a sure sign of being unprepared. No, you don't have to bring your interviewer an expensive bottle of wine, but you should be sure to bring along the following things: a watch, a pen, a notebook, and—most importantly—an extra copy of your resume. If the interviewer happened to misplace your resume, show them how prepared you are when you take out the extra copy you brought along. Finally, so that you are not juggling all these things around, bring a briefcase or a leather-bound folder with you to complete the look of professionalism.

The Crucial Introduction

The first few moments of the interview can really set the mood for the duration of your conversation. If you come off as being shy and intimidated, an interviewer may not want to dig so deep and ask you the really difficult questions (a.k.a. the questions that get you the job). Even if you are extremely shy, now is not the time to retreat. It's human nature to judge a person by the first impression so, in the case of the job interview especially, you want to make sure it's a good one.

Making a strong impression is easy, as long as you know the things an interviewer is looking for. First things first: EYE CONTACT! Establishing eye contact is probably one of the most important parts of your introduction. You want to make sure that you look the interviewer directly in the eye as you're being introduced and/or are shaking hands. At the same time, you don't want to seem like you're crazy, so don't stare at this person. Similar limitations are placed on the handshake; while you don't want to shake this

person's hand so lightly that they need to check to see that your hand is actually there, you also don't want to send them to the emergency room with a fracture. A firm grip with a quick shake or two of the hand is appropriate; don't hold on for dear life.

The first few minutes will also often consist of such small talk as "How was your ride in?" "Did you have any problem finding us?" Expect this kind of small talk and be ready to respond without sounding dumbfounded by the question at hand or being garrulous. When you walk into the interviewer's office, wait until they tell you to be seated before just plopping down. There are definite rules of etiquette to observed in these instances; just remember those words that your parents used to tell you: "Be on your best behavior."

Interview Formats

Generally, interviews will fall into one of two categories: structured or unstructured. The structured interview is probably the one you think of most often when you think of interviewing for a job; this is when the interviewer asks a prescribed set of questions and you retort with brief answers. In an unstructured interview, the questions are more open-ended. The interviewer is asking you questions that are specifically designed to get you talking and reveal more about yourself than you would if just asked the same old standard questions. What the interviewer is looking to do is find out more about you, your character, your skills, your background, and your aspirations. While these styles are certainly distinct, interviewers do not need to limit themselves to one style. In fact, it is common practice for a recruiter or hiring professional to start out with some basic objective questions and finish the interview with more open-ended inquiries. Be on the safe side and anticipate both.

Setting a Tone

While your qualifications (as seen as your resume) were certainly what got you in the door, it is your personality and attitude that will dictate whether you go any further in a company. Don't waste

Come Overprepared!

As hiring managers and recruiters are often under a lot of pressure to review candidates and get a position filled quickly, it shouldn't surprise you if you are left in the waiting room for a few minutes.

That said, it may be a good idea to bring along some reading material. That way, when you're told "it's going to be another few minutes," you can show them how understanding you are by sitting quietly and reading.

your time and energy trying to project the perfect image, as you'll most likely come off as being nervous. Instead, think of yourself as a calm, cool, and collected individual and try to relax and let a little bit of your true personality seep out. In the end, you have no control over the outcome of an interview; you could easily win an interviewer over and still not get the job, or you could botch the entire interview and still receive an offer. The only thing you do have control over is what you do and say while you're in an interview. Remember, the key qualities that an interviewer is looking for are:

Adaptability
Competence
Confidence
Dedication
Dependability
Easygoing Manner
Enthusiasm
Resourcefulness

Think of these qualities in every answer you give and every thing you say, and you should have no problem projecting the image of a confident and competent candidate.

Show Off Your Knowledge

At some point in the interview, the interviewer will proceed to tell you a bit more about the position and the company in general. If you have done your research, this information should seem like second nature to you. Where appropriate, you may want to show-case your knowledge of the company, the position, and/or the industry, without sounding like a show-off. A great way to build rapport with the interviewer (and leave an impression) is to engage them in an intelligent conversation. Again, if you have done your research, it is likely that you will be able to discourse on something that the interviewer mentions. Without interrupting (or correcting this person), try your best to tactfully mention your familiarity with the topic and hope it grows into a conversation between equals.

Make an Impression

Do you know how many candidates a recruiter and/or hiring manager has interviewed in his or her lifetime? Depending on the number of years they've been in the business, it could be hundreds. What can you do to make sure that your name, face, and resume stand out from the hordes of others? Try your hardest to make an impression.

When an employer begins to describe the activities of the company and the typical duties that your desired job will entail, listen carefully. Think of ways in which you have demonstrated aptitude at these sort of duties and draw parallels between the company's needs and your own experiences. Describe your experiences in the interview the same way you would on a resume: emphasize your results and achievements, and don't be modest. On the other hand, don't exaggerate to the point of incredulity either.

If you are interviewing for a competitive position or with a large company, the first interview is the most difficult. This is where the company chooses those who are a definite NO and sends them a complimentary thank you letter. It is for this reason that making a great impression, especially during the first screening interview, is so important. Focus on a few of your greatest strengths and keep highlighting them throughout the interview.

Don't Be Negative

No matter how much you hate your current job or how much you despise one of your former bosses, an interview is not the appropriate forum in which to talk about this. In fact, you should try your hardest to make sure that nothing negative comes out of your mouth at all! Considering the fact that you are seeking new employment, the interviewer is obviously aware that you are somehow unhappy in your current position. That said, keep the slanderous

Chatterboxes Need Not Apply

One of the most difficult parts of the interview is trying to figure out how much of an answer the interviewer wants. Will a quick yes or no do, or are they looking for you to retrace all of your achievements, starting with your first birthday? It is not at all wrong to ask the interviewer this question. If you're really unsure of how detailed an answer they are seeking, just ask!

remarks or disparaging comments to yourself. The only thing this will convey to the interviewer is the possibility of a future attitude problem, which probably won't place you too high on the "Must Hire" candidate list.

Emphasize the Positive

In keeping with the previous point, you want to make sure that you emphasize the positive points of your experience. Turn all those "bad jobs" into "learning experiences" and really think about what you learned from them. For example, instead of saying "I hated my position as a telemarketer because I was forced to bother people night and day," say "I realized that cold-calling wasn't my strong suit. Though I really enjoyed being able to interact with people, I decided that my talents could be better utilized in a face-to-face situation." Even the worst job taught you some sort of lesson; figure out what it was and discuss that.

Answering Difficult Questions

Having an impossible question (one which you don't have an answer to) thrown at you is probably one of the worst things that could happen during an interview. While it's always a terrifying experience, rest assured that it happens quite often. In fact, some recruiters will ask these types of questions, knowing full well you can't answer it. Their intention is not to embarrass you or have you go running and screaming out the door, they are simply testing you. Especially if you're applying to a high-pressured job, the recruiter wants to see how you respond to pressure. Do you stumble and stutter nervously? Do you try and make something up? Or do you admit that you do not know? The easiest way to end the situation is to actually think about it for a few seconds and, if you can't come up with an answer, simply say (without an apology) "I don't know" or "I cannot answer that question." Just make sure that you remain confident in your response, even when you don't have an answer.

Prepare Your Own Questions

Near the end of the interview, the interviewer will probably ask you if you have any questions. Even if you know everything there is to know about this company and/or position, have something prepared to ask. If you look back sheepishly and say "Nope! I think you answered 'em all," you're not likely to be remembered. Make sure that you have a few questions ready. That way, if the interviewer should happen to answer a few during the course of your conversation, you'll have a backup plan all ready.

The worst thing you could ever do is ask the interviewer a question that has already been answered. Not only will they think that you are inattentive, but they may think that you are incapable of absorbing large amounts of information in a short period of time. Also, you want to avoid reading the questions directly from list you have written.

If you have done your research, this is another part of the interview where you can subtly demonstrate your knowledge. By asking questions that pertain to this particular company, you are showing the interviewer that you know what you're talking about. But don't allow your questions to turn into an interrogation; avoid asking questions the interviewer may find difficult or awkward to answer. Steer clear of questions that don't pertain directly to the job. For example, while it may interest you to know whether or not all the company's catalogs are printed on recycled paper, now is not the time to ask. Ask intelligent questions that will underscore your interest in the position as well as a long-term career with the company.

Ending the Interview

The end of the interview should not come as a surprise to you. The interviewer will probably ask if you have any further questions and tell you that he or she is done. If the interviewer doesn't offer up the next step of the process, ask. Find out whether the company will contact you or if it will be up to you to get in contact with them. How long will it be before they make a decision? Make sure to write down whatever it is this person tells you so that you can be sure of the agreed upon next step. If the interviewer doesn't

Talking Money

When it comes to the interview, one of the worst questions you can ask is "How much will I be paid?" Even more tactful incarnations of this question ("What type of salary would accompany this wonderful position?") are inappropriate. While some employers will tell you the salary up front (and whether or not it is negotiable), others will wait until the final stages of the game. If the interviewer asks you what type of salary you are looking for, make sure you give them a range instead of an actual figure. "$25,000 - $30,000" is much easier to negotiate than "$29,657.43."

offer you a business card, ask for one. If he or she is fresh out, be sure to write down the interviewer's name (you can ask for the correct spelling), title, and phone number (if you don't have it already). Keep this information alongside the names and titles of anyone else you may have met with in the company.

Giving "Thanks!"

Well, you've survived at least one interview—Congratulations! But wait, you're not done. Instead of sitting by the phone and waiting for the call, it's time to send a little note of thanks to the interviewer and anyone else with whom you spoke at the company. In addition to showing your appreciation for their time, the follow-up letter allows you the chance to (tactfully) mention any details you may have forgotten. If the interview didn't go as smoothly as you planned, now is the time to win back some points. Be polite and make sure to express your continued interest in the position, as well as your ability to perform the duties the job requires. Make sure to proofread the letter carefully and, if you're still unsure of how to spell the person's name, call the company receptionist and ask. While a hand-written letter on a piece of nice stationery is the best way to do it (provided your writing is legible), sending a quick e-mail is okay too. If the interviewer's e-mail address is listed on their card, use it. If not, don't ask for it. Make sure to write and send this thank-you letter immediately following the interview so that your meeting is still fresh in the interviewer's mind. It will help them put a face to the letter . . . and maybe a face to the position.

Keep in Touch

After sending a follow-up letter, allow the interviewer five to ten days to receive it. If, at that time, you still have not heard anything, now is the appropriate time to get in touch again. The best way to express your continued interest is with a brief telephone call. Make it short; ask whether or not a decision has been made and when the applicants will be notified of a decision. If, during the course of

Some Common Interview Questions You May Be Asked

Tell me about yourself.

Why did you leave your last job?

Why are you leaving your current job?

What is the most exciting part of your current job?

Where do you see yourself in five years?

How much overtime are you willing to work?

If I asked a previous employer to tell me something about you, what do you think they would say?

Tell me about a difficult situation that you have faced in the workplace and how you handled it.

What are your greatest strengths?

What are your weaknesses?

Describe a situation where you took initiative and went beyond your normal responsibilities.

Why should we hire you?

your interview, the interviewer provided any possibilities for a follow-up conversation (like reading an article or a book), make sure to mention how much you learned from the piece and thank them for their recommendation. Again, always be honest. If the interviewer recommended something for you to read but you still haven't gotten around to it, don't lie and tell them how much you enjoyed it. They'll know.

Moving Right Along

If you don't receive a phone call the day after interviewing, don't fret. As it can often take companies several weeks (maybe even a month or longer) to interview all possible applicants, it may be a while before you hear any news. Don't sit around waiting for their phone call. Make sure you spend this time wisely; send your resume out to other firms and set up other interviews. Even if you have your heart set on working for one specific company, it always helps to have a backup plan. Keeping the job search going is also important because, should you have a number of opportunities on the table, you are in a much better position to negotiate.

Dealing with Rejection

Just as a cover letter and a resume are always part of the job search process, so is rejection. Disheartening as it is, rejection is inevitable; we will all experience it at some point. Still, how you prepare for it in the job market is important, as it is not something you should take personally. Don't swear off a company or start up an ABC Company boycott just because they didn't hire you; turn rejection around and make it work for you. One way you can do this is by contacting each of the interviewers who rejected you and thanking them for their time. You can also ask that they keep you in mind for any future openings. If you feel comfortable, you may even want to ask the interviewer for help. Ask them if they have any suggestions for how you might have a better chance of getting a job in the industry, or ask them for the names of any people or companies they may know of that are hiring.

Before you do contact a rejecting employer, be aware of two things. First, don't ask them why they didn't hire you. In addition to being completely out of line, this is a question that will definitely make the interviewer feel a bit uncomfortable. Second, if you do decide to ask for suggestions, make sure that is not the only thing it sounds like you called for. Engaging this person in a friendly (but brief) conversation that eventually leads to offering suggestions will make them much more willing to talk to you.

Second Interviews and Beyond

If you've made it through the first interview (and done well), chances are the employer will call you in again before offering you the position. Very few companies will offer a job without conducting a series of interviews beforehand. The purpose of the first interview is to narrow down the number of candidates that the company will then seriously consider. That is why the goal of the first interview is to stand out and be remembered. When going back for later interviews, there is a bit of a different strategy involved.

By getting through the first interview, a candidate has proven that he or she has several strengths that could benefit the company. Hence, in the second interview and beyond, employers will be looking (specifically) for your weaknesses. Your ultimate goal here is to present yourself as a well-balanced candidate and the right person for the job. In later interviews, try to figure out the underlying concern at hand for each of the questions you are asked. In your answer, try to dispel that apprehension. If you are interviewing with people who are in a position to reject your hiring but not push it forward, try your hardest to build a strong rapport.

While most professional positions will require at least two interviews, you can usually count on at least three interviews for a higher-level job. There are even some firms out there who are famous for conducting a minimum of six interviews before offering a position. The good news in all this is that, with each subsequent

Thank You Required

While the thank-you letter is a relatively new part of the whole job search process, it is quickly becoming a step that is expected and almost required by certain employers. Sending a quick thank-you or follow-up letter reinforces your enthusiasm for a position and restates your desire to be hired, even after the interview. Don't take chances. Stay in the good graces of each employer you interview with, and always send a thank-you letter.

interview, the competition is less and you should begin to feel more relaxed and comfortable with the company's business.

Bring Out the Zingers!

One of the other ways in which a second interview differs from a first is that the questions are not so straightforward or expected. Questions are always much more specific, and they can become very technical. What the company is trying to do is test your depth of knowledge of the field, including how well you're able to apply your education and work experience to your everyday work life. While the first interview is likely to be a screening interview that is conducted by a human resources professional or a recruiter, the second interview will most likely be with your future boss, a professional peer group, or a group of executives who oversee the work group you're being considered for.

Following are some of the most challenging questions you could be asked during a second interview (and some good ways to respond). If you think you could answer these questions with just a split second to think, you should be prepared to field just about any question the interviewer may throw at you.

Tell me about yourself.

I am a production assistant for a local morning talk show with a B.A. in communications and three years of solid broadcasting and public relations experience. I have extensive experience developing and researching topics, pre-interviewing guests, and producing on-location television segments. I have a tremendous amount of energy and love to be challenged. I'm constantly taking on additional responsibilities so that I may learn new things. I have watched your station for quite some time now and have always been impressed with your innovative approach to broadcasting and programming. I'd definitely like to be part of that winning team.

★ This is the perfect opportunity to sell yourself to an employer in just a few seconds. You need to "package" yourself in to one small paragraph where you mention your experience, skills, accomplishments, goals, and personal qualities. Declare your interest in the company and how you could make a difference if you were hired. If you're a recent college graduate with not too much real world experience, be sure to mention your educational qualifications and emphasize the classes you took that pertain to the job.

Tell me about a project in which you were disappointed with your personal performance.

In my last job with a manufacturing company, I had to analyze all the supplier bids and present recommendations to the vice president of logistics. Because the supplier bids weren't in an organized format, my analysis often consisted of comparing dissimilar items. This caused some confusion in my final report, and by the time I'd reworked it and presented it to the vice president, we'd lost the critical time we'd needed to improve our approval process for these bids. In hindsight, I should have taken a different approach to the problem and not tried to make it so complex or all-inclusive. Ever since, I've paid much more attention to making recommendations in a timely manner.

★ Describe the barriers you've come across in past experiences and how you've worked around them. How have your skills come into play? In hindsight, what could you have done differently? Most importantly, turn this roadblock into a lesson and tell the interviewer what you learned from having gone through the experience.

Tell me about the most difficult work or personal experience you've ever faced.

A coworker, with whom I was very close, was going through a very difficult time and had begun to abuse drugs and alcohol. After a long talk, he decided that the best thing for him was to attend a rehabilitation center. For the next six months, I had to take on much of this person's work in addition to my own. While the long hours and pressure were not the ideal situation, I know that he would have done the same for me and I never once regretted it. It's very important to me to have that kind of

trust among the members of my work group and I am glad that I was able to help someone out in their time of need.

★ The ultimate goal of this question is to find out how you hold up under pressure. Ideally, you want to describe a situation, either personal or professional, that involved a great deal of conflict and challenge and, as a result, placed you under an unusual amount of stress. Explain, specifically, what the problems were, and what you did to resolve them.

What was your greatest challenge in your last job?

After years of working completely with paper, my company decided to have a new e-mail system installed. As many of the longtime employees had limited or no computer experience, it was very difficult to get them to embrace this new system. After what seemed like a million pep talks on the need for less paper in everyone's job, I came up with a plan. I created a temporary e-mail account with one daily riddle on the system; everyone who responded to the riddle got his or her name put in a weekly drawing. Each week, we would draw someone's name and award them with dinner for four at a great local eatery. The employees learned the benefit of e-mail and how they could use it in their everyday work.

★ When thinking of a challenge in your last job, think specifically of a problem that existed that you helped to solve. While the interviewer may not come right out and ask how you helped to overcome this challenge, an answer that touches on your involvement in solving the problem is exactly what they're looking for. If you've had very little work experience, it's fine to think of a minor challenge that you were faced with and how you overcame it; you didn't have to save your company from a hostile takeover to get the job.

How have you handled criticism of your work?

The first time I had a complaint from a client, I was devastated. It was impossible for me to keep the complaint separate from my professional service of the account. The client was upset about the downtime in ATM machines. I learned that showing empathy usually calms an unpleasant situation. I also learned that no client is going to be happy with everything, even if that client's overall experience is positive. I know that I should not take things personally and, instead, put myself in that person's shoes and see if I can't do something to help them feel better.

★ With this question, the interviewer is looking to learn something about your accountability and professional character. If you can think of a specific project or work habit that caused you a problem until you faced up to it and overcame it, talk about that experience. Alternatively, you might describe a time you responded objectively and professionally to particularly harsh or unreasonable criticism of your work.

What might your current boss want to change about your work habits?

Because I'm a morning person and my boss is a night owl, we often put in our extra time at opposite ends of the day. I prefer to come into the office at least an hour early, usually by seven, to get a jump start on my work. My boss, on the other hand, likes to come in after nine and work late into the evening. If there were one thing she could change about me, she'd probably make me into a night owl, too, so I'd be there during the same hours she is.

★ The interviewer is looking to find out how well you'll fit in with your future boss and coworkers and will also want to feel confident that he or she has uncovered any surprises about your corporate style. One good way to answer this question is to point out minor differences of preference. Alternatively, you may want to describe a weakness of yours that you and your boss have worked on and improved.

Tell me about a situation that frustrated you at work.

I was frustrated once when a client, who had insisted on purchasing a high-growth stock, called in a panic because the stock had dropped more than twenty points in one day. I had a hard time convincing him to ride it out rather than cut his

losses. I think what frustrated me most was that this happened despite my attempts from the beginning to explain the short-term volatility of that stock.

★ This is another question designed to probe the candidate's professional personality. The interviewer will want reassurance that you're able withstand pressure on the job. Describe how you've remained diplomatic, objective, or professional in a difficult situation.

Tell me about one of your projects that failed.

I've always been somewhat of a workaholic and have the attitude that I can tackle anything and achieve good results. After a rather destructive hurricane, my insurance company was inundated with claims. I immediately thought I was completely capable of handling all the claims in my area, and dove right in to a series of eighteen-hour workdays. After about a week, I realized that there was no way I could complete all of the claims on time and on my own, and I had to begin delegating some of the responsibility to my investigators. What I learned was that, no matter how efficient and competent you are, there are always situations where you need to ask for help from others.

★ Make sure that you demonstrate the ability to be humble when answering this type of question. One of the worst answers you can come up with in a situation such as this one is "I can't think of anything" or "I've never had a project fail." Show the employer how much you can learn from your mistakes. In hindsight, what could you have done differently? How has your leadership style changed because of the experience?

Tell me about a time when your employer wasn't happy with your job performance.

When I first began working as a paralegal, I handed in two letters with typos in them during my first week on the job. I am not sure why my work was sloppy; perhaps it was my nervousness at beginning a new career and actually working instead of going to school. After that first week, however, my boss did tell me regularly how happy she was with my work.

★ Try to think of a relatively minor incident to answer this question. Also, show your willingness to accept responsibility for the problem—don't blame others or make excuses. Simply describe what happened and what you did to successfully resolve the situation.

Have you ever been passed up for a promotion you thought you deserved?

A couple times in my early career, I thought I was unfairly passed up for a promotion. However, in retrospect, I now realize that I probably wasn't ready to perform those jobs. In fact, the additional training I received remaining where I was proved invaluable in the last few years, as I've made significant progress moving up the corporate ladder. I've also learned to appreciate that being ready for a promotion doesn't necessarily mean it will happen. There are many external factors, aside from a person's performance and capabilities, that need to be taken into consideration.

★ The interviewer wants to gauge the candidate's self-confidence as well as his or her objectivity about personal or professional limitations. Be sure to give evidence here that you have enough patience to learn what is important before you get bored in one position or frustrated because you haven't been promoted. After you've mastered your own job, would you stay motivated long enough to be productive?

Have you ever been fired?

When I was in college, I was fired from a summer internship. I was working for a software consulting company and, midway through the summer, a new president was appointed because of some financial difficulties. As one of his first orders of business, he requested the resignation of my entire work group. I was swept out with everyone else, though my work performance had never been criticized.

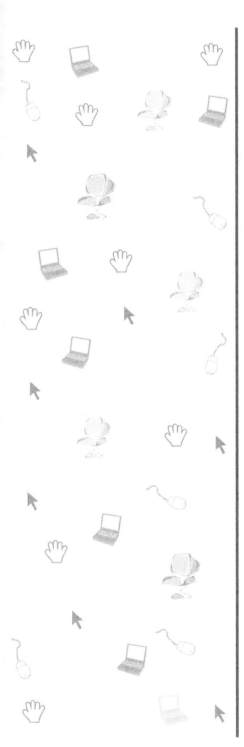

★ If you've never been fired, this should be an easy question to answer. If you have been fired, you'll need to be prepared to discuss the situation in detail and possibly answer a series of specific follow-up questions. If the termination was the result of a situation beyond your control, like corporate downsizing, most interviewers will be understanding. If you were fired due to poor performance or some other personal problem, you'll need to admit your fault and convince the interviewer you've corrected the problem. Although this may be a difficult question to answer (and one that makes you, ultimately, nervous about your overall impression), you should be completely honest. If you aren't, and the recruiter finds out as much from your references, you may be subject to an immediate dismissal, or your job offer may be revoked.

Why have you changed jobs so frequently?

My frequent job changes over the last five years have been due to the rapid changes in my profession. My jobs have been based on government contracts, and over the last several years congressional appropriations have been up and down, causing some companies' contracts to be canceled, while other companies land huge, unexpected contracts. The unpredictability creates some good opportunities, but also causes a lot of uncertainty. Because your business is based mostly on consumer products and not on government products, I welcome the opportunity to work in an environment where the business cycle is more stable and predictable.

★ Be candid when answering this question. Personal growth, a larger budget, or other career-enhancing experiences are all valid reasons for moving on. Convince the interviewer that you're interested in his or her company for the long haul.

Why did you stay in your last job so long?

I was in my last job for over seven years. During that time, I completed an advanced technical degree at an evening university and also had two six-month assignments in which I was loaned out to different departments. As a result, I acquired some addi-

tional skills that normally aren't associated with that job. Therefore, I think I've made good progress and am ready to accept the next challenge.

★ The interviewer may be curious about your interest in personal improvement, tackling new assignments, and so on. He or she may also be concerned about whether you have a tendency to get too comfortable with the status quo. Demonstrate how you've developed job responsibilities in meaningful new ways.

Tell me about your least favorite manager or professor.

Well, I've been pretty fortunate as far as managers go, and I didn't have any problems with my professors. In my first job out of college, I worked with a manager who was pretty inaccessible. If you walked into his office to ask a question, you got the sense that you were bothering him, so we just learned to get help from each other instead. I wouldn't say he was my least favorite manager, because he was good in a lot of ways, but I would have preferred that he'd been more available to us and given us more direction.

★ Answering this question will be a little bit like walking across a minefield, so be careful! Keep in mind that the interviewer doesn't really want to learn about your former supervisors; he or she wants to learn about the way you speak about them. Though the interviewer may bait you to make a negative statement about your former employer, doing so can create a host of problems. Even if your claim is completely true and entirely justified, the recruiter may conclude either that you don't get along well with people or that you shift blame to others. The best way around this dilemma is to choose an example that's not too negative, touch upon it briefly, then focus the rest of your answer on what you learned from the experience.

Who's the toughest employer you've ever had to work for and why?

That would be Mrs. Rogers at the Brady Project. She would push people to their limits when things got busy and she was a

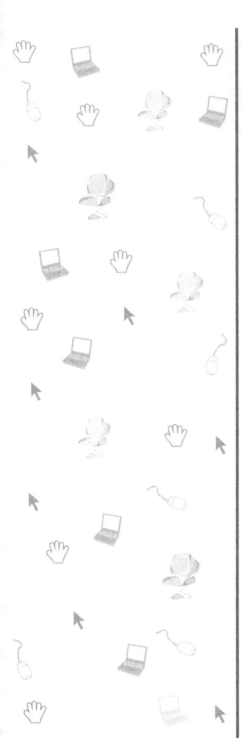

stickler for detail. But she was always fair, and she rewarded good, hard work. I'd definitely call her a tough boss, but I'd also call her a good boss.

★ Again, make sure not to make any negative statements about your previous employers. Turn the question around with a positive, upbeat response. Make sure to mention the positive aspects of this boss in addition to the qualities that made them so tough.

What are some of the things your supervisor has done that you disliked?

The only thing I really don't like is to get feedback in front of others. I want to hear good or bad feedback in private, so that I have time to think and react to the issue without other distractions. I believe that's the fair way to improve learning or to change future behavior.

★ Again, avoid being overly negative about your ex-boss or manager. Discuss a relatively minor example with which the interviewer is likely to empathize. Put a positive spin on your answer by describing what you learned from this difficult situation.

How do you handle tension with your boss?

The only tension I've ever felt was once when we both got too busy to keep each other informed. My boss overcommitted me with a short deadline, not knowing I was bogged down with another client problem. I believe firmly in the importance of staff meetings, so coworkers can respect the demands on each other's time.

★ The safest ground here is to describe an example of a miscommunication in your early relationship with a boss and how you resolved it. The interviewer will want to know how you avoided a recurrence of the problem.

Would you be able to work extended hours as necessary to perform the job?

I'm accustomed to working long hours during the week. I usually work until at least six-thirty, because I get a lot done after the office closes at five. I can make arrangements to be available on weekends, if necessary, though I do prefer to have at least twenty-four hours' notice.

★ Your response should match closely the position you're applying for and should reflect a realistic understanding of the work and time required. Ask about seasonality of your work if you're unsure, and show a willingness to work occasional extended hours.

Prove to me that your interest is sincere.

I know that there are a lot of people out there who would like to work in television because of large income potential or the opportunity to be on camera, but my reasons go far beyond that. To me, communication is an art form, and the television industry is the ultimate test of how well one communicates. Working in television isn't like working for a newspaper where, if a reader misses a fact, he or she can just go back and reread it. A television news story can go by in a flash, and the challenge is to make sure the audience understands it, learns from it, and, in a broader sense, can use the information to better their lives or their situations. It's the way television can evoke action that's always made me want to be a part of the industry. I'm particularly interested in this station because I like your focus on the community. Though the on-air products have a great look, the stations seems to remain focused on the tradition of local news and what matters to its audience. The special reports that emphasize town politics, that go on location each week to a different town for a live shot, that explain the big issues facing a community, make the viewer feel that the station is a part of the community. In my opinion, this is a great way to maintain a loyal audience.

★ Being unprepared to answer this question can eliminate you from further consideration. On the other hand, if you're able to demonstrate a strong interest in the company and the position, you'll have an advantage over the competition.

What would you do if I told you I thought you were giving a very poor interview today?

Well, the first thing I would do is ask you if there were any specific part of the interview that you thought I mishandled. After that, I'd think back and try to remember if there had been any faulty communication on my part. Then I'd try to review possible problems I had understanding your questions, and I'd ask for clarification if I needed it. Finally, if we had time, I'd try to respond more fully and appropriately to the problem areas you identified for me.

★ Interviewers like to ask stress questions like these to see how well you hold up under pressure. Your best bet is to stay calm and relaxed; don't allow your confidence to be shaken.

How would you respond to a defaulted form Z-65 counterderivative renewal request if your manager ordered you to do so, and if the policy under which the executive board resolves such issues were currently under review?

★ Being asked an impossible question such as this one is actually a good sign. The recruiter is looking to see how you will respond to this question, they're not really looking for an answer. If you're asked a tough question that you can't answer, think about it for a few seconds. Then, with a confident smile, simply say something like "I don't know, but if you hire me, I'll be happy to find out for you."

Special Situations

When you find yourself in what is deemed a "special situation," interviewing can be even more stressful. Special situations can include a lack of paid job experience, extended absence from the workplace, concerns about possible discrimination because of age or disability, or trying to enter a field in which you have no practical experience. Don't let such a thing stress you out too much.

The key to improving your chances of getting a job when you're in one of these special situations is to emphasize your strengths. Focus your interview on your marketable skills (whether they were acquired in the workplace or elsewhere) and highlight impressive achievements, relevant education and training, and/or related interests. Downplay or avoid discussing any information that may be construed as a weakness.

Questions for Career Changers

Career changers have one advantage over a candidate just entering the job market—they usually have a ton of experience. Even if you've spent the last 10 years working for an insurance company, you've gained skills and experience that will benefit you in any career. Instead of emphasizing your job history, emphasize the skills you've acquired that apply to the job you're seeking. Some questions that may come up in the course of your interview follow.

Why do you want to leave your current position?

My current position has allowed me to learn a great deal about the plastics industry, and I am very glad to have had the opportunities I've had at Chloe Company. However, I've also found that my interests really lie in research and development, which Chloe has recently decided to phase out over the next two years. That is why I am so interested in your organization. As I understand, Severine Industries places a great deal of importance on research and development, and is also a highly respected leader in the industry.

★ The interviewer's foremost concern with career changers will always be why they want to switch careers. But, people do it every day, so don't think you won't get the job just because you don't have any hands-on experience in the field. Show the interviewer that your decision to switch careers has been based on careful consideration. Explain why you decided on this particular position and how the position will allow you to further your skills and interests.

Why would you want to leave an established career at an employment agency for what is essentially an entry-level position in marketing?

During my many years at the agency, I have acquired many valuable skills. At the same time, I feel as if I've stopped growing. There's only so far you can go in such a career, and I am nearing the end of the career path. I am no longer challenged by my work, and being challenged is what keeps me motivated. I've thought about this for a long time, as switching careers is not an easy decision to make. Still, I am confident that I am doing the right thing by looking for a job within another industry, even if it means starting over. My interest in marketing arose last year when a local family lost their home to a fire. A bunch of the people from my community decided to pitch in and help this family raise enough money to rebuild their home. I helped by designing and distributing posters, placing advertisements in local newspapers, and selling T-shirts outside grocery stores and shopping malls. When I began to see the result of what my work was doing, I became very excited about this task. I learned that you can have a great product and a great cause, but if nobody knows about it, you're dead in the water. I felt as if the work I was doing was making a difference—and I was good at it, too. Since then, I have taken two introductory marketing courses and am planning to enroll in a part-time degree program this fall. Also, I'll be able to use many of the skills I've acquired working at an employment agency to benefit me in a marketing career as well. After all, working in an employment agency is marketing—marketing the agency to corporate clients and job seekers, and marketing the job seekers to corporate clients.

★ The interviewer wants to determine two things: the candidate's motivation for choosing a new career and the likelihood that the candidate will be comfortable in a position where he or she will probably have less power and responsibility than in previous jobs. To dispel the interviewer's fears, discuss your reasons for

Knowing Your Way

One of the best ways you can spend your time before an interview is by taking a few minutes to find the place (that is, of course, assuming it is a local company). If you are not sure where the company is located, don't be afraid to ask when setting up the interview. Even if the recruiter has given you a detailed set of directions, you may want to have a map handy anyway. There are plenty of online sites where you can obtain a map of a certain address, or even acquire the driving directions from one place to another by simply typing in the address of Point A and Point B. Check out the following sites to print out a map:

DeLorme Cyber Maps
www.delorme.com

Map Blast
www.mapblast.com

Expedia Maps
maps.expedia.com

MapQuest
www.mapquest.com

Lycos Road Maps
www.lycos.com/roadmap.html

Yahoo! Maps
maps.yahoo.com

switching careers and be sure to show that you have a solid understanding of the position and the industry in general. Many candidates expect to start their new career in a position comparable to the one they held previously. The truth is that most career changers must start in a lower, if not entry-level, position in their new company to gain basic experience and knowledge in the field.

Questions for Candidates Re-entering the Job Market

There's no doubt about it: if you've been out of the workforce for an extended period of time, you will face some troubling issues upon your re-entry. You may feel anxious, wondering if you've still got what it takes to make it out there, and it's not uncommon for employers to feel the same way. The first thing you should do before looking to re-enter the workforce is to make sure all your skills, technical and otherwise, are up to date. Read some articles on the industry and make sure the techniques, computer programs, etc. being described are all familiar to you. If you think your own skills could use a little tweaking, consider retraining by taking courses or learning a new computer program. The main things you will want to focus on during your interview are the jobs you've had previously and the skills they called for, the ways in which you've kept up your learning during your absence (reading trade journals, doing freelance work, attending seminars, networking with industry professionals), and the skills you've learned at home that can be transferred to the workplace.

Your resume indicates that you have not worked in the past few years. Would you mind explaining?

I have spent the last five years raising my son, Liam, who's now in kindergarten. Leaving the workplace was a very difficult decision for me, but as this was our first child, I didn't think I would be able to commit to my career one hundred percent, knowing what responsibilities I had at home. Since I didn't think it would be fair to my employer to give any less than 100 percent, I believe it was the right decision for me at the time. Now that my son is old enough to be in school, I feel refreshed and am completely ready to devote myself to a full-time career.

★ Whatever the reason for your hiatus, be honest. Discuss the decisions behind your absence, whether they were to stay at home and raise a family or recuperate from a debilitating injury. Be sure to emphasize the reasons why you want to return to work and why you think you are ready. Most importantly, stress your eagerness to resume your career.

Illegal Questions

There are plenty of questions that an interviewer is not allowed to ask, by law, and you should be aware of these in case one comes up during an interview. Federal law prohibits employers from discriminating against a candidate because of sex, age, race, nationality, or religion. If you are asked a question that seems to probe one of these private matters, it is most likely an illegal question. For instance, an interviewer may not ask you about your age or your date of birth. However, he or she may ask you if you are over the age of eighteen, as that may apply to the job. If you're asked an illegal question during an interview, don't jump and scream "Police!" or demand that the interviewer retract the question. The truth is, many employers simply don't know what is legal and what is illegal to ask an applicant.

One strategy you can employ is to get to the heart of the question. For example, if an employer asks you about your plans to have children, they may be concerned that you won't be able to fulfill the travel requirements of the job. Try to get to the heart of the matter by saying "I'm not quite sure I understand." If you can determine the interviewer's concerns, you can allay them with a reply like "I'm very interested in developing my career. Travel is definitely not a problem for me—in fact, I enjoy it tremendously."

On the other hand, you may choose to answer the question or to point out that the question is illegal and decline to answer it. Avoid reacting in a hostile fashion. You can always decline a job

How Would You Like Other People to Think of You?

I like people to think I'm there when they need me. But more than that, I want to be thought of as fair, considerate, and evenhanded. I want everyone I come in contact with to be able to say afterward that it was a positive experience.

offer. The responses below outline some of the many ways in which you could go about answering what is, essentially, an illegal question.

What religion do you practice?

1. *I make it a point not to mix my personal beliefs with my work, if that's what you mean. I assure you that I value my career too much for that.*
2. *I'm not quite sure what you're getting at. Could you please explain how this issue relates to the position?*
3. *That question makes me a bit uncomfortable. I'd really rather not answer it.*

How old are you?

1. *I'm in my fifties and have over 30 years of experience in this industry. My area of expertise is in . . .*
2. *I'm not quite sure what you're getting at. Could you please explain how this issue relates to the position?*
3. *That question makes me a bit uncomfortable. I'd really rather not answer it.*

Are you married?

1. *No.*
2. *Yes, I am. But I keep my family life separate from my work so that I can put all my effort into my job. I'm flexible when it comes to travel and late hours, as my references can confirm.*
3. *I'm not quite sure what you're getting at. Could you please explain how this issue relates to the position?*
4. *That question makes me a bit uncomfortable. I'd really rather not answer it.*

Do you have children?

1. *No.*
2. *Yes, I do. But I keep my family life separate from my work life so that I can put all my effort into my job. I'm flexible when it comes to travel and late hours, as my references can confirm.*

3. *I'm not quite sure what you're getting at. Could you please explain how this issue relates to the position?*
4. *That question makes me a bit uncomfortable. I'd really rather not answer it.*

Students and Recent Graduates

One of the ways in which inexperienced applicants most often kill their chances of employment is by making too many negative comments during an interview. A college student or recent graduate should never make disparaging comments during an interview—even if its completely true and fully justified. If a recruiter asks why you had an unsatisfactory grade in a particular course, don't say "The professor graded me unfairly," or "I didn't get along with the professor." Tell the truth.

A recruiter would rather hire someone who gets and deserves an unsatisfactory grade in a course than someone who has trouble getting along with others or makes a habit out of shifting blame. Just remember that you can greatly increase your chances of being hired by projecting a positive, upbeat attitude. This is one of the easiest and best ways that you can stand apart from the rest of the candidates. You can project your excitement by smiling from time to time during the interview (though don't overdo it with an ear-to-ear grin throughout the entire interview), by responding to interview questions with enthusiasm, by demonstrating experience about your past accomplishments, and by showing optimism about the prospect of starting your career.

Questions Recent Graduates Are Likely to Be Asked

Whether you just finished college or just received your high school diploma, recent graduates are usually treated to a different set of interview questions than those given to seasoned professionals. Still, while the whole work thing seems like a Catch-22 you need experience to get a job, you need a job to get experience—emphasizing

your strengths and educational achievements can be just as impressive as talking about past work experiences. No matter what your level of experience, just remember to always answer an interviewer's question with enthusiasm and confidence; be sure to make eye contact while you speak and really listen to what they say in response.

About Your Grades

Why are your grades so erratic?

As I am never one to shy away from a challenge, many of the electives I selected throughout my education were classes that were primarily filled with students who were majoring in the subject. For example, though I was an English major, I decided that taking a bunch of physics courses would be a great way to round out my education. Though I did well in the classes, I did find them much more challenging than the majority of my classmates, who were majoring in the subject.

★ Again, it is important that when asked a seemingly negative question, you don't get defensive and don't place blame. Instead, try to put a positive spin on the question—talk about the challenges you were faced with and how you overcame them.

About Academics

What was your favorite class?

Outside of my major, one of the classes I particularly enjoyed was an introductory course in economics. It was a completely new subject area to me, and I really enjoy new challenges. I was particularly fascinated with macroeconomic theory, where complex mathematical equations can be combined with psychology to explain past economic events and predict future trends.

What was your most challenging class?

Initially, I was completely overwhelmed by the introductory chemistry course I took last year. No matter how hard I studied, I seemed to be getting nowhere. I even failed the first three quizzes. After that, I decided to try a brand new approach. Instead of just studying by myself, I organized a small study

Money Talks

As much as the recruiter talks about the position, the company, and all these other vital details, you're waiting to hear that magic word: SALARY! Unless the interviewer brings up salary, it is completely uncouth for you to mention it. If there is not a set salary for the position, an interviewer is likely to ask you the kind of money that you are looking for first. Your best bet is to give them a salary range. But, before you calculate your range, you should probably figure out what the average person in your position is making in the area you're looking to work in (that's right, location plays a big part in determining the kind of money you can ask for). To find out the normal pay scale for a variety of positions in your field, check out any of the following Web Sites:

Absolute Career
www.absolutecareer.com

Career Spectrum
www.careerspectrum.com

Career Campus
www.careercampus.com

JobStar
jobsmart.org

group. I also began to get help after class from my professor from time to time. I found that more time spent in the lab was critical. I ended up receiving a B+ in the course, and I felt I had achieved a solid understanding of the material. More than that, I learned that tackling a new field of study sometimes requires a new approach, not just hard work, and that the help of others can be crucial.

★ The interviewer is trying to figure out how well you respond to difficult situations. Demonstrate that you won't fold in the face of difficulty and that you're willing to put in extra effort to meet a challenge.

What are the steps you take to organize yourself for a large project, like writing a term paper?
My first step is to read as much as I can on the subject at hand and write up a tentative one-page outline. Then I gather all the appropriate books for reference and begin compiling notes onto index cards. I organize the index cards as logically as possible and begin forming my thesis statement in my mind. After that, I compose a revised and much more detailed outline. Finally I put my thoughts on paper, following both my outline and index cards.

How do you prepare for a major examination?
The first thing I usually do is read through the notes and other information I have on the areas I feel particularly weak in. After I feel I have mastered that, I skim through all of the notes and information that pertain to the upcoming exam a few times, and test myself on the information at hand.

Why did you decide to major in history?
Choosing to major in history was a difficult decision to make; I was so attracted to the areas of government, international relations, and economics, that I had to make up my mind between them. But, because the study of history seemed to encompass all three of these areas, I thought it would be the best choice. Plus,

because I majored in economic history, I was lucky enough that I could combine all these interests. I was also lucky in the fact that so many of the professors in the department were exceptionally knowledgeable and stimulating.

★ Show that you have solid, logical reasons for choosing your major. If you can't defend your choice of major, the interviewer will wonder how much thought you've put into choosing a career. You should also be sure that your reasons for choosing your major are compatible with your career choice. For instance, if you're applying for a position as a banker, don't say you were an English major because you love literature and writing.

About Extracurricular Activities

Why did you participate so little in extracurricular activities?

I really wanted to expend as much energy as possible on my academic studies. I came from a high school in a small town, where I received mostly A's, but I wasn't well prepared for college. I had to study much harder than I ever had before. When I was not studying, I really enjoyed taking some time to explore the city and develop relationships with my classmates and dorm mates.

★ The interviewer may be worried that if you don't have many outside interests, you may eventually suffer from burnout. Employers like candidates who are well-rounded and have interests outside work. If you didn't participate in formal extracurricular activities in college, you still may want to talk about some of your interests, like reading or exercising, that you participated in on a more informal level. For instance, you may have a passion for running, even if you weren't on the college track team.

I see you made the football team as a sophomore. Why didn't you play varsity football during your junior or senior years?

While I enjoyed the comradeship and being part of the team, I did find practices and drills to be tedious and unchallenging. I was always assigned to play guard, and how many different

ways can you block a rusher? Instead, I joined the Drama Club and was able to give more time to my studies. While I didn't become a great actor, it was an enriching experience.

About Tough Academic Situations

Your transcript reads "incomplete" for the second half of your sophomore year. Why?

I was suspended from school for the second half of the semester for being at a party where there was excessive drinking and damage to school property. While I didn't cause any damage to school property myself, I did accept responsibility for the incident, paid the penalty, and definitely learned my lesson. I was very grateful for the opportunity to return to school. I applied myself with vigor to my studies and have never been involved in any other incident.

I see that you failed two classes your last semester of freshman year and then took a year off before returning to school. Is there some sort of connection here?

Four years ago, as a freshman, I didn't know what I wanted to study, what career I wanted to pursue, or what direction I was headed in. The year off from school was one of the most constructive experiences of my life. After working as a dishwasher in a restaurant for much of the year, I developed a lot of respect for the value of a college education. I came to school completely refreshed, embarked on a major in English, and committed myself to pursuing a career where I could use my mind a little more and my hands a little less.

About Work Experience

Did you enjoy your summer job as a dishwasher at the Blackstone Grille?

I wouldn't want to do it for the rest of my life, but it was fine for a summer job. The work was more interesting than you might think, I enjoyed my coworkers, and I had a great rapport with my boss!

I see you worked as a lifeguard one summer, mowed lawns another summer, and babysat for two other summers. Which job did you find the most interesting?

Actually, by far the most interesting job I held wasn't a summer job but a part-time job I had at school. I did research for my political science professor's just-published book, The Disaffected Electorate. *It's based on extensive surveys that show that most people feel state and federal politicians aren't responsive to their constituents. I conducted hundreds of door-to-door interviews to compile the information and helped tabulate the results. It was fascinating to be part of this study almost from start to finish, and at the same time it was dismaying to see, from the results, how disenfranchised people feel.*

About a Lack of Work Experience

I see that, while you returned home each summer, you held jobs with different companies each time. Why didn't you ever return to work at the same company?

My career goal is to get a job in business after graduation. Because I attend a liberal arts college, I can't take any courses in business. So even though I was invited back to each summer job I held, I thought I could develop more experience by working in different positions. Although I didn't list high school jobs on my resume, I did work for almost three years at the same grocery store chain.

I see that you did quite a lot of traveling during summer breaks rather than take a summer job. Do you expect to do more traveling once you graduate?

I figured that once I graduate from college, I'll be spending the next 40 years of my life working, so I might as well get in some extended travel while I have a chance. I hope to begin a career position immediately upon graduating, and I plan to stay with that company for some time.

About Plans for the Future

Where would you like to be in five years?

I plan to remain in the banking industry for the foreseeable future. I hope that within five years, I'll have developed a successful track record as a loan officer, first perhaps with consumer loans, then switching to business loans. Ideally, I'd hope that within five years I'd also have advanced to servicing middle-market-size companies.

Do you have any plans for graduate school?

Definitely not on a full-time basis. At some point I might like to take courses at night that could contribute to my work performance.

I see that you grew up in Hawaii. That's pretty far away. Do you plan on relocating there at some point in the future?

No. I'd prefer to be based in a large mainland city, like here, but I'd be perfectly happy to go wherever my career might take me.

About Your Work Preferences

Why do you want to work in retailing?

I've been fascinated by the retail trade as long as I can remember. To me, each store is a stage or theater for its merchandise; the same merchandise can be sold in an infinite variety of ways. I know it's a challenging field, too. Merchants need to think about current fashion trends, the needs of local consumers, building a niche in the market, and all the other aspects of running a business. Also, retail is a field that's changing quickly, and I want to see firsthand in what direction retailing is going.

What other types of positions are you interested in, and what other companies have you applied to work for?

Actually, I've definitely decided to pursue a career as a restaurant manager, so I'm applying only for restaurant management training programs. I've recently had interviews with several other large national fast-food chains, including Chaco Chicken, the Peach Pit, and Minella's Diner.

Have you thought about why you would prefer to work with our firm over the other companies you've applied to?

Yes. I like your policy of promotion from within. I think the company's growth record is impressive, and I'm sure it will continue. Your firm's reputation for superior marketing is particularly important to me, because I want to pursue a career in marketing. Most important, it seems that your firm would offer a lot of opportunities—not just for possible advancement, but also to learn about many different product lines.

Chapter 12
Computerized Job Interviews

J ust when you thought your computer couldn't rear its head once more in the job search process, along comes the computerized job interview. Computerized interviews are used by companies like banks, hospitals, hotels, and retailers which traditionally hire large volumes of workers. In order to save time and money, many of these companies are now having interested applicants meet with a computer rather than a human resources representative. Though it's a fairly new technique, don't be surprised to see many more companies (including smaller companies that can't spare the time to interview hundreds of people) employing some sort of computer assisted interview.

The mission of the first interview is the same with a computer as it is with another human being. The only difference is that it is the computer that does the asking. Prepare to be asked questions about your work and educational backgrounds, as well as your skills and qualifications. Questions are usually posed in a true/false or multiple-choice format, though some programs will give you a time limit to type out your answer. When you've completed the interview, the computer provides the recruiter with a summary of the your answers. Among other things, this summary might recommend a face-to-face interview and give the interviewer a list of follow-up questions.

Structured Interviews

Computerized job interviews are based on the principle of the structured job interview. As previously discussed, structured interviews are interviews where each candidate is asked the same list of questions so that the company can fairly screen the applicants and decide who they would like to bring back in for a second interview. Supporters of the structured interview like this format because it brings a consistency to the hiring process; it's a consistency that can often be lacking in the cases where an unstructured interview format is used. By asking each candidate the same question, they essentially can compare apples with apples. Another advantage of the computerized interview is that the companies that create these programs have taken the time to carefully word each question so that nothing illegal is being asked. A final advantage of the structured interview is that it is more efficient; it gathers more information in a shorter period of time.

What to Expect

Computer assisted interviews start out in the exact same way as a traditional interview. You get a call from a recruiter or personnel professional and schedule a mutually convenient time to come into the office to meet. You meet with a human resources representative (yes, a real live person) and are then "introduced" to your interviewer . . . Mr. IBM. The human resources representative is likely to stick around for a few moments to make sure that you don't have any questions, and then it's just you and the computer. If you know *anything* about using a computer, you should have no problem navigating the computer interview program. Because they're designed to test job seekers at every level, they are a very basic and easy to navigate program. In general, you're given a time limit of about 30 minutes (about the same time as a face-to-face interview) in which to complete the interview. When you've finished, the computer will then provide the hiring manager with a summary that will recommend the next step, should they want to take one.

Computer assisted interviews generally consist of about 100 questions that relate to your educational and work background. The following series of questions are questions you might expect to find in a computer-assisted interview. They are taken from the ApView computer-assisted interview from SHL Aspen Tree Software:

Are you currently employed?
A. Yes
B. No

Why did you leave your last job, or why do you want to leave your present job?
A. I was dismissed
B. I was laid off

C. To take a better job

D. Relocation

E. To go to school

F. I am not leaving my present job

G. Other reason

How often do/did you experience conflict with your coworkers?

A. Often

B. Sometimes

C. Rarely

D. Never

E. Cannot say

What kind of recommendation do you think your present or most recent supervisor would give you?

A. Outstanding

B. Above average

C. Average

D. Below average

E. I don't know

On previous jobs, were you able to develop new or better ways of doing the work assigned to you?

A. Most of the time

B. Usually

C. Sometimes

D. Seldom

E. Never

While the first computerized interview programs consisted entirely of multiple-choice or true/false questions, the programs are advancing as more and more companies depend on them for the screening process. Many programs require that a candidate type out an extended, written answer instead of choosing the most relevant answer from a premanufactured list. ApView, for example, allows its customers the option of asking open-ended questions instead of, or

Dress for Success

If an employer calls to tell you that you have been invited in for a computerized first interview, don't take this as an invitation for informality. Even if the typical handshake is being replaced by a mouse click, you always want to be properly attired in a business suit. As you will be interacting with live humans at some point (who will be noting your appearance, etc.), you always want to be dressed for success.

in addition to, multiple choice questions. Written answers are reviewed by a human resources professional (not the computer), so do be sure to answer any open-ended questions exactly how you would if someone were sitting in the chair across from you. As most computer programs are tailored to a specific company or position, it is important that you do all of the research you normally would when preparing for an interview.

The Importance of Accuracy

Accuracy is key in a computerized interview. You should answer every question just as you would in a face-to-face interview. Don't exaggerate your skills and accomplishments and think that the computer won't know you're lying. While the computer may not be able to measure your body language and pick up on hints that you may be lying (as a recruiter can), a computer is able to quickly notice any inconsistencies in your answers . . . and you can best believe this will be reported. Remember, a computer-assisted interview is just the first step; if you're selected for a face-to-face interview, the interviewer will see from your application and resume that you were lying to the computer, which will eliminate you from contention.

Don't Confess Your Sins

While you certainly don't want to lie to a computer, you don't want to be *too* honest either. Studies have shown that—because they are not looking at another human—people are likely to be more honest with a computer than they would be with a human. People are likely to disclose information about themselves to a computer that they wouldn't dream of telling a human interviewer, especially in sensitive areas. So, before you start unveiling the skeletons in your closet, remember that your answers will be sent to a human interviewer as soon as you leave. That said, keep in mind that you *never* want to tell a computer anything you wouldn't tell a human interviewer.

Time Flies . . . When You're Lying?

Studies have shown that, on the average, it takes a human being longer to respond to a question when telling a lie than it does when telling the truth. That said, one of the things a computerized interview program does is measure the time it takes for you to respond to a question. When a computer summarizes your answers for a recruiter, it also highlights those questions that took you an abnormally long time to respond to.

What the Computer Tells the Company

Once you've completed the interview, the program analyzes your responses and presents a summary to a recruiter. The recruiter reads the report and decides whether or not to call you in for a second interview. Based on your answers, the computer can also provide the recruiter with a list of follow-up questions that should be asked in a second interview. Another key feature of the computerized interview program is its ability to flag any inconsistencies or contradictions in your answers. Needless to say, if a recruiter has reason to believe that an applicant is somehow lying, it is not likely that they will be called in for a second interview. Always be candid and completely truthful in your answers, and such contradictions should never arise.

Advanced computer programs even allow employers to create a standardized "employee profile" for their company. The computer then analyzes your answers in comparison with this model, and decides whether or not you would be a good fit to the company. By comparing your answers with those of successful hires, the computer can predict—usually with measurable success—whether or not you'll be a successful employee.

Internet Job Interviews

Using the Internet as a platform to administer screening interviews is a method that is quickly gaining popularity. And why not? We use the Internet to do everything else in our everyday lives, so why not interview? Internet interviewing is especially beneficial in long-distance job searches. For example, say you're applying for a position with a company in Boston but you live in Seattle. If you're online, you can complete a screening interview from the comfort of your own home. Not only does this save the company time, but it saves you money from having to travel to an interview. Faultfinders say that a telephone screening is a better way, but companies who employ the method don't seem to be listening.

Advantages of a Computer-Assisted Job Interview

+ Candidates report being less nervous when interviewing with a computer rather than an actual person.
+ It simplifies the initial screening process and makes it more effective.
+ Companies who employ the use of computer-assisted interviews report higher productivity, improved customer service, lower employee turnover, less employee absenteeism, and less theft in the workplace.

Again, the process of an Internet interview starts out like any other: you're contacted for an initial screening interview, but instead of a telephone or face-to-face interview, you're provided with a password that gives you access to the company's in-house computer system. Log on, and you'll be engaged in what is essentially a computer-assisted interview. You'll be asked basic questions about your experience, and the computer will create a report for the recruiter.

Scenario-Based Interviews

As the name implies, a scenario-based interview involves more situational interviewing than the structured, computerized multiple-choice interviews discussed above. Scenario-based interviews are used to see how candidates behave in simulated work situations. Learning Systems Sciences, a leader in this type of computerized interview, reports that their clientele consists primarily of banks and retail establishments, including many large department store chains. Like the structured, computerized job interviews, these interviews are most often used to screen candidates for entry-level positions that traditionally have high turnover rates. Candidates who pass these simulations are brought in for a face-to-face interview.

Many companies prefer this type of interviewing, because instead of asking someone, for instance, how he or she feels about customer service (and getting a canned answer), the employer can see how a candidate will perform in tough situations. For instance, the computer screen might show an irate customer yelling about a product he bought that he believes is faulty, and the candidate must try to placate the customer.

Instead of having a candidate key in one of a set of preformulated answers, the computer records the candidate's voice, allowing the recruiter to hear how he or she handled the situation. Did the candidate remain calm and polite, or did he or she sound harried and rude? Candidates are usually graded on a decided-upon scale. For instance, a candidate might get extra points for apologizing to a customer but could lose points for not sounding sincere.

Disadvantages of Computer-Assisted Interviews

- Some people report that the questions are biased against certain groups, especially minorities and women.
- A computer lacks the ability to take special circumstances into account, like a history of unemployment due to disability, and will provide the recruiter with a negative report.
- A computer is not a person; it cannot measure eagerness, enthusiasm, or willingness to work hard. Alternatively, it also cannot measure negativity or pessimism.

Computerized Assessment Tests

Assessment tests are nothing new to the world of job hunting. For years, applicants have been asked to take all kinds of tests to evaluate their suitability. The reasoning behind these tests is simple: hiring new employees is time-consuming and expensive. By carefully screening applicants with both structured, computer-assisted interviews and computerized assessment tests, recruiters can greatly reduce the chances that a new hire will leave after only a few months.

Employers generally use three main types of assessment tests: skills, integrity, and personality. The purpose of each of these tests is pretty basic. Skills tests determine if you have the ability to do a particular job, integrity tests help determine whether you'll be a trustworthy employee, and personality tests tell the interviewer if your disposition is suited for a particular position. Depending on the nature of the position, you may be asked to take one, two, or all three tests. Most positions require some type of skills test—for example, a math test for accountants and a typing test for administrative assistants. Some computer programmers are even asked to write a short program as part of their pre-employment testing. If you're applying for a position where you'll be dealing with goods or money, you'll probably be required to take an integrity test. Personality or psychological tests can be used in virtually any situation but are especially common if you're interviewing for a management position or one where you'd be working with sensitive material.

Skills tests can often be part of the initial screening process, but personality and integrity tests are usually one of the last steps of the interviewing process. If you're asked to take a computerized assessment test, your interviewer will likely take you to a room with a computer. After you receive instructions on how to use the program, the test will be administered, usually with a time limit. Depending on the nature of the test, you may answer multiple-choice or true/false questions or transcribe written information into a computer program. Integrity and personality tests typically contain upwards of one hundred questions. Most are of the multiple-choice, yes/no, true/false, always/sometimes/never variety. Once your time is up, the computer will score your work and, if applicable, compare your answers to a specified profile. It then generates a report that tells the recruiter how a candidate fits in relation to other candidates.

Computerized Skills Tests

Skills tests are the most straightforward types of computerized assessment tests. Basically, they measure your aptitude for performing a specific task or duty. Anyone who has done any temporary work will be familiar with many computerized skills tests. These tests determine your proficiency in word processing, spreadsheet, and database programs. You're asked to do some basic exercises using the various applications and are tested on your accuracy. With some tests, especially those for word processing programs, you have a certain amount of time to format and write a document, for example. Then the computer tests not only your accuracy but how much you managed to accomplish in that time. Similarly, a spreadsheet test might judge you on how quickly and accurately you can enter data and perform different functions.

An accountant or engineer might be tested on his or her mathematical or logical reasoning skills. A computer programmer might need to write a few lines of code or debug a problematic program. A test may measure the applicant's reaction time or memory.

Scoring

Computerized skills assessment tests are measured on your raw score, which is then compared to a mean, or average score, of everyone who has taken the test. For instance, if you scored a seventy-five and the mean is sixty-eight, this will show the employer that you have above-average skills.

Strategy

Unfortunately, there's no real way to prepare for skills tests. The best you can do is prepare for the type of test, like a typing or math test, by brushing up on those skills.

Advantages of Scenario-Based Interviews

+ It gives candidates a realistic idea of what to expect of a job.
+ Companies that employ scenario-based interviews report a lower turnover rate along with improved overall quality in their employees.

Computerized Integrity Tests

Integrity tests measure your honesty and morals. The Pinkerton Stanton Survey, for instance, is designed to measure the moral standard by which you live. This doesn't just mean whether someone is likely to embezzle company funds or steal from the cash register. An applicant's level of honesty and moral standard can also help determine whether someone is likely to be tardy, socialize excessively during work hours, leave early, take long lunches, "borrow" office equipment, and so forth.

Integrity tests allow employers to measure a candidate's reliability, work ethic, and trustworthiness. These traits are important indicators of performance. For instance, a recruiter might question the candidacy of an applicant who, on his integrity test, stated that it's all right to steal sometimes.

Strategy

When taking an integrity test, try to avoid absolutes, like "always" or "never." No one is likely to believe you if you say you've never in your whole life lied or have never gotten so much as a parking ticket. Simply be honest, but don't reveal more than you have to.

Computerized Personality Tests

Personality tests are the most complex of all computerized assessment tests. They're generally used to see if a candidate's personality is suited to the job. Tests like Pinkerton's Adult Personality Survey measure traits like work motivation, adaptability, and trustworthiness. The results of a personality test are then compared against a standard, or norm, developed from those who have previously taken the test. For instance, if you're applying for a position as an insurance underwriter, your scores will be measured against a norm group of successful underwriters.

Companies like personality tests because they allow them to see if you'll fit in. This benefits both you and the employer, because if you're not happy with your job, it hurts both you and the company. If you decide to leave after only a few months, the company has wasted time and money to train you, and you've wasted time in a job you didn't like.

Another Pinkerton test, the Stanton Profile, is a hybrid personality/skills test that measures work preferences to determine general employability. The score is measured against the minimum requirements of a particular job. For instance, the test will ask you a question regarding your adaptability. This is a good trait for an administrative assistant but less important for someone working in a stockroom, who will likely be doing the same tasks day after day.

Strategy

While preparing for skills and integrity tests is difficult, preparing for personality tests is nearly impossible. First, many people aren't sure whether they should let their "true" selves answer questions or if they should answer based on the kind of personality they think the company is looking for. Experts differ on the subject. Some suggest you use your work personality; others say you should just be yourself.

While it's good to look at traits that have made others successful, first look at what's gotten you where you are. If you've spent any time in the workforce, you know that your work personality differs from your personality outside work. Therefore, use what you've learned in the workplace—what is and isn't acceptable workplace behavior—to answer the questions.

Avoid Absolutes

As with the integrity tests, try to avoid using absolutes like "always" and "never." A large number of "always" and "never" answers might make it look as if you're lying—or, worse, be a signal of extreme behavior. Employers look for moderation and tend to stay away from extremists.

Chapter 13

The Job Offer

While it seems like getting a job offer is probably the most exciting part of the entire process, it can really be a nerve-wracking experience. As it's likely that you will be interviewing with several companies at once, it is also possible that you will be offered more than one job at once. Deciding which offer to accept can pose a number of questions and concerns. On the one hand, if you've been looking for a job for quite some time, you're likely to find yourself screaming "YES! I'LL TAKE IT!" before the recruiter even finishes stating the offer. On the other hand, you may be worrying that something better will come along just as you accept the offer (that's just your luck, right?).

As job seekers are faced with far too many conflicting emotions at the last stage of the game, it's easy to see how so many people can make unnecessary and costly mistakes. It is far too often the case that eligible job seekers—with a lot to offer any company—sell themselves short. They don't believe they will be hired anyplace else (and they don't feel like spending the time looking), so they accept an offer without even exploring their options. On the opposite end of the spectrum, there are those job seekers who have wildly unrealistic expectations of what they are worth as an entry-level employee. For those job seekers who go straight for where the money is, they're overlooking some very important aspects of a job that will come back to haunt them later. You can help avoid making these last-minute blunders by answering the following questions.

Do You Want This Job?

If you are going to seriously consider a job offer, make sure it is a job you want. Are you willing to live and work in the area in question? Is the work schedule and job lifestyle one you will enjoy? If you're just graduating, is the job in the field you'd like to pursue?

Will It Help Your Career?

Determining whether or not a specific job will help in the progress of your career is a much more important question than what your starting salary should be. In some organizations, you may be given a lot of responsibility right away but then find that there's nowhere else to go. Make sure you know whether or not the company offers room for advancement. Are there periodic performance reviews and, if so, when are they conducted?

Is the Environment a Comfortable One for You?

You wouldn't want to live in a climate that didn't suit you, so, similarly, you shouldn't work in an environment that will hinder your productivity. One of the main goals of the entire interview process is to determine whether or not you and your personality will be a good fit to the work environment of the position. You'll want to consider specifics, including office or workstation setting, privacy, proximity to other staff, amount of space, noise level, and lighting. What is the level of interaction among coworkers? While some organizations strongly encourage teamwork, others promote individual accomplishment. Think about which approach works better for you. Remember: if you don't like the work environment before you accept the job, you probably won't like it as an employee.

Okay, So What About the Money?

Questions about salary and benefits are often frightening to those new to the workplace, as they're not issues they've had to consider before. Talking salary with a potential employer does not have to be a scary experience. As long as you prepare for the inevitable mention of the topic, you should do just fine.

Again, before talking salary with a company, you should be well aware of what the going rate is for someone with your background (education, experience), in your position, and in your geographical area. If you find out that the median salary is $27,000, tell a recruiter (if and when asked) that you were looking for between $25,000 and $30,000. While an employer will be quick to alert you to any set salary requirements and whether or not your needs exceed it, it is best not to seem self-important (or completely clueless) by requesting $100,000 a year for a $30,000 a year job.

Negotiating a Salary

Depending on the company you're dealing with and the position you're applying for, a company will do one of two things when asked to negotiate a salary: stand firm or negotiate. You can easily determine whether or not a company is willing to negotiate on a salary simply by asking, "Is that salary negotiable?" The question is a very common follow-up to the big salary disclosure, and it is not a question that should be taken the wrong way.

If a company says that they are willing to negotiate a salary, your next move is to justify the increase. You want to assure them of your interest in the position but explain why the said salary probably wouldn't be enough. Rather than saying you just want more money or that you are worth it, give solid evidence as to why more money is needed. For example, explain why their offer doesn't sufficiently cover your living expenses or moving expenses.

Remember, as the term tells us, "negotiating" is not a one-sided battle where the job seeker names a price and the employer says yes or no. This is not employee *Priceline.com*. Negotiating entails *you* listening to the employer and giving their negotiation consideration (even if it's not as much as you were looking for). Set realistic expectations for salary and it's much more likely that an employer will be willing to match it.

How Much Should You Expect?

Again, average salaries change with just about every aspect of the job. The previous chapter mentioned some of the online sites to visit where you could research salaries. Other ways in which you can find out a realistic salary is to read the trade journals for your industry, read the newspaper help-wanted ads, browse through some online job posting boards, or ask the question in an online discussion group of industry professionals and see what similar jobs are offering. If possible, talk to current employees. The U.S. Department of Labor's *Occupational Outlook Handbook* lists salaries and other information about a variety of jobs. It can be found at your local library.

Get It in Writing

If you're satisfied with the offered salary but haven't talked about benefits yet, now is the time to do so. After you have discussed all the aspects of the new job, ask if you can have everything outlined in writing. If an employer is reluctant to provide you with a written outline of the job offer, you may want to rethink the decision to accept the offer.

In the End, It's Your Happiness That Matters

Sure, a six-figure salary is an enticing perk a job may offer, but it's important to remember that salary isn't the only aspect of the job that will determine your satisfaction. Finding a job that you enjoy and can grow with is just as important. Similarly, finding a job that lets you showcase your skills and be yourself is equally important. If the starting salary of a job is fairly low, but the job seems to present a great and unique opportunity, think about the benefits of taking this job.

Still, if there's a great opportunity being offered but you just can't get past the low salary, you may want to take a while to think about it. Rather than start out a job with a negative attitude, it is best to shop your skills around and wait until all the pieces come together and the perfect job opportunity makes itself available to you. Trust your instincts and consider your happiness above everything else.

Five-Year Planning

A recruiter asks: What do you reasonably expect to be earning within five years?

My expectation is that my contributions to the company will be recognized and rewarded accordingly. Because salary levels are based on many factors—including the company's profitability and the general industrial business cycle—I could not give an exact figure. However, I can say that as I take on greater responsibilities I would expect to be compensated accordingly."

★ If asked a question like this, the last thing you want to do is speculate to the point of sounding arrogant. Turn the question around and ask the recruiter what is typical for the career path. Leave it to the recruiter to determine the appropriate time frames for promotions.

Glossary

ADSL: An acronym for Asymmetric Digital Subscriber Line; a quicker way of using the non-voice part of a telephone line to send data; also known as a DSL.

ARPANET: An acronym for Advance Research Projects Agency Network; the first computer network developed by the United State Department of Defense; the original ancestor of the Internet.

ASCII: An acronym for American Standard Code for Information Interchange; the most basic code for written documents, ASCII documents contain no special formatting like boldface or italics; invented so that computers could communicate with one another easily, regardless of the writing program they are using.

Access: The ability to connect to a service or resource and receive information.

ActiveX Control: An add-on program that enhances the capabilities of an Internet Explorer browser; similar to a plug-in.

Address: A combination of letters and/or numbers that allows you to reach another user online; *you@email.com* would be an example of an e-mail address.

Agent: A software program that searches out information and brings it back to your computer.

American Standard Code for Information Interchange: See *ASCII*.

Archie: A software program that allows you to find files on an anonymous FTP site.

Attachment: A file consisting of text, pictures, sound, or video that is sent with an e-mail message.

Backbone: The central line or series of connections that forms the main pathway in a network; the backbone connects all the networks together.

Bandwidth: The amount of information you can actually send through a connection; bandwidth is usually measured in bits per second (BPS).

Baud: The scientific unit of measurement for data transmission speed.

Binary File: A non-ASCII, non-text file.

BinHex: A method used to convert binary files (non-ASCII, non-text) into an ASCII format.

Bit: Short for binary digit; a bit is the smallest measurement of data; the speed at which data is transmitted is often measured by bits per second (BPS).

Bookmark: A way of saving your favorite Web sites so that you don't have to type the address in again and again.

Browser: A software program that locates Internet resources and displays them to users.

Byte: A measurement of eight bits of computerized data.

Cache: The area of a computer's hard drive that stores the most recently accessed Web sites.

Chat: Sending messages back and forth in real time; messages appear instantly as they are written.

Click: To press on the mouse button and cause another action to occur.

Client: A software program that allows a computer to communicate with another computer or server and to gain access to its files and programs.

Commercial Online Service: A company selling Internet access, but offering a variety of other services as well, such as e-mail, chat rooms, news and information, and shopping.

Communications Software: A software program that enables you to use your modem; communications software controls the exchange of information between your modem and a remote modem.

Computer-Assisted Job Interview: A job interview conducted by a computer; the test usually consists of a series of true/false and multiple-choice questions.

Computerized Assessment Tests: Tests administered by a computer that help determine job fit; tests usually fall into one of the following categories: skills, personality, and integrity.

Configure: Adjusting the software settings so that a computer can connect to the Internet using an ISP.

Cookie: Information that a Web page automatically stores on your hard drive once you've viewed it; cookies will help a Web site recognize you when you visit again.

Cyberspace: A general term often used to refer to the nonexistent space that the Internet and all its functions inhabit; the term originated in William Gibson's 1984 novel *Neuromancer*.

DSL: An acronym for Digital Subscriber Line; a quicker way of using the non-voice part of a telephone line to send data; also known as an ADSL.

Database: An organized collection of electronically-stored information; a database's construction allows it to be searched quickly and easily.

Discussion Group: An Internet-based meeting place where computer users from all over can get together to chat, discuss shared interests, or post and read messages.

Domain Name: An Internet site's registered name; the end of the domain name (.com, .edu., etc.) is the top-level domain that alerts you to what kind of site it is; the beginning of the domain name is the second-level domain, it is usually the name of the company or organization.

Download: Copying a file or software program that was retrieved online or from another computer onto the hard drive of your own computer.

E-mail: A shortened version of "electronic mail"; messages are sent from one computer to another.

E-mail Discussion Group: A type of discussion group found on the Internet; also referred to as "mailing list" or "list serve."

Electronic Resume: A resume that can be sent via some function of the Internet (e-mail, for example); so that they are easy to read and search, electronic resumes are stripped of any formatting.

Emoticons: Punctuation used to symbolize emotions; emoticons are used in e-mail and newsgroups.

Encryption: The jumbling of messages and/or information so that they cannot be read without a decoding device.

Ethernet: One of the most common ways to network the computers in a LAN; can handle about 10 million BPS.

FAQs: An acronym for Frequently Asked Questions; common questions and answers that are asked in newsgroups and on Web sites.

FTP: An acronym for File Transfer Protocol; allows you to access and retrieve or send information over the Internet that is housed in a certain Web site; used in both private and public domains.

Filtering: Censoring questionable material by blocking access to it on the Internet, in newsgroups, or via e-mail. Parents often filter adult material so that their children are not exposed to it and companies filter to monitor their employees.

Filtering Software: The software used to censure questionable material.

Finger: A program that allows you to retrieve information about a user, simply by typing in their e-mail address; while fingers normally only retrieve non-personal information, many Web sites do not allow incoming finger requests.

Flame: An angry or hostile e-mail message or newsgroup posting.

Flame War: The result of various angry or hostile messages being sent back and forth in an online discussion group.

Forum: The specific name given to discussion groups on CompuServe, AOL, and Delphi; a meeting place where participants can post and read messages.

Frame: An independent part of a Web page; not all browsers are able to display frames.

Freeware: Public domain software files that are available, free of charge, to computer users.

GIF: Acronym for Graphics Interchange Format; a file format that is often used to display images on the Web.

Gigabyte: A measurement one thousand times larger than a megabyte.

Gopher: Originated the idea of making the Internet a more user-friendly tool for non-computer-people; Gopher can be broken down into its two major search engines, Veronica and Jughead; Gopher is often referred to as the grandparent technology of the Web.

Graphical Browser: A browser that allows users to use a mouse instead of the keypad.

HTML: An acronym for Hypertext Markup Language; the language used to create a Web page.

HTTP: Acronym for Hypertext Transfer Protocol; the command that moves hypertext pages over the Internet; any Web address begins with http://

Hit: A term that is most often used on the World Wide Web; when a Web site claims to have had one million hits, they are essentially saying that one million people have visited their Web site.

Home Page: A Web site's front page; home pages often serve as the index or "table of contents" of an entire site.

Host: A computer that provides some sort of service(s) to other computers in a network; functions could include access to particular files or access to the Internet.

Hypertext: A series of linked pages on a related topic; created by using HTML.

ISDN: An acronym for Integrated Services Digital Network; a quicker way to move data over a telephone line; both ends are digital, not analog.

ISP: See *Internet Service Provider.*

Icon: A picture that will execute a command when you click on it.

Intelligent Agent: A software program that locates information and understands context.

Interface: The onscreen look of the page that allows users to interact with their computers.

Internet: A network of computer networks that contains innumerable computers worldwide; each computer in the network has the ability to communicate with every other computer in the network.

Internet Explorer: A web browser made by Microsoft.

Internet Relay Chat: A system allowing for real time communication; often referred to as IRC.

Internet Service Provider: A company selling dial-up access to the Internet; also known as an ISP.

Intranet: A sort of personalized Internet system; intranets are found in companies so that information can be exchanged by coworkers, but is not available for public viewing.

JPEG: An acronym for Joint Photographic Experts Group; a file format that is often used to display images on the Web.

Jughead: The smaller of Gopher's two main search engines; Veronica is the other search engine.

Keyword: A word or phrase that is used to search a database or document of files.

Kilobytes: A measurement equal to one thousand bits of data; modem speed is measured in kilobytes.

Link: A word, phrase, or icon you can click on to automatically connect to another Web site.

List Serve: A type of discussion group found on the Internet; also referred to as "mailing list" or "e-mail discussion group."

Local Area Network: Also referred to as a LAN, one of the basic kinds of networks; in a LAN, computers are usually within a close physical proximity of one another, like in an office.

Log In: To connect with a remote computer or computer network; the phrase can be used interchangeably with "log on."

Lynx: A text-only browser; many UNIX-based operating systems use Lynx.

MPEG: An acronym for Motion Picture Experts Group; a file format that is often used to view video clips on the Internet.

MacTP: The software a Macintosh computer needs to use the Internet; similar to the TCP/IP a PC needs to connect.

Mailing List: A type of discussion group found on the Internet; also referred to as "list serve" or "e-mail discussion group."

Megabyte: A measurement equal to one million bytes; referenced as MB.

Meta-List: A "list of lists" found on the World Wide Web with a number of links to other Web sites or Internet resources.

Modem: An electronic device connecting a computer to a telephone line, allowing for communication between computers; modems can be either internal or external.

Moderator: The person who monitors a discussion group or special interest group on the Internet and ensures that information being posted is relevant to the topic at hand.

Mosaic: The first graphical browser; allows users to point and click a mouse to navigate the Web.

Multimedia: Term used to refer to the employment of several different kinds of media in a single application.

Netiquette: An established set of manners that should be used when communicating via the Internet; so that you do not insult someone in your communication, it is important to learn netiquette.

Netizen: An Internet user who always displays proper netiquette.

Netscape Communicator: A software package that includes the Netscape Navigator browser, an e-mail and newsreader program, tools for building a home page, and other features.

Network: A set of computers that are physically connected—most often through hardware—to assist in the sharing of information; the two basic kinds

of networks are a Local Area Network (LAN) and a Wide Area Network (WAN).

Newbie: Internet slang for someone who is new to the Internet and the World Wide Web.

Newsgroup: An online discussion group found in the Usenet area of the Internet; the Internet's most popular type of discussion group.

Newsreader: A software program that allows you to read and post messages to newsgroups.

Online: To link, via modem, to another computer or computer network; to say that you are "online" generally means that you are accessing the Internet.

PGP: An acronym for Pretty Good Privacy; a software program that jumbles the text of an e-mail to protect one's privacy.

POP: An acronym for Point of Presence; the location that an Internet service provider can connect to with a local telephone call.

PPP: An acronym for Point-to-Point Protocol; an account with an Internet service provider.

Page: A document with text, pictures, or sound. Pages can be found on the World Wide Web.

Password: A secret word; passwords can allow you access to your computer, the Internet, a particular Web site, etc.

Plug-Ins: Used to enhance the ability of your browser by allowing you to hear sounds, experience virtual reality, etc.; plug-ins are purchased as software.

Post: As a noun, a post is a message or item you find and read online, like a job listing or a message on a newsgroup; as a verb, post means that you have sent a message or item to a newsgroup or Web site so that it can be read by others.

Protocol: A set of rules that determine how computers exchange information.

Pull-Down Menu: A list of several choices that drops down when you click on it.

Push Technology: A system that sends customized information directly to a computer because of a user's previously stated preference.

QuickTime: A file format that is often used to show short video clips on the Internet; developed by Apple Computer.

SET: An acronym for Secure Electronic Transaction; a standard used by credit card companies and online retail sites that jumbles information, making online shopping a safe transaction.

SIG: See *Special Interest Group*.

SLIT: An acronym for Single Line Internet Protocol; an account with an Internet service provider; an older version of a PPP.

SSL: An acronym for Secure Socket Layer; a system that jumbles information to protect one's privacy, they are often used by retail Web sites to ensure safe shopping.

Search engine: A software program that searches out topics, words, and phrases on the Web and in newsgroups and displays them as a link on your computer.

Server: A central computer or software program that serves as the hub of a network; functions of the server could include sending e-mail or accessing a Web site.

Shareware: A software program that is free for an initial trial period; if you continue using the software, you are charged a fee by the developer.

Site: The specific Internet location where users can find information; if the information is found on the World Wide Web, it is referred to as a Web site.

Spam: Junk e-mail.

Special Interest Group: A type of discussion group found when using a commercial online service; includes bulletin boards and forums; also known as an SIG.

Status Indicator: An icon that appears on your browser to indicate whether or not the browser is active.

TCP/IP: Acronym for Transmission Control Protocol/Internet Protocol; the set of rules that computers abide on the Internet to communicate with one another.

Tags: Codes employed in HTML that are used to execute certain functions; tags can be used to create links, or employ boldfaced or italicized print.

Telephony: A technology that allows for voice communication over the Internet; telephony may involve using microphones or computers, not telephones.

Telnet: The smallest of the Internet's four parts.

Thread: A collection of messages that are on the same topic; threads are found in newsgroups and bulletin boards.

Toolbar: A horizontal row of icons and verbal commands; each button will execute a different command.

UNIX: An operating system for computers; invented before Windows, UNIX was used heavily in the past and is still used today.

URL: An acronym for Uniform Resource Locator; the address of a site on the Internet.

Upload: The process of transferring files from your computer to another computer.

Usenet: An abbreviation of Users' Network; comprised of the thousands of newsgroups found on the Internet.

Veronica: The larger of Gopher's two search engines; Jughead is the other search engine.

Virtual: Something that is close to being real; for example, the term "virtual reality" refers to a computer-generated program that feels like it is real, though it is not.

Virus: A computer program that runs unexpectedly on a computer; depending on the severity of the virus, these programs can impair your computer's ability to perform normal tasks interminably or even wipe out all your pre-existing programs.

WYSIWYG: An acronym for "What You See Is What You Get"; a Web-authoring tool that allows you to preview what a Web page will look like before you finish creating it; pronounced "wizzy wig."

Web Browser: A software program that enables users to navigate the World Wide Web.

Web site: A collection of information and pictures that are linked together because they belong to the same individual, company, institution, or organization.

Wide Area Network: Also referred to as a WAN; one of the basic kinds of networks; in a WAN, computers are often scattered across several cities, states, or even countries; the Internet would be considered a Wide Area Network.

World Wide Web: One of the four parts that comprise the Internet; the World Wide Web is very graphics-oriented, rich in images, sound, and video.

Index

We Have EVERYTHING!

Available wherever books are sold!

Everything **After College Book**
$12.95, 1-55850-847-3

Everything **Astrology Book**
$12.95, 1-58062-062-0

Everything **Baby Names Book**
$12.95, 1-55850-655-1

Everything **Baby Shower Book**
$12.95, 1-58062-305-0

Everything **Barbeque Cookbook**
$12.95, 1-58062-316-6

Everything® **Bartender's Book**
$9.95, 1-55850-536-9

Everything **Bedtime Story Book**
$12.95, 1-58062-147-3

Everything **Beer Book**
$12.95, 1-55850-843-0

Everything **Bicycle Book**
$12.95, 1-55850-706-X

Everything **Build Your Own Home Page**
$12.95, 1-58062-339-5

Everything **Casino Gambling Book**
$12.95, 1-55850-762-0

Everything **Cat Book**
$12.95, 1-55850-710-8

Everything® **Christmas Book**
$15.00, 1-55850-697-7

Everything **College Survival Book**
$12.95, 1-55850-720-5

Everything **Cover Letter Book**
$12.95, 1-58062-312-3

Everything **Crossword and Puzzle Book**
$12.95, 1-55850-764-7

Everything **Dating Book**
$12.95, 1-58062-185-6

Everything **Dessert Book**
$12.95, 1-55850-717-5

Everything **Dog Book**
$12.95, 1-58062-144-9

Everything **Dreams Book**
$12.95, 1-55850-806-6

Everything **Etiquette Book**
$12.95, 1-55850-807-4

Everything **Family Tree Book**
$12.95, 1-55850-763-9

Everything **Fly-Fishing Book**
$12.95, 1-58062-148-1

Everything **Games Book**
$12.95, 1-55850-643-8

Everything **Get-a-Job Book**
$12.95, 1-58062-223-2

The ultimate reference for couples planning their wedding!

- Scheduling, budgeting, etiquette, hiring caterers, florists, and photographers
- Ceremony & reception ideas
- Over 100 forms and checklists
- And much, much more!

$12.95, 384 pages, 8" x 9¼"

Personal finance made easy—and fun!

- Create a budget you can live with
- Manage your credit cards
- Set up investment plans
- Money-saving tax strategies
- And much, much more!

$12.95, 288 pages, 8" x 9¼"

For more information, or to order, call 800-872-5627
or visit www.adamsmedia.com/everything

Adams Media Corporation, 260 Center Street, Holbrook, MA 02343